The Laws of the State of New Mexico
Affecting Church Property

To Roman —

In happy remembrance
of many good times —

Manny

The writing of this dissertation was conducted under the direction of the Rev. John J. McGrath, A.B., LL.B., J.C.D., as major professor, and was approved by the Very Rev. Clement V. Bastnagel, S.T.L., J.U.D., and the Rev. Meletius M. Wojnar, O.S.B.M., S.T.L., J.C.D., as readers.

A MI *PAPÁ* Y *MAMÁ*,
CON CARIÑO

FOREWORD

During the course of slightly more than four hundred years, New Mexico has been under the sovereignty of five different governments: Spanish, Indian, Mexican, Confederate, and American. Although perhaps "unique" is not quite *le mot juste* with which to characterize New Mexico, it has had more than one hundred governors, and has experienced rebellions, invasions, battles, sieges, massacres. Ecclesiastically its history is much more impressive: from suffraganship under the Archdiocese of Seville in Spain to a Metropolitan See in its own right, it has been nurtured by the Catholic Faith for nearly five centuries.

It is an ancient land, this. Indications of human occupation as long as twenty thousand years ago have given name to the Folsom and Sandia Man. Spanish explorers traversed New Mexico eighty years before the Pilgrims on the Mayflower sighted the New England coast. A crucifix is, of course, not tolerated in the court room today; but there was a time, centuries ago, when, for all practical purposes, the Inquisition of the Holy Office was the tribunal of last resort. Until the American occupation in 1846, the law of the land was basically a code of laws promulgated by the Visigoths in 693. And corporations subsisted as fictitious legal entities existing only in intendment and consideration of law years before Sir Edward Coke so defined them.

Today, title to church property in New Mexico can be held by corporations aggregate, corporations sole, and in fee. In an attempt to ascertain how church property was held prior to the American occupation, brief synopses of the civil, ecclesiastical, and legal histories have been presented, with special reference to the administration, ownership, and tenure of such realties. To complete a proper *mise en scène* for the main part of this work, it has been deemed opportune to present a study of the nature of corporations at Anglo-American law and in the mind of Innocent IV, who lent initial impetus to the Fiction Theory—the theory considered orthodox in Anglo-American jurisprudence.

The primary purpose of this study is to compare Canon law with the law of the State of New Mexico regarding their provisions concerning corporations created for religious and charitable purposes, and regarding the acquisition, tenure, and administration of church property, in an effort to determine how and to what extent these two systems of law are parallel in their legislation, and to what degree the Church is affected in those instances where such parallel does not exist.

The writer is deeply grateful to His Excellency, the Most Reverend Edwin V. Byrne, D.D., Archbishop and Metropolitan of Santa Fe, for the opportunity to undertake graduate studies in Canon law. He also wishes to thank the members of the Faculty of the School of Canon Law of The Catholic University of America for their invaluable and kind assistance during the course of these studies and in the preparation of this work. A special note of gratitude is owed Reverend John J. McGrath, A.B., LL.B., J.C.D., and Professor Stephan G. Kuttner, J.U.D., S.J.D., J.C.D., LL.D.

TABLE OF CONTENTS

CHAPTER III

CHAPTER IV

CHAPTER I

BRIEF OUTLINE OF THE CIVIL AND ECCLESIASTICAL HISTORY OF NEW MEXICO [1]

This historical sketch is necessarily just that—a sketch. Consequently, and at the risk of sounding pedestrian, the writer must note at the outset that the history of New Spain in general and of New Mexico in particular is unintelligible if ever one loses sight of the fact that until the American occupation in 1846 there was no separation of Church and State. One example will suffice to set off that fact in ample relief: some eight bishops and archbishops held the high office of viceroy between 1611 and 1809.[2]

For our purposes, the history of New Mexico may be divided into four periods, as follows:

1. The years of exploration: 1539 to 1598.
2. The years of colonization to the end of Spanish rule: 1598 to 1821.
3. The Mexican period: 1821 to 1846.
4. The Territorial period to Statehood: 1846 to 1912.

[1] The facts hereinbelow narrated are generally accepted as such; nonetheless, verification thereof may be made by reference to Bancroft, *The Works of Hubert Bancroft* (39 vols., Vol. XVII, *History of Arizona and New Mexico*, San Francisco, 1889); Read, *Illustrated History of New Mexico* (translated from the 2. Spanish ed. by Eleuterio Baca, Santa Fe: New Mexican Printing Co., 1912); Twitchell, *The Leading Facts of New Mexican History* (5 vols., Cedar Rapids, Iowa: The Torch Press, 1911-1917); Prince, *A Concise History of New Mexico* (Cedar Rapids, Iowa: The Torch Press, 1912); Cuevas, *Historia de la Iglesia en Mexico* (3 vols., 3. ed., El Paso: Editorial "Revista Católica," 1928); Defouri, *Historical Sketch of the Catholic Church in New Mexico* (San Francisco: McCormick Brothers, 1887) [hereinafter cited Defouri]; Salpointe, *Soldiers of the Cross: Notes on the Ecclesiastical History of New Mexico, Arizona, and Colorado* (Banning, California: St. Boniface School, 1898) [hereinafter cited Salpointe].

[2] Cf. Bancroft, Vol. XI, *History of Mexico* (4 tomes, San Francisco, 1883), Tome III, 20, 108, 127, 167, 186, 256, 456; Tome IV, 76.

ARTICLE 1. THE YEARS OF EXPLORATION: 1539 TO 1598

Alvar Nuñez Cabeza de Baca was the first Spanish explorer whose name appears in New Mexico history, although it is by no means certain that he ever entered its present boundaries. He was a survivor of the ill-fated expedition of Panfilo Narvaez to the west coast of Florida. With three companions he traversed on foot the vast unexplored region from the Gulf of Mexico to the Pacific Ocean, and thence in 1536 he proceeded to Mexico City,[3] where he reported on the region of large houses and populations to the far north. One of Cabeza de Baca's companions, a Negro named Estevan, did eventually reach the Zuñi country in western New Mexico, as a guide to the expedition of the Franciscan Fray Marcos de Niza in 1539.

The stories told by Cabeza de Baca and Fray Marcos de Niza, added to the prevailing rumors of gold and silver to be found in the north, culminated in the famous expedition in 1540 of Francisco Vasquez Coronado, the first of the *conquistadores*. This ambitious expedition started north from Compostela in western Mexico, bound for the famous Seven Cities of Cibola. Progress was slow, and, after many sanguinary encounters with the Indians, Coronado finally arrived at the fabled "cities" of gold: Gran Quivira, a region of Indian villages of golden straw huts. Coronado, greatly disappointed and badly injured, started with his army homeward to Mexico in April, 1542, leaving behind the Franciscan friars Juan de Padilla, Luis de Escalona, and Juan de la Cruz, all three killed by the Indians. Despite its fiasco, the Coronado expedition was one of the most remarkable adventures in history.

Almost forty years elapsed before there was an attempt to regain New Mexico. In 1581 the Franciscan friar Augustin Rodriguez, accompanied by the Franciscans Francisco Lopez and Juan de Santa Maria and twelve soldiers commanded by Francisco Sanchez Chamuscado, proceeded by way of the Rio Grande

---

[3] Mexico City had been conquered in 1521 by Cortes. It was he who, in 1525, promoted the building there of the first church in the Spanish colonies.—Cf. Mendieta, *Historia Eclesiástica Indiana* (edited by Joaquin Garcia Icazbalceta, Mexico, D.F.: Antigua Librería, 1870), p. 222 (hereinafter cited Mendieta).

as far as Galisteo. Chamuscado returned to Mexico; the three Franciscans remained, and were killed by the Indians.

ARTICLE 2. THE YEARS OF COLONIZATION TO THE END OF SPANISH RULE: 1598 TO 1821

It was Juan de Oñate who completed the conquest and established the first permanent settlement in New Mexico. Oñate crossed the Rio Grande near El Paso and proceeded up the river, meeting with little or no opposition. At Santo Domingo, a conference was held with Pueblo representatives, who swore allegiance to the Spanish Crown [4] on July 7, 1598. Across the Rio Grande from San Juan, Oñate established the first capital of New Mexico and gave it the name of San Gabriel. The Oñate conquest culminated in the storming of Acoma in January, 1599, in which hundreds of Indians were killed.

Ecclesiastically the territory that is now New Mexico was successively subject to Seville, Mexico City, Michoacan, Guadala-

---

[4] In the year 1511, a board was created by Ferdinand II (1479-1516) and remodeled by Charles V (1516-1556) in 1524 for the exclusive superintendence of the affairs of the Spanish colonies in America, known as the Supreme Council of the Indies (*Consejo Supremo de las Indias*). It held its sessions in Madrid, and its powers were both judicial and executive. Civil, military, ecclesiastical, and commercial matters came within the sphere of its action. The Spanish colonies in America were divided into four Viceroyalties: Mexico, Peru, Rio de la Plata (Buenos Aires), and New Granada. In 1528 a Royal Audience (*Audiencia Real*) was established in Mexico City, the Viceroy being *ex officio* president thereof. This judicial body possessed a great deal of power and influence; it had control over all other tribunals, ecclesiastical as well as civil, and enjoyed the privilege of corresponding directly with the sovereign and with the Council of the Indies. New Mexico was a province within the intendency (*intendencia*) of Mexico City; it remained under the jurisdiction of the Audience of the latter until 1728, when it was transferred to that of Guadalajara. During the Spanish period, the province of New Mexico was immediately ruled by a Captain-General as governor, whose immediate superior was the Viceroy; the latter, in turn, answered to the Council of the Indies.—Cf. Mayer, *Mexico: Aztec, Spanish and Republican . . . , and Notices of New Mexico and California* (2 vols., Hartford: S. Drake & Co., 1851), II, 14-15 (hereinafter cited Mayer); cf. also Reynolds, *Spanish and Mexican Land Laws: New Spain and Mexico* (St. Louis: Buxton & Skinner Co., 1895), pp. 25-30 (hereinafter cited Reynolds).

jara, and Durango.[5] However, for all practical purposes, no
bishop exercised active authority to any extent over New Mexico
prior to the first part of the 18th century.[6] It must be borne in
mind that the ecclesiastical history of New Mexico during the
Spanish period is essentially the history of the Franciscan missions established and maintained by the Order of Friars Minor.[7]

The New Mexico missions were established in 1598; they were

[5] The Spanish colonies were initially placed under the jurisdiction of the
Archdiocese of Seville in Spain. Mexico City was created a diocese in
1530, from the dismemberment of which the diocese of Michoacan was
erected in 1536. In 1546 Mexico City was made an archdiocese, at which
time the Mexican territory was withdrawn from the metropolitan jurisdiction of Seville and placed under that of the Province of Mexico City.
The diocese of Michoacan was divided in 1548, and the new diocese of
Compostela was formed; however, the seat of this diocese was transferred
to Guadalajara in 1560. Guadalajara was dismembered and the diocese of
Durango was erected in 1620.—Cf. *Bulario de la Iglesia Mejicana: Documentos Relativos a Erecciones, Desmembraciones, etc., de Diócesis Mejicanas,* compilados por Jesus Garcia Gutierrez (Mexico, D.F.: Editorial
"Buena Prensa," S.A., 1951), pp. 179, 189, 591.

[6] Cf. Scholes, "Problems in Early Ecclesiastical History of New Mexico,"
New Mexico Historical Review, VII (1932), 43. [Hereinafter this publication will be cited *N.M.H.R.*]

[7] In two Bulls, the *Alias felicis* of Leo X, April 25, 1521, and the famous
Exponi Nobis of Adrian VI, May 10, 1522, the Franciscans, *inter alios,* had
been given full liberty to undertake the work of evangelization in the
Indies and were granted numerous privileges and concessions. The Franciscan superiors could exercise quasi-episcopal powers, and enjoyed the
faculty to confirm, to confer minor orders, to consecrate churches and
ornaments, to issue indulgences, and to dispense from certain matrimonial
impediments. The Bull *Exponi Nobis* contained the famous statement
that these powers were to be exercised in areas where there were no bishops,
or when the Franciscans found themselves two days distant (*"dietae"*)
from a bishopric, and that these Franciscan superiors were to have
"omnimodam auctoritatem Nostram in utroque foro." In 1533, Paul III,
in the Bull *Alias felicis,* confirmed these earlier concessions and abolished
the two-day limitation thereon. The complete texts of the above-mentioned Bulls may be found, in order of reference, in Mendieta, pp. 183-196;
and in Hernaez, *Colección de Bulas, Breves, y Otros Documentos Relativos
a la Iglesia de América y Filipinas* (2 vols., Bruselas: Vromant, 1879), I,
378-379, 385-386, 390-391 (hereinafter cited Hernaez).

erected into a custody in 1616,[8] named the Custody of the Conversion of St. Paul in New Mexico (*Custodia de la Conversión de San Pablo del Nuevo Mexico*), which had for its first custodian Fray Estevan de Perea.[9]

By 1608, Oñate had been succeeded as governor by Pedro de Peralta, who founded Santa Fe and moved the capital there from San Gabriel.

Fray Alonso de Benavides was elected custodian in 1623 and was, moreover, appointed Commissary of the Inquisition of the

---

[8] The traditional date of 1621 can no longer be defended. Students of history will find a scholarly disquisition *in re* in Scholes, "Problems in Early Ecclesiastical History of New Mexico," *N.M.H.R.*, VII (1932), 44 ff.

[9] A brief outline of Franciscan organization follows. The Minister-General presided over the entire Order, and he was assisted in the administration of Franciscan affairs in the Spanish colonies by a Commissary-General for the Indies, with residence in Madrid. Then, within the Americas, two lesser Commissaries-General were appointed, one for New Spain and another for Peru. Areas of missionary endeavor were divided into provinces, each such unit being governed by a Provincial. A custody (Lat. and Span. *custodia*) may be described as an administrative unit which did not have the status of a full-fledged province. Most of the custodies were parts of and subject to a regularly constituted province; thus, a custody was a semi-independent unit, autonomous and self-governing in local matters, but still subject to the general control of the province of which it formed a part. A custody was immediately governed by a custodian (Lat. *custos*, Span. *custodio*). The normal process of development was for the custodies to develop into full-fledged provinces. Within each province and custody were the convents (*conventos*), each of which housed a group of friars under the direction and supervision of a Guardian. The Custody of the Conversion of St. Paul in New Mexico remained under the control of the Province of the Santo Evangelio, Mexico City, down to the end of the Spanish period. The powers exercised by the custodian in New Mexico were very extensive. Not only did he enjoy authority over the friars, but he was prelate of the entire community, civil and ecclesiastical, for he enjoyed quasi-episcopal powers, as granted by the Bulls of Leo X, Adrian VI, and Paul III. He was ecclesiastical judge ordinary for the entire province (in the civil sense), and sometimes Commissary of the Inquisition. Thus, the custodian wielded great power and influence; in fact, except for the civil governor of the province, the custodian was the most powerful personage in New Mexico, and, in some cases, he was actually more influential than the governor.—Cf. Scholes, *ibid.*, pp. 34 ff.

Holy Office in New Mexico. He arrived in New Mexico late in December, 1625, and on January 25, 1626, the first Edict of the Faith was read in the Santa Fe church. Massive mission churches and convents were built in Indian pueblos during the first decades of the century. To add to difficulties, there were repeated clashes between ecclesiastical and civil authorities, mostly over the treatment of the Indians.

After several uprisings, the troubles with the Pueblos reached a climax in 1680, when under the leadership of Popé, a San Juan Indian, they arose simultaneously and attacked the Spanish settlements north of Santa Fe, murdering twenty-one Franciscans, seventy-three soldiers, and more than three hundred others. They then drove the Spaniards out of Santa Fe after a five-day siege.

At least four attempts were made between 1681 and 1693 to reconquer New Mexico. Finally, in 1693, Don Diego de Vargas Zapata Lujan Ponce de Leon reconquered Santa Fe and the province. In the years which followed, there were constant Indian raids, many bloody encounters, and not a few charges and counter-charges by ecclesiastical and civil authorities against each other.

The Spanish Cortes abolished the Inquisition in 1813,[10] and then by decree of August 17, 1820, it suppressed the Society of Jesus throughout the monarchy in one fell swoop.[11]

ARTICLE 3. THE MEXICAN PERIOD: 1821 TO 1846

On September 28, 1821, Mexico declared its independence from Spain. By law of April 16, 1834, the Mexican government ordered all missions of the Republic to be secularized.[12] And "after . . . the expulsion of the Spanish Franciscans, the wants of the par-

---

[10] *Legislación Mexicana: Colección completa de las disposiciones legislativas expedidas desde la independencia de la República (1687-1889)*, ordenada por Manuel Dublan y Jose Maria Lozano, edición oficial (19 vols., Mexico, D.F.: Imprenta del Comercio, 1876-1890), I, p. 399, n. 109 (hereinafter cited *Legislación Mexicana*).

[11] *Legislación Mexicana*, I, p. 522, n. 223.

[12] *Legislación Mexicana*, II, p. 689, n. 1395.

ishes at first so flourishing under the saintly Friars were supplied by secular priests sent from Durango." [13]   It was during this period, in 1832, that the bishop of Durango appointed the Reverend Juan Felipe Ortiz, a native of Santa Fe, Vicar General Forane of New Mexico.[14]

New Mexico remained under Mexican sovereignty for only a quarter of a century.[15]   In 1835, President Santa Ana sent Colonel Albino Perez to govern New Mexico. Perez met with opposition. A conspiracy among the Indians, fomented by prominent New Mexicans, brought the northern Pueblos and many settlers to Santa Cruz with the aim of capturing Santa Fe and installing a rebel regime. Perez was beheaded. On August 10, 1837, the insurrectionists took possession of the Governor's Palace and installed a Taos Indian, Jose Gonzales, as governor. The following month, General Manuel Armijo, although suspected of having been one of the main instigators of the rebellion, gathered a military force and proclaimed a counter revolution. Gonzales was shot. Armijo was then confirmed as governor and for eight years ruled New Mexico with a heavy hand.

[13] Defouri, p. 27.

[14] Besides the visits the Franciscans received from their own superiors, they also had those of the bishops of Durango, who had jurisdiction over all the missions of New Mexico. The territory received the pastoral visitation of Bishop Benito Crespi in 1725, that of Bishop Martin Elizacochea in 1737, and in 1760 that of his successor, Bishop Pedro Tamaron. In 1817 the province was visited by the vicar general of Bishop Juan de Castañiza, followed in 1833 and 1845 by the episcopal visitations of Bishop Antonio Zubiria.—Cf. Salpointe, pp. 128, 165; cf. also Sister Mary Ramona, S.C.N., "The Ecclesiastical Status of New Mexico (1680-1875)," *The Catholic Historical Review,* XIV (1928-1929), 525-568. Writing in 1812, a Spanish priest observed that conditions in New Mexico were lamentable, priests and people not knowing whether or not there was a bishop since they had not seen one in over fifty years.—Pino, *Noticias Históricas y Estadísticas de la Antigua Provincia del Nuevo Mexico . . . (1812),* adicionadas por el Lic. D. Antonio Barreiro en 1839, y ultimamente anotadas por el Lic. D. Jose A. de Escudero (Mexico, D.F.: Imprenta de Lara, 1849), p. 31.

[15] The Province of New Mexico was erected into a Territory by the Mexican Federal Constitution of 1824.—Mayer, II, 15.

ARTICLE 4.   THE TERRITORIAL PERIOD TO STATEHOOD:
1846 TO 1912

On May 13, 1846, President Polk declared war on Mexico.
The Army of the West was under the command of General
Stephen Watts Kearney, who, on August 18th, entered Santa Fe
unopposed. From the Palace of Governors, on the following day,
he issued a proclamation by which he took formal possession of
of New Mexico. A code of laws, known as the Kearney Code,
was promulgated, but it was not until the Treaty of Guadalupe
Hidalgo was ratified on May 30, 1848, that New Mexico was
formally ceded to the United States. Congress provided for a
territorial form of government, and the first territorial legislature
met in June, 1851.

Indian raids continued to harass New Mexico, numerous
skirmishes being fought with Apaches, Navajos, and Utes. There
was strife between military and civil authorities, and there was
dissension among the clergy, finally settled by Bishop John B.
Lamy, who arrived in New Mexico in 1851.

By decree of July 19, 1850, Pope Pius IX had made New
Mexico a Vicariate Apostolic,[16] and on the 23rd day of the same
month appointed for it as Vicar Apostolic, *in partibus,* with the
title of Bishop of Agathonica, the Reverend John B. Lamy.[17]
Pope Pius IX, by decree of July 29, 1853, raised the Vicariate
Apostolic of New Mexico to a diocese with Santa Fe as the see
city and as a suffragan see of the archdiocese of St. Louis,[18]

[16] Archives of the Archdiocese of Santa Fe, 1850 diocesan document
(File 1), No. 1. [Citations in this work to the archives of the Archdiocese
of Santa Fe will follow the actual system of classification used in the
Chancery Office as developed by Fray Angelico Chavez, O.F.M., in his
descriptive index therefor, *Archives of the Archdiocese of Santa Fe:
1678-1900* (Washington, D.C.: Academy of American Franciscan History,
1957). Thus, all such references shall hereinafter be cited as *Santa Fe,*
followed by the date of the document in question and by the pertinent file
designation. Since the Chavez catalogue is arranged in chronological order
within each primary division (Mission, Diocesan, *Patentes,* etc.), reference
thereto becomes invitingly facile, and hence no further reference to Chavez
will be made.]

[17] *Santa Fe,* 1850 Diocesan 2, 3.

[18] *Santa Fe,* 1853 Diocesan 12.

with Bishop Lamy as its first bishop.[19] Four years later, on February 15, 1857, Bishop Lamy held the first synod of the diocese of Santa Fe. The second synod, again under Bishop Lamy, was celebrated on September 16, 1861.[20]

Early in the Civil War, southern New Mexico was occupied by Confederate forces. In January, 1862, General Hopkins H. Sibley defeated the Federals at Valverde. Albuquerque and Santa Fe fell to the Rebels, but not for more than a month.

A third synod was held under Bishop Lamy in 1874.[21] On February 12, 1875, the diocese of Santa Fe was erected into a Metropolitan See, and Bishop Lamy was made its archbishop, with the Vicariates of Arizona and Colorado as suffragans.[22] In quick succession, the fourth, fifth, and sixth synods were held under Archbishop J. B. Salpointe in 1888, 1891, and 1893.[23]

New Mexico had striven for statehood for over half a century. Several efforts had failed, until in 1911 President Taft signed the resolution admitting New Mexico as the 47th state of the Union, thus ending a sixty-year struggle for statehood. On January 6, 1912, President Taft signed the proclamation admitting New Mexico to the Union.

[19] *Santa Fe*, 1853 Diocesan 13.

[20] *Santa Fe*, 1861 Diocesan 6. Four provincial councils had been held in Mexico City in 1555, 1565, 1585, and 1770.—Cf. Vera, *Apuntamientos Históricos de los Concilios Provinciales Mexicanos* (Mexico, D.F.: Tipografía Guadalupana, 1893), pp. 9-37; cf. also Mansi, *Sacrorum Conciliorum Nova et Amplissima Collectio* (53 vols. in 60, Parisiis, 1901-1927), XXXIV, 1015-1228 (hereinafter cited Mansi). However, this former ecclesiastical legislation "left little if any influence upon the early synodal enactments of the dioceses created out of this once immense Spanish domain."— Guilday, *A History of the Councils of Baltimore* (New York: The Macmillan Co., 1932), p. 28.

[21] *Santa Fe*, 1874 Diocesan 10.

[22] *Santa Fe*, 1875 Diocesan 12. In 1859, the Territories of Arizona and Colorado had been annexed to the diocese of Santa Fe.—Cf. Salpointe, pp. 224, 228.

[23] *Santa Fe*, 1888 Diocesan 1. The seventh synod was held in 1958 by Archbishop Edwin V. Byrne.

CHAPTER II

LEGAL BACKGROUND OF NEW MEXICO, WITH SPECIAL REFERENCE TO THE ADMINISTRATION, OWNERSHIP, AND TENURE OF CHURCH PROPERTY

ARTICLE 1. PAPAL CONCESSIONS TO THE SPANISH CROWN

Soon after the return of Columbus to Spain, Ferdinand and Isabella applied to the Holy See to confirm them in their recent discoveries, and to invest them with an extent of jurisdiction like to what was formerly conferred on the kings of Portugal. It was an ancient opinion, perhaps as old as the crusades, that the Pope, as Vicar of Christ, had competent authority to dispose of all countries inhabited by heathen nations in favor of Christian potentates.[1] The Roman Pontiff did give the Spanish monarchs a number of very important concessions; however, Spain did not rest her title alone on the grant of the Pope. She, with other European nations, also claimed and exercised the right of discovery—a right which was deemed sufficient to maintain a title to any part of the world.[2]

Section 1. Alexander VI: "Inter Caetera" (1493)

By means of the very famous Bull, *Inter caetera*, issued on May 4, 1493, Alexander VI gave to Ferdinand and Isabella and to their successors title to the lands discovered, or thereafter to be discovered, by them. The Pope begins by praising the zeal of the Spanish monarchs in the propagation of Catholicism; he cites the liberation of Granada and the expedition of Christopher Columbus; and exhorts Ferdinand and Isabella to continue their

---

[1] Prescott, *History of the Reign of Ferdinand and Isabella* (2 vols., 3. ed., New York: American Publishers Corp., 1838), I, 370.

[2] Cf. Hall, *The Laws of Mexico: A Compilation and Treatise Relating to Real Property, Mines, Water Rights, Personal Rights, Contracts, and Inheritances* (San Francisco: A. L. Bancroft & Co., 1885), p. 2, § 2 (hereinafter cited Hall).

zeal in propagating the Faith. To this end Alexander VI gives the Spanish monarchs title over the Indies, with the conditional obligation of carrying on the conversion of the aboriginal population. The salient part of the Bull follows:

> . . . Motu proprio . . . omnes insulas et terras firmas inventas et inveniendas, detectas et detegendas . . . , quae per alium regem aut principem Christianum non fuerint actualiter possessae . . . , cum omnibus illarum dominiis, civitatibus, castris, locis et villis, iuribusque et iurisdictionibus ac pertinentibus universis, vobis, haeredibusque et successoribus vestris (Castellae et Legionis Regibus) in perpetuum, tenore praesentium, donamus et assignamus: vosque et haeredes ac successores praefatos illarum dominos cum plena, libera et omnimoda potestate, auctoritate et iurisdictione facimus, constituimus et deputamus.[3]

Section 2. Alexander VI: "Eximiae Devotionis" (1493)

On the same day, May 4, 1493, by virtue of a second Bull, *Eximiae devotionis*, Alexander VI gave the Spanish monarchy all the concessions, privileges, and rights that former popes had conceded to the kings of Portugal in lands discovered beyond the seas. The most noteworthy of these concessions was the right of patronage.[4]

Section 3. Alexander VI: "Eximiae Devotionis" (1501)

Eight years later, on November 16, 1501, Alexander VI granted to the Crown, through a third Bull, *Eximiae devotionis*, the right to collect the tithes (*diezmos*) in the American colonies, with the condition that the Crown provide revenues for the establishment of churches and missions. This grant reads, in part, as follows:

> Nos . . . vobis et successoribus vestris . . . , ut, in insulis praedictis, ab illarum incolis et habitatoribus . . . , postquam illae acquisitae fuerint (ut praefertur), assignata prius realiter et cum effectu, iuxta ordinationem tunc Dioecesan-

---

[3] For the complete text of *Inter caetera*, cf. *Magnum Bullarium Romanum, a Beato Leone Magno usque ad S.D.N. Benedictum XIII* . . . , editio novissima (8 vols., Luxemburgi, 1727), I, 454; cf. also Hernaez, I, 12.

[4] The text of this Bull may be found in Hernaez, I, 15. Cf. *infra*, Section 1, Article 5, this chapter, for a discussion on the right of patronage.

orum locorum, quorum conscientias super hoc oneramus, ecclesiis in dictis insulis erigendis, per vos et successores vestros praefatos, de vestris et eorum bonis dote sufficiente, ex qua illis praesidentes earumque rectores se commode sustentare, et onera dictis ecclesiis pro tempore incumbentia perferre, ac cultum divinum . . . debite exercere, iuraque episcopalia persolvere possint, Decimam . . . percipere et licite ac libere valeatis, auctoritate Apostolica, tenore praesentium, de specialis dono gratiae indulgemus.[5]

Section 4.   Julius II: "Universalis Ecclesiae" (1508)

Pope Julius II, on July 28, 1508, granted to the Spanish Crown the right of universal patronage over the Church in the Indies by virtue of the Bull, *Universalis Ecclesiae*.[6]

On the basis of the foregoing concessions, the Crown established an unparalleled control over ecclesiastical organization in America.

ARTICLE 2.   SPANISH LAW FOR AMERICA: CODE OF THE INDIES

The laws which were enacted in Spain for the government of the colonies were issued in the form of *cédulas, decretos, resoluciones, ordenamientos, reglamentos, autos acordados,* and *pragmaticas*.[7]   Naturally enough, these laws soon became so numerous that it was difficult for the authorities to keep informed on the divers subjects incident to administration. To remedy this, a complete compilation of the laws governing the colonies was ordered; but it was not completed until 1680, under the reign of Charles II (1665-1700). This code is known as the *Recopilación de las Leyes de los Reynos de las Indias,* which represents a digest of the *cédulas, decretos,* etc., issued at different times for the government of the American colonies.

[5] For the complete text of *Eximiae devotionis,* cf. Hernaez, I, 20.

[6] The concessions were indeed vast: "Nos . . . ius patronatus et praesentandi personas idoneas ad . . . metropolitanas ac cathedrales ecclesias et monasteria ac dignitates . . . ac quaecumque alia beneficia ecclesiastica et pia loca in dictis insulis et locis . . . Ferdinando Regi et Ioannae Reginae . . . , auctoritate Apostolica, tenore praesentium, concedimus."—Cf. Hernaez, I, 24, for the complete text of the present Bull.

[7] Schmidt, *The Civil Law of Spain and Mexico* (New Orleans: Thomas Rea, 1851), p. 93 (hereinafter cited Schmidt).

The *Recopilación de las Indias* was limited in its range. While this code regulated, to a greater or lesser extent, the ecclesiastical, military, political, and fiscal affairs of Spanish America, it was a mere enumeration of exceptions to the civil laws of Spain.[8] And it was expressly stated in the *Recopilación de las Indias* that in cases wherein the laws and provisions of this code failed to provide, the laws of the Spanish kingdom, particularly as found in the *Recopilación, Siete Partidas,* and *Leyes de Toro* [9] should obtain.[10]

Prior to the time of Philip IV (1621-1665), all laws enacted in Spain applied equally in the Spanish American colonies. But at this time it was provided that no law enacted for the government of Spain should apply to America unless accompanied with a *cédula* so declaring it, sent out by the Council of the Indies. It necessarily follows, therefore, that many laws subsequently enacted for Spain did not apply to America; the converse is also true, that many laws enacted especially for America were not in force in Spain. But after the assembly of the Cortes in Spain in 1810,[11] all laws in force in Spain also obtained in the American colonies, without special enactment.[12] Consequently, "it may be claimed with authority, that the civil laws of Old Spain were in

[8] Schmidt, p. 95.

[9] These are all codes of Spanish civil law. Cf. the subsequent Article in this chapter for a consideration thereof.

[10] ". . . En lo que no estuviere decidido por las leyes de esta recopilación, para las decisiones de las causas y su determinación, se guarden las leyes de la Recopilación y Partidas de estos reynos de Castilla, conforme a la ley siguiente."—*Recopilación de las Leyes de los Reynos de las Indias, mandadas imprimir y publicar por la Magestad Católica del Rey Don Carlos II* (9 Books in 4 vols., 2. ed., Madrid: Antonio Balbas, 1756), lib. II, tit. 1, ley 1 (hereinafter cited *Recopilación de las Indias*). Also: "Ordenamos y mandamos, que en todos los casos . . . en que no estuviese decidido . . . por las leyes de esta recopilación . . . , se guarden las leyes de nuestro reyno de Castilla conforme a la de Toro . . ."—*Ibid.*, ley 2.

[11] On April 14, 1809, the Spanish possessions in America were declared to be no longer colonies, but integral parts of the Spanish monarchy, and given direct representation in the Central Council of the Government of the Kingdom.—Reynolds, p. 29.

[12] Blackmar, *Spanish Institutions of the Southwest* (Baltimore: Johns Hopkins Press, 1891), p. 62 (hereinafter cited Blackmar).

most cases the laws of New Spain." [13]   Besides studying the provisions of the *Recopilación de las Indias,* then, one must make a summary investigation of the old Spanish law in order to have a complete understanding of the decrees and mind of the legislator with reference to any given matter within Spanish America in general, and New Mexico in particular.   Before instituting such a study in regard to church property, then, one must gain some understanding of the Spanish civil codes, because one remarkable feature in the legislation of Spain is that at no time was any attempt made, upon the promulgation of a new code, to abrogate the old one.   Hence, all the different codes of Spain must be examined in order to determine the law on any given subject.

ARTICLE 3.   THE SPANISH CODES OF LAW [14]

The Spanish system of law was developed with Roman law as a foundation and with many ideas taken from the Visigoths and the Moors who, during successive periods, occupied the Spanish peninsula.[15] Their legal system has always been, and still is, a structure of statute law; the common law institution of *stare decisis* is unknown under the Spanish system.

For the purpose of outlining the background of the Spanish legal system as it existed throughout the time that New Mexico was subject thereto, one may divide its development and evolution into four periods, as follows:

1.   Spain under the Romans: to 415.
2.   Spain under the Visigoths: 415 to 710.
3.   Spain under the Arabs: 710 to 1492.
4.   Spain after the expulsion of the Arabs: 1492 to 1805.

Section 1.   Spain Under the Romans: to 415

During the first period, naturally enough, Roman law governed the Spanish peninsula, which was in fact a province of the

[13] *Loc. cit.*

[14] Unless otherwise noted in specific instances, the synopsis on the Spanish codes of law in this Article has been condensed from the treatment thereof in Schmidt, pp. 85-89, and Madden, *Political Theory and Law in Medieval Spain* (New York: Fordham University Press, 1930), pp. 29-41.

[15] Kerr, *A Handbook of Mexican Law* (Chicago: Pan American Law Book Co., 1909), p. 1.

Roman empire. This period comprises a space of about six centuries, if counted from the close of the Second Punic War until the conquest by the Visigoths.

Section 2. Spain Under the Visigoths: 415 to 710

The laws of the Visigoths supplanted Roman law, but this change was gradual, inasmuch as the conquerors and the conquered were for a long time governed by their own peculiar legislation. At the middle of the seventh century, the Roman and Visigothic laws coalesced: the king of the Visigoths, Chindaswinth (642-653), promulgated the resultant new code. This remarkable code was published under the title of *Forum Iudicum*, appeared later as the *Liber Iudicum*, and is commonly known as the *Fuero Juzgo*. It is considered by jurists to be the source of Spanish jurisprudence.[16] An analysis of the *Fuero Juzgo* shows that "it is infinitely more rational, mild and philosophical than all other attempts at legislation of the same period, and that it contains provisions which retain their force and efficacy even at this day." [17] It is claimed, and not without reason, that the *Fuero Juzgo* was, to a large extent, the result of the councils of Toledo in which the interests of the whole country were represented.[18]

[16] Cf. Blackmar, p. 26; cf. also Ziegler, *Church and State in Visigothic Spain,* The Catholic University of America Theological Studies, n. 32 (Washington, D.C.: The Catholic University of America, 1930), pp. 101-105.

[17] Schmidt, p. 86.

[18] Blackmar, p. 26. It is interesting to note that "the first book of the *Fuero Juzgo,* entitled *de instrumentis legalibus* and intended as an introduction to the compilation, had its source in the fundamenal ideas of [Saint] Isidore's [of Seville] *Etimologiae.* Under two titles, *de legislatore* and *de legibus,* it consists of an exposition of the philosophy of law and government, enumerating the duties of the lawgiver and laying down the characteristics which law should possess and the ends it should attain. Although at the present time these principles appear as commonplace, they were an attempt to bind rulers by ethical standards and to subordinate them to the conceptions of the divine law and the requirements of the common welfare. These formulas are characteristic of the idea of legislation depending on something essentially higher than the mere will of the prince. Much of this exposition is taken almost verbatim from the definitions of Isidore."—Vance, *The Background of Hispanic-American Law* (New York: Central Book Co., 1943), pp. 49-50.

Section 3.   Spain Under the Arabs: 710 to 1492

Under the subjugation of the Moors, Spain still retained its ancient laws, although it became subject to the Moslem sway. Various small States were formed, and the feudal laws were introduced to a greater or lesser extent.

When the power of Castile finally became predominant, its monarchs promulgated general codes, among which the *Fuero Viejo,* towards the end of the tenth century, was more particularly designed to define and sanction the prerogatives of the nobility.   Alfonso X (El Sabio, 1252-1284) prepared a general code, as an introduction to which he caused the *Fuero Real* to be published in 1255. The general code, known as the *Siete Partidas,* did not become the law of the land until nearly a century after its first appearance, when it was promulgated by Alfonso XI (1312-1350). The latter monarch also published the *Ordenamiento de Alcalá,* a code intended primarily to regulate the form of judicial proceedings.

In consequence of the great number of codes published during this period, the jurisprudence of Spain became exceedingly complicated.   A reform was badly needed, but none was effected.

Section 4.   Spain After the Expulsion of the Arabs: 1492 to 1805

Ferdinand and Isabella attempted to introduce some order into the system of legislation, but the *Ordenamiento Real* and the *Leyes de Toro* published by them for this purpose, instead of producing the desired effect, tended rather to increase the confusion.

Philip II (1556-1598) promulgated the *Nueva Recopilación,* a general code which furnished some guide to the general law of the kingdom.   It was far from being satisfactory, however.   From its publication, in 1567, to 1805, when the *Novisima Recopilación* made its appearance, the *Nueva Recopilación* was modified from time to time by means of royal decrees which were published as supplements thereto under the title of *Autos Acordados.*

It must be observed that the *Fuero Viejo* was so modified and changed by subsequent enactments that it can no longer be consulted for any useful purpose.   And all that remains useful in the *Ordenamiento Real,* the *Autos Acordados,* and *Leyes de Toro* has been incorporated into the *Novisima Recopilación.* The general legislation of Spain, during the Spanish period in New Mexico, is therefore to be found in the *Fuero Juzgo, Fuero Real, Siete Partidas,* and in the *Novisima Recopilación.* In consulting these codes, one experiences no difficulty as to the authority of the *Novisima Recopilación,* which is the latest authority. But when this code is silent, "there exists some diversity of opinion as to which of the remaining codes ought to prevail, some authors giving preference to the *Partidas,* others to the *Fuero Juzgo,* or the *Fuero Real.*" [19]

ARTICLE 4. PROVISIONS OF SPANISH LAW REGARDING CHURCH PROPERTY

In general, the Spanish codes of law treat the question of church property under three main divisions: gifts, administration in general, and alienation. These vehicles, it must be understood, are more or less wide, and patient of greater or lesser elasticity. It is to be remembered, too, that the right of the Church to acquire, hold, and administer goods and property was fully recognized by the civil law. Consequently, nowhere in the tremendous mass of Spanish legislation is explicit mention made of the fact that the Church has a right to temporal possessions. That was presumed. Indeed, the primary concern of the civil law in matters of ecclesiastical property was to provide that the

[19] Schmidt, pp. 88-89. In order to present some idea of the mass of Spanish legislation in force, at least theoretically, in New Mexico during Spanish rule, the writer is subjoining a list of the different codes, with an account of the year of promulgation, and of the number of books, titles, and laws they contain.

Year	Code	Books	Titles	Laws
693	Fuero Juzgo	12	55	560
992	Fuero Viejo	5	33	229
1255	Fuero Real	4	72	549
1263	Siete Partidas	7	182	2479
1348	Ordenamiento de Alcalá	7	32	125
1490	Ordenamiento Real	8	115	1133
1567	Nueva Recopilación	9	214	3391
1745	Autos Acordados	9	110	1134
1805	Novisima Recopilación	12	330	4036
1680	Recopilación de las Indias	9	218	6447

Church's possessions be fully guarded and that its rights thereto
be guaranteed. Moreover, Spanish legislation was not concerned
with the manner in which church goods and property were held.
In regard to ecclesiastical property in general from the beginning
of the Christian Era, "although there is a controversy about the
precise manner in which property was held, it appears that
ecclesiastical authorities, as individuals, acquired actual ownership of the necessary goods and likewise managed all of the
possessions. It was understood by all the faithful, however, that
the property was held by the ecclesiastical society as such." [20]

Section 1. Concerning Gifts

The main concern of Spanish legislation in regard to the
temporal goods of the Church was that ecclesiastical property
should be properly safeguarded and remain in the ownership of
the Church. The *Liber Iudicum* provides as follows:

> Si famulorum meritis iuste compellimur debite compensare
> lucra mercedis, quanto iam copiosius pro remediis animarum
> divinis cultibus, et terrena debemus impendere, et impensa
> legum soliditate servare. Quapropter quaecumque res
> sanctis Dei basilicis, aut per principum, aut per quorumlibet
> fidelium donationes conlatae reperiuntur, votive ac poten-
> tialiter pro certo censemus, ut in earum iure inrevocabili
> modo legum aeternitate firmentur. [21]

The Visigoths, then, provided that all temporal goods ceded to a
church by anyone—from a monarch on down to the humblest
member of the faithful—must be regarded as owned by that
church.

It is remarkable that the other codes [22] repeat the provisions

[20] Wiggins, *Property Laws of the State of Ohio Affecting Church Property,* The Catholic University of America Canon Law Studies, n. 367
(Washington, D.C.: The Catholic University of America Press, 1956), pp.
6-7 (hereinafter cited Wiggins).

[21] Lib. V, tit. 1, ley 1. All citations in this work from the *Fuero Juzgo*
are from *Los Códigos Españoles, Concordados y Anotados* (14 codes in 12
vols., Madrid: La Publicidad, 1847-1851) [hereinafter cited *Los Códigos
Españoles*].

[22] It must be noted, *semel pro semper,* that the following codes are silent
in regard to ecclesiastical goods: *Fuero Viejo, Leyes del Estilo, Espéculo,
Leyes para los Adelantados Mayores, Leyes Nuevas,* and the *Ordenamiento*

of the *Fuero Juzgo* almost verbatim *in re,* with little more than slight changes in phraseology.[23] The *Novisima Recopilación* adds nothing substantial to the provisions of the *Fuero Real,* and the latter merely adds to those of the *Fuero Juzgo* that the goods of a church are in the dominion thereof: ". . . que . . . sean . . . en su poder." [24]

Section 2. Concerning Administration in General

The *Fuero Juzgo,*[25] the *Fuero Real,*[26] the *Ordenanzas Reales de Montalvo,*[27] and the *Novisima Recopilación* [28] all firmly establish the precept that the temporal goods of the Church are to be well safeguarded. And, in particular, bishops are charged with the obligation of making a complete inventory of the goods of their bishoprics as soon as they take canonical possession thereof. This written inventory is to be given to the successor in office, with the view of forestalling any and all kinds of dispossession by the heirs of the decedent bishop during the interregnum. The following are the provisions of the *Fuero Real* in this matter:

> . . . Because the Holy Church is to be loved and honored by us above all mundane things . . . , We wish to indicate how ecclesiastical goods are to be safeguarded. Wherefore, We direct that as soon as the bishop, or the one elected has been confirmed [in office], wishes to take possession of the goods of the church or of his bishopric, he do so before the chapter of his church; and these are to consign to writing an account of all the goods which he receives, be they chattels, real

de las Tafurerias. It must also be remembered that the eighty-three laws of the *Leyes de Toro* are now included in the *Novisima Recopilación;* accordingly, the provisions of the former code as such will not be considered separately herein.

[23] Cf. *Fuero Real,* lib. I, tit. 5, ley 1; *Ordenanzas Reales de Castilla de Montalvo,* lib. I, tit. 2, ley 1; *Ordenamiento de Alcalá,* tit. 32, ley 53; *Novisima Recopilación,* lib. I, tit. 5, ley 1. [The source for all references to, and all citations from, Spanish civil law codes in this work is *Los Códigos Españoles.*]

[24] *Fuero Real,* lib. I, tit. 5, ley 1.

[25] Lib. V, tit. 1, ley 2.

[26] Lib. I, tit. 5, ley 2.

[27] Lib. I, tit. 2, ley 2.

[28] Lib. I, tit. 5, ley 2.

property, privileges, or legal instruments (*cartas*) of the churches, as well as [an account] of what the church owes or of what is owed thereto; [all] in such wise that the bishop's successor in office will be in a position, by means of said inventory, to demand the goods of the church: and [in order that] if [the successor] find that some item on said inventory has been sold or unlawfully alienated, he will be able to demand its return to the church, giving the buyer the price paid therefor, if it appears that said consideration accrued to the church; but if the consideration was not placed in the church's treasury, the church is to demand what is its own and is not to be held to pay the price; [in such instances] the heirs of the bishop who alienated the thing are to remunerate [the buyer] ... And We direct that the foregoing provisions also obtain with regard to monasteries and abbacies.[29]

If it is true that Spanish law fully recognized the right of the Church to acquire and administer temporal goods, it is also true that such recognition and acknowledgment was predicated of a given church or diocese as moral personalities, as canonical corporations. Such is patently evidenced by the fact that the bishop was considered to hold the goods of his diocese in trust and that, upon his death, his natural heirs were estopped from dispossessing the moral personality of its patrimony.

A further argument showing that the particular canonical corporation as such owned and had the inherent right to administer its temporal goods is adduced from the fact that Spanish law was careful to draw a clear distinction between the ecclesiastical corporation and the administrator thereof. The law provided that clerics and religious, as physical persons, could own and administer their own personal estates. In the matter of the acquisition of property by clerics, the law distinguished between property acquired personally by the clerics *quocumque iusto titulo* and property acquired *intuitu ecclesiae*. In the former case, the clerics acquired personal dominion thereto and could freely dispose thereof, even by testament. And if they died intestate, their natural heirs within seven degrees of consanguinity succeeded to the estate; if the decedents left no heirs within that range, the church which they served succeeded.[30]

29 *Fuero Real*, lib. I, tit. 5, ley 2. [Translation by the writer.]

30 *Fuero Juzgo*, lib. IV, tit. 2, ley 12; *Siete Partidas*, Part. I, tit. 6, ley 53.

There is one big difference, however, between property owned by a church as a canonical corporation and property held personally by clerics: the former was immune from taxation,[31] while the latter was subject to the assessments (*contribuciones*) levied against all other landed property.[32] Although the term *mortmain* as such did not originate until the publication of the *Magna Charta* in 1215 in England,[33] the definition of *manus mortua* was certainly realized in Spain almost from the beginning: church corporations did not pay the taxes imposed upon physical persons, and every acquisition of property by the former was in fact a detriment to the royal treasury (*hacienda real*). The term *manos muertas* is a commonplace in the *Recopilación de las Indias*.

Religious communities, too, were regarded by Spanish law as corporations capable of acquiring property [34] and administering such goods:

> ... Those religious communities which, in accordance with the dispositions of the Council of Trent (cap. 2, sess. 25, *de Regularibus*), are capable of acquiring temporal goods may administer said properties through their religious superiors (*oficiales*), with the express condition that all direct and indirect illicit trading (*negociaciones*) proscribed by the sacred canons be avoided.[35]

Section 3. Concerning Alienation

In the matter of unlawful alienation of church property, the king trusted no one—not the prelates, not even himself.[36] No one, then, could unlawfully alienate church property. Even the following exception in favor of the king carried a saving clause:

[31] *Ordenamiento Real*, lib. I, tit. 3, ley 27; *Siete Partidas*, Part. I, tit. 11, ley 1; *Novisima Recopilación*, lib. I, tit. 9, leyes 1, 2, 3, 6, 7, 8, 12, 14; lib. VI, tit. 18, ley 3.

[32] *Siete Partidas*, Part. I, tit. 6, ley 53.

[33] Wiggins, pp. 22-23.

[34] *Fuero Real*, lib. I, tit. 5, ley 2.

[35] *Novisima Recopilación*, lib. I, tit. 28, ley 8. [Translation by the writer.]

[36] This distrust was apparently not without foundation. The desamortization and sequestration of church property by royal decree will be considered in subsequent Articles.

The king may not appropriate the treasury or [other] goods of the churches; but in the event of war or other great calamity, the king may take said treasury, on the condition that he afterward restore the whole amount to the churches.[37]

It is interesting to see the evolution of Spanish law in the matter of unlawful alienation of church property by the trustee of the canonical corporation in question. The *Fuero Juzgo* provides as follows:

If any bishop or priest or any other cleric should sell or otherwise assign anything belonging to the church without the consent of the other clerics, We decree that such transfer is null and void, if it was not effected in accordance with the norms established by the decrees of the Popes.[38]

The provisions of the *Novisima Recopilación*[39] are substantially the same as those of the *Fuero Real:*

No bishop, abbot, or any other prelate may sell or otherwise alienate anything with which he has become possessed *intuitu ecclesiae;* if, however, he acquires or inherits something *intuitu personae physicae*, he may dispose of it as he will.[40]

In comparing the language of the *Fuero Juzgo* with that of the *Fuero Real* regarding this matter, one cannot help being impressed with the merging of conservatism with an evolution which prevents the law from becoming something dead, soulless. In comparison, the *Fuero Real* is crisp, clear-cut, incisive.

The foregoing observations obtain with even more emphasis when the provisions of the *Siete Partidas* are examined. This remarkable code rules as follows:

Alienation is any act or contract which men enter into, or perform among themselves, by which the ownership of property passes from one person to another . . . The property of a church should not be alienated except for the following special reasons. First, on account of some important debt which the church owes, which it cannot discharge in any other way. Second, to liberate its parishioners from captivity, where they have not property with which to liberate

37 *Novisima Recopilación,* lib. I, tit. 5, ley 8. [Translation by the writer.]

38 Lib. V, tit. 1, ley 3. [Translation by the writer.]

39 Lib. I, tit. 5, ley 2.

40 Lib. I, tit. 5, ley 3. [Translation by the writer.]

themselves. Third, to give food to the poor in time of famine. Fourth, to build the church. Fifth, to purchase property near at hand to increase the size of a cemetery. Sixth, for the benefit of the church, where something which was not good was sold or exchanged in order to purchase what is better.

For any of these six reason [*sic*] the property of a church can be alienated, and in no other way, unless it has some real estate which is not profitable: for property of this kind can be transferred to any person for a certain space of time, in return for a consideration paid for it, as stated above; although no other urgent necessity may exist, why this should be done for any of the six above-named reasons.[41]

And:

Prelates have the power to alienate the property of their churches for any of the six reasons stated in the preceding law. But it is understood that this should be done with the consent of their chapters, and that they should do it in the following way. For instance, where the church has personal property which comes under the above-named conditions, it should be sold before real estate; and with regard to chattels, such as are not sacred should be sold before those that are; and if it should become necessary to sell holy objects, such as chalices, crosses, and vestments of any kind, they should be sold to some church which desires to purchase them, rather than to any man: and where a church buys them they can be sold for the purpose for which they are made, but if they are sold to an individual, and are of metal, they should be melted before they are delivered to him. Where movable property is not sufficient for the purpose, then real estate of this kind can be sold, and that which is of least value should first be disposed of.

Although prelates can sell, or convey the property of the church for any of the above-named reasons, yet lands which emperors, kings, or their wives have given to churches cannot be alienated in any way whatsoever.[42]

The *Siete Partidas* also provides that a church can claim its property from those who unlawfully alienate it, or from anyone in whose possession it may be found.[43]

[41] *Siete Partidas,* Part. I, tit. 4, ley 1. [Translation by Scott, *Las Siete Partidas,* translation and notes by Samuel P. Scott (New York: Commerce Clearing House, Inc., 1931), p. 182 (hereinafter cited Scott).]

[42] *Siete Partidas,* Part. I, tit. 14, ley 2. [Translation by Scott, p. 183.]

[43] Part. I, tit. 14, ley 12.

It is against the background which has been delineated that the development of the Church in New Mexico must be viewed. At the same time, however, we must not lose sight of the fact that our forefathers were not so much interested in the legal niceties involved in connection with the operation and affairs of canonical corporations as they were with the very demanding and tangible problems of a livelihood, of living their Faith in the face of so many obstacles, of communicating that Faith to the infidels.

ARTICLE 5. PROVISIONS OF THE *Recopilación de las Indias* REGARDING CHURCH PROPERTY

As an *avant-propos* to the matter here under discussion, it is essential that an earlier observation be recalled, viz., that the *Recopilación de las Indias,* albeit quite extensive, was limited in its range in the sense that its provisions constituted mere exceptions to the civil law of the mother country. Where, therefore, the laws of this code failed to make due provision, the laws of Spain were operative.[44] It follows as a natural consequence, then, that the civil law codes furnished the ultimate basis upon which the *Recopilación de las Indias* was radicated, and that the latter is unintelligible if one prescinds from the jurisprudence established by the former. The situation might be likened somewhat to that existing in our country, particularly in yesteryears, where the English common law is looked to in the case of lacunae in Anglo-American jurisprudence. Perhaps a more reasonable facsimile exists at Canon law: there are numerous exceptions to the common law of the Church in vogue and force in missionary areas of the world; nonetheless, the Code of Canon Law, and not the exceptions thereto, constitutes the basic jurisprudence of the Church even in such areas, and therefore recourse to the Code of Canon Law must be had wherever a hiatus exists in the special laws to which reference has been made.

Section 1. *"Real Patronazgo": Right of Patronage*

As previously stated,[45] Pope Julius II in 1508 granted to the Spanish Crown the right of universal patronage over the Church

---

[44] Lib. II, tit. 1, leyes 1, 2.

[45] Cf. *supra,* p. 12.

in the Indies by virtue of the Bull, *Universalis Ecclesiae*.[46] Reference to that grant is made in the *Recopilación de las Indias*, wherein it is decreed that the right of patronage belongs to the Crown *in solidum*.[47]

Briefly, the right of patronage comprehends the sum total of the privileges which, together with certain burdens, are granted by the Church to Catholic founders of a church, chapel, or benefice.[48] In that body of privileges, the most noteworthy is that by which the patron presents a cleric to a vacant church or a vacant benefice.[49] Actually, rudiments of the right of patronage existed in the Church almost from the beginning; [50] however, the Code of Canon Law [51] abolishes henceforth the right of patronage,[52] without prejudice, however, to such right if it was acquired before the promulgation of the code.[53]

[46] For the text of this Bull, cf. Hernaez, I, 24.

[47] Lib. I, tit. 6, ley 1.

[48] Canon 1448.

[49] Canon 1455, 1°. For treatises on the right of patronage, reference may be made to Wernz-Vidal, *Ius Canonicum ad Normam Codicis Exactum* (7 vols. in 8, Romae: Apud Aedes Universitatis Gregorianae, Vol. II, 3. ed., 1943; Vol. IV, Pars II, 1935), II, 341-373 (hereinafter cited Wernz-Vidal); Vermeersch-Creusen, *Epitome Iuris Canonici* (3 vols., Vol. II, 6. ed., Mechliniae-Romae: H. Dessain, 1940), II, 543-553 (hereinafter cited Vermeersch-Creusen); Coronata, *Institutiones Iuris Canonici* (5 vols., Vol. II, 4. ed., Taurini-Romae: Marietti, 1951), II, 404-425 (hereinafter cited Coronata); Cappello, *Summa Iuris Canonici* (3 vols., Vol. II, 4. ed., Romae: Apud Aedes Universitatis Gregorianae, 1945), II, 531-534; Abbo-Hannan, *The Sacred Canons: A Concise Presentation of the Current Disciplinary Norms of the Church* (2 vols., rev. ed., St. Louis: B. Herder Book Co., 1957), II, 673-684 (hereinafter cited Abbo-Hannan); Woywod-Smith, *A Practical Commentary on the Code of Canon Law* (2 vols., revised by Callistus Smith, revised and enlarged edition, New York: Joseph F. Wagner, Inc., 1948), II, 175-183 (hereinafter cited Woywod-Smith); Godfrey, *The Right of Patronage According to the Code of Canon Law,* The Catholic University of America Canon Law Studies, n. 21 (Washington, D.C.: The Catholic University of America, 1924).

[50] Wernz-Vidal, II, 345. The First Council of Orange (441) gave impetus to this institution.

[51] Canon 1450.

[52] "The Church wanted to encourage people of means to devote a portion of their wealth to the service of God—and thus indirectly relieve the

In New Spain, appointment to all dioceses [54] and other benefices [55] was reserved to the Crown.

In actual practice the Crown exercised direct power of appointment in the case of archbishops, bishops, and cathedral chapters. The nominations of archbishops and bishops were sent to the Pope, who formally installed the appointees in office. Appointment to lesser benefices was made by the viceroys and provincial governors, acting as vice-patrons, from a list of nominations made by the local prelates. The person chosen was then presented to the bishop, who installed him in office. The Crown permitted private individuals to endow local ecclesiastical foundations, such as chaplaincies, and to exercise patronage over them, but this form of private patronage was under the strict control of civil authority.[56]

One may well ask at this point whether the right of patronage as enjoyed by the Spanish Crown remained intact after the Council of Trent. The answer is in the affirmative, for the Council of Trent explicitly made an exception in favor of the right of patronage in regard to cathedral churches and also in favor of the right of patronage previously enjoyed by emperors and kings, when for all other instances it abrogated the right of patronage. In the words of the Council,

---

poor people from the burden of building and endowing churches and other places of divine worship—by giving them certain rights over the church or benefice they had founded or endowed. Frequently the rights granted to founders were not used by them or their successors to the best interests of the Church, and in many instances they insisted absolutely on their rights but neglected their obligations."—Woywod-Smith, II, 174.

[53] In the United States, the Second Plenary Council of Baltimore, confirming earlier decrees of the Provincial Councils of Baltimore, did not allow the granting of the right of patronage.—*Concilii Plenarii Baltimorensis II in Ecclesia Metropolitana Baltimorensi a die VII ad diem XXI Octobris A.D. MDCCLXVI habiti et a Sede Apostolica Recogniti Acta et Decreta* (2. ed., Baltimorae: Joannes Murphy, 1880), tit. IV, cap. un., n. 184, p. 111.

[54] Lib. I, tit. 6, ley 3.

[55] Lib. I, tit. 6, ley 4.

[56] Scholes, "Church and State in New Mexico: 1610-1650," *N.M.H.R.*, XI (1936), 12.

. . . Patronatus omnes . . . exceptis patronatibus super cathedralibus ecclesiis competentibus, et exceptis aliis, quae ad imperatorem, et reges, seu regna possidentes, aliosque sublimes, ac supremos principes iura imperii in dominiis suis habentes, pertinent . . . , in totum prorsus abrogata, et irrita cum quasi possessione, inde secuta intelligantur.[57]

Section 2. Administration of Church Property

First of all, the Crown left no lacunae in its rigid control of all building programs for religious and charitable purposes: an injunction was issued by Philip II in 1574, and in it provision was made that no church, monastery, hospital, or other pious foundation could be founded or erected without the express permission of the king.[58] This building permit was to be obtained from viceroys and governors, and these, in turn, were instructed to keep the king *au courant* in such matters.[59]

It was the desire of the Crown that its viceroys and governors see to it, without prejudice to the above-mentioned supervision, that in every Indian village (*pueblo*) there be built a church wherein the Indians could be instructed and receive the sacraments.[60] Furthermore, it was prescribed that the churches be well built, and that the cost be apportioned into three parts: one-third to be underwritten by the royal treasury; one-third by the *Encomenderos*;[61] and the remaining third by the Indians.[62] In

[57] Conc. Trid., sess. XXV, *de ref.*, cap. 9.—Mansi, XXXIII, 187.

[58] Lib. I, tit. 6, ley 2.

[59] Lib. I, tit. 2, ley 1.

[60] Lib. I, tit. 2, ley 6.

[61] An *encomendero* was the lord vested with an *encomienda,* the latter being "a right granted by royal grace to the deserving of the Indies to receive and collect for themselves the tributes of the Indians that shall be given them in trust, for their life and life of one heir . . . with the charge of looking after the spiritual and temporal welfare of the Indians and of dwelling in and defending the provinces where they are given them in trust and of doing homage and making personal oath to fulfill all this."—From a *cédula* of Philip II, 1571 translated by Simpson, *The Encomienda in New Spain* (Berkeley: University of California Press, 1929), frontispiece. Much has been written about the Encomienda System. Without a doubt, some *encomenderos* were guilty of abuses, of gross injustices. This is not the place, nor is the writer competent, to pass judgment in this matter; how-

addition, the Indians were directed to build rectories contiguous
to their parish churches; these rectories were ordinarily given
in trust to the clerics concerned,[63] and could not be alienated or
converted to other uses.[64]

Once a church had been built, the *encomendero* on whose *encomienda* it lay was charged with the duty of providing that the
church be decently maintained as such. A *cédula* of Charles V
dated May 10, 1554, provides as follows:

> We decree that the *encomenderos* have an obligation to
> provide [the churches with] whatever is necessary for divine
> worship, such as ornaments, wine, and wax, and to provide
> whatever is needed by the ministers; all in accordance with
> the judgment and dispositions of the bishop [in the mat-
> ter].[65]

As might be expected, the Crown meted out properties and
land grants to its vassals in order to encourage discoveries and
settlements in the Indies; [66] but it is interesting to note that as
early as October 25, 1535, Charles V felt the financial detriment
incident to *manos muertas* militating against the royal treasury
every time landed property was ceded to the Church. To forestall an accumulation of real property immune from taxation, he
decreed that

> The lands shall be apportioned without excess among the
> discoverers and old settlers, and their descendants, who must
> remain on the land, and the most qualified shall be pre-

---

ever, one viewpoint may not be ignored: ". . . [The Encomienda System]
probably represented, at the beginning, at least in theory, the most efficient
and rapid way of civilizing the Indians."—Lacas, "The Encomienda in
Latin-American History: A Reappraisal," *The Americas,* VII (1952), 262.

62 Lib. I, tit. 2, leyes 2, 3.

63 Lib. I, tit. 2, ley 19. The law reads, ". . . [que] sean [estas casas]
de los clerigos que tuvieren la iglesia." The extremely complex question of
ownership and tenure of church property during the Spanish, Mexican, and
American periods will be treated, respectively, in Sections 1, 2, and 3, Article 6, this chapter.

64 *Loc. cit.*

65 Lib. I, tit. 2, ley 23.   [Translation by the writer.]

66 Lib. IV, tit. 12, ley 1.

ferred; and they can not sell the lands to a church nor monastery, nor to any ecclesiastical person, under the penalty that they shall lose them, and that said lands may be apportioned to others.[67]

Residential bishops were given the faculty by the Crown to divide, unite, or suppress benefices whenever conditions and circumstances so warranted, provided that the vice-patron of the benefice concerned gave his consent.[68]

Whenever a residential bishop died, the pontifical estate was to pass on to the church (diocese) of which he was ordinary at the time of his death.[69] In the case of clerics, apparently some bishops had exercised undue influence in the matter of the disposition of these clerics' personal estates. In any event, Charles I decreed as follows on January 30, 1538:

> Some prelates of Our Indies have assumed a right to the estates of the . . . clerics . . . of their dioceses, and have succeeded thereto *ex testamento* and *ab intestato*. We . . . direct . . . each and every prelate to allow . . . clerics . . . to draw up their last wills with the liberty granted them under law, and to distribute their goods to whomever they will, in accordance with the ancient custom in vogue in the Kingdom of Castile, whereby the goods left by a cleric *in sacris* on his death . . . are to pass to the decedent's heirs *ex testamento* and *ab intestato* . . . And We order Our viceroys and governors . . . not to allow prelates . . . to intermeddle in these matters.[70]

Reference has already been made [71] to the Bull *Eximiae devotionis*, issued in favor of the Spanish monarchy by Alexander VI on November 16, 1501,[72] whereby the Crown was given the right

[67] Lib. IV, tit. 12, ley 10. [Translation by Hall, p. 20, § 41.]

[68] Lib. I, tit. 6, ley 40. Noteworthy is the fact that a *cédula* of Philip II, issued on May 26, 1573, made all benefices in Indian pueblos curate (*curata*).—Lib. I, tit. 6, ley 41. A benefice is curate or non-curate according as the care of souls is or is not attached thereto.—Canon 1411, 5°.

[69] Lib. I, tit. 7, ley 40.

[70] Lib. I, tit. 12, ley 6. [Translation by the writer.] Cf. also lib. II, tit. 32, ley 8.

[71] Cf. *supra*, p. 11.

[72] The text of this Bull may be found in Hernaez, I, 20.

to collect the tithes (*diezmos:* "the tenth part") in the American colonies. These tithes were collected by the officials of the royal treasury; the sums collected were expended according to a general scheme ordered by the Crown.[73] It was the usual custom to divide the tithes into four equal parts, of which one was paid to the bishop and one to the cathedral chapter.[74] The remainder was divided into nine parts, or *novenos,* of which the Crown retained two and the remaining seven were distributed among the clergy of lesser rank, hospitals, and the general fund of the particular diocese.[75] The *dos novenos,* or king's share, were frequently used for pious purposes.[76]

Section. 3. *Laws Affecting Holdings of Religious*

Like the secular clergy,[77] religious communities, too, needed a royal permit to build churches and monasteries:

> Wherever necessary for the conversion and instruction of the native population and for preaching the Holy Gospel, We order that monasteries of religious be founded and built, with the proviso that We be consulted and Our license be obtained prior to the construction of any church, convent, or hospice for religious . . . In seeking the aforementioned license, the consent of the diocesan prelate must be obtained in accordance with [the provisions of] the Council of Trent, and that of the viceroy, the Audience within the respective district, or the governor . . . And if any of the above-mentioned edifices be constructed or be in the process of building, either *bona fide* or *in fraudem legis* without the required license, the viceroys, Audiences, or governors will provide that they be demolished forthwith without entertaining any excuse.[78]

[73] Lib. I, tit. 16, ley 1.

[74] Lib. I, tit. 16, ley 23.

[75] Lib. I, tit. 16, ley 24.

[76] Cf. Scholes, "Church and State in New Mexico: 1610-1650," *N.M.H.R.,* XI (1936), 12.

[77] Lib. I, tit. 6, ley 2.

[78] Lib. I, tit. 3, ley 1. [Translation by the writer.] As a matter of fact, "occasionally ecclesiastical buildings were actually torn down by royal command as the result of violation of the patronage."—Scholes, "Church and State in New Mexico: 1610-1650," *N.M.H.R.,* XI (1936), 13.

Once royal license for building had been obtained through the proper channels, the royal officials parceled out the lands on which the building in question was to be constructed. But the governors were instructed "not to permit [religious] to appropriate more land than is absolutely necessary for the foundation and reasonable living quarters for the religious: definite boundaries are to be defined within which the foundation is to be made, executed, and perfected." [79]

The cost of the religious foundation was to be borne by the royal treasury wherever the *encomienda* within which the foundation lay was incorporated in the Royal Crown, and by the *encomenderos*, Crown, and Indians according to their means wherever the *encomienda* was not so incorporated.[80]

Needless to say, rigid supervision was also exercised by the Crown over religious communities in matters touching on other aspects of the right of patronage. Thus, for example, all provincial superiors, chapters, visitors, and guardians elected by the Orders were obliged to present their letters patent of office to the civil authorities.[81]

Philip II had occasion to remind religious that they were not to presume to own property as individual persons.[82] The religious of the Order of St. Francis were also reminded that in accordance with their Constitutions and Rule even the Order as such was incapable of owning anything.[83] It was also provided that, when the residential bishop made his episcopal visitation to the churches administered by religious, he be allowed to conduct a canonical visitation of the parochial churches, the Blessed Sacrament, the Holy Oils, the ornaments, the books, the confraternities, and the monies which the religious were administering. Furthermore, an inventory of everything belonging to the church was to be made; it was understood, of course, that such inventory of goods was the property of the church which the religious

[79] Lib. I, tit. 3, ley 2.   [Translation by the writer.]

[80] Lib. I, tit. 3, ley 3.

[81] Lib. I, tit. 15, ley 3.

[82] Lib. I, tit. 14, ley 50.

[83] Lib. I, tit. 15, ley 25.

administered. This, however, did not apply to those places which the religious held as their own.[84]

ARTICLE 6.   OWNERSHIP AND TENURE OF CHURCH PROPERTY IN NEW MEXICO

Section 1.   Under Spanish Rule: 1539 to 1821

The problems incident to an inquiry into the acquisition, tenure, and ownership of property—personalty and realty—by the clergy in general and ecclesiastical corporations in particular during the Spanish rule are indeed intriguing, albeit extremely complex and numerous.   Obviously, however, the scope of the present study resists anything beyond a relatively brief consideration of the main propositions and juridical consequences entailed.   Even many propositions not entirely collateral cannot be entertained, except perhaps in the most laconic of terms. And yet the instant discussion is not without its practical import: the policies and *de facto* extant situations which obtained in the matter at the end of the Spanish period were, in the main, incorporated into Mexican law.   The American government, in turn, honored the provisions and *res gestae* of the previous sovereignties.

But if the very intricate and complex question of ownership and tenure of church property in New Mexico during the Spanish rule is not to become hopelessly confused, one must constantly appeal to the legal axiom, *distingue tempora, et concordabis iura.* One cannot afford, then, to forget to view the many propositions entailed from the proper foci of the divers times and circumstances involved.   For without such efforts, one will be unable to reconcile the grey of the *de facto* extant status with the black and white of what perhaps should have been.

Specifically, the problem herein primarily pertinent is reducible to the question of who owned the church property during the mission era and how that property was held.   The complexity of the problem, attributable in no small measure to the various papal grants in favor of the Crown, is further aggravated in the case of New Mexico by the fact that the Franciscans held all

[84] Lib. I, tit. 15, ley 29.

church property until the 19th century, when the missions were secularized.

In connection with the *Inter caetera* and other grants by Alexander VI and Julius II, there are at least two points which instantly arise to claim recognition as apparently germane to the problem at hand. The first is the theoretical question of determining in an absolute manner precisely what, if anything, was granted the Crown by way of legal title to realties. The number of those who would claim that nothing was given is legion,[85] and they would rest their case on the *Nemo plus iuris* principle.[86] Since, as a matter of actual fact, the Crown had a potent enough title to the colonies derived from actual possession, the academic question as stated can best be left to savants in history and political science.[87]

The second question which arises in connection with the papal grants to the Crown is whether or not the Holy See thereby abdicated its right and the right of inferior ecclesiastical corporations to acquire, hold, and own property in the colonies. And the answer is decidedly in the negative. It will be recalled that the Spanish civil codes took for granted and presumed that the Church had an inherent right to acquire, hold, own, and administer property as means necessary to its primary end.[88] Indeed, the primary concern of Spanish civil law in matters of ecclesiastical property was to provide that the Church's possessions be fully guarded and that its rights thereto and dominion thereof be guaranteed.[89]

[85] Cf., e.g., Prescott, *op. cit.*, I, 370.

[86] "Nemo plus iuris in alium transferre potest, quam sibi competere dignoscatur."—Reg. 79, R.J., in VI°.

[87] Cf. Ehler-Morrall, *Church and State Through the Centuries* (London: Burns and Oates, 1954), p. 100; Gomez, *Las Leyes de Indias y el Derecho Ecclesiástico en la América Española e Islas Filipinas* (Medellin, Colombia: Ediciones Universidad Católica Bolivariana, 1945), pp. 21 ff.

[88] Cf., e.g., *Fuero Juzgo*, lib. V, tit. 1, leyes 1, 3; *Novisima Recopilación*, lib. I, tit. 5, leyes 1, 2, 8; lib. I, tit. 28, ley 8; *Fuero Real*, lib. I, tit. 5, leyes 2, 3.

[89] Cf. *Siete Partidas*, Part. I, tit. 4, ley 1; tit. 14, leyes 2, 12.

Since the *Recopilación de las Indias,* by its own provisions,[90] constituted mere exceptions to the Spanish civil laws, and since the former nowhere attempted to abrogate, or derogate from, the right of the Church to temporal goods as recognized by the latter, it follows that the Crown recognized that right in its colonies as well.[91]   True, the Crown exercised quasi-plenipotentiary powers over ecclesiastical matters by virtue of the universal right of patronage which it enjoyed by papal grant.   However, the right of patronage did not carry with it an abdication of the right of the Church to dominion over temporal property.   It is also true that the *Inter caetera* of Alexander VI bestowed title to the colonies on the Crown.   But it is equally certain that the Alexandrinian Bull must be considered in its proper context of time and circumstances.   It is a law of human nature that a voluntary act is posited by a free agent upon consideration of the attending circumstances: *rebus sic stantibus.*   More concretely and specifically, the *Inter caetera* (as well as subsequent grants) must be viewed against the benevolent attitude of the Spanish monarchs (particularly Ferdinand and Isabella) in general and against the existing jurisprudence of Spanish civil law in particular on the matter of church property.   Furthermore, sight must not be lost of the avowed *raison d'être* for the divers papal grants to the Crown, viz., to carry on the work of evangelization *in partibus infidelium.*   How, then, can a kingdom divided against itself stand?   And since the Crown was only too ready to legislate in accordance with rights, such as that of patronage, granted to it by the Holy See, would the Crown not have legislated *ab initio* in accordance with any abdication of the right to dominion over church property had it been on the receiving end of such forfeiture? [92]

[90] Lib. II, tit. 1, leyes 1, 2.

[91] Cf. *Recopilación de las Indias,* lib. I, tit. 2, ley 19; lib. I, tit. 7, ley 40; lib. IV, tit. 12, ley 10.

[92] Actually, Spanish jurists have never been in agreement concerning the nature and extent of the prerogatives of the right of patronage, and the court in Madrid sometimes ruled in accordance with the opinion of one faction, at times with that of another.—Cf. Mora, *El Clero, El Estado y la Economía Nacional* (Mexico, D.F.: Empresas Editoriales, S.A., 1950), p. 55.

And as a matter of fact, the Crown, while it attempted to curtail the acquisition of property by the Church as *manos muertas,*[93] allowed ecclesiastical corporations in general to become possessed of, and to exercise dominion over, both chattels and realty.[94] It is an incontrovertible historical fact that ecclesiastical corporations, such as dioceses, parishes, religious communities, and the Inquisition of the Holy Office, owned much property in the colonies.[95] Actually, the most conservative estimate in this regard which the writer has encountered claims that the secular and regular clergy owned at least one-half of the total value of the landed property in that huge expanse of what was then Mexico.[96]

[93] It is claimed that the divers measures taken by the Crown to attack the institution of mortmain and to initiate the desamortization of the goods thereof began with Law 12, Title 2, Book IV, of the *Fuero Juzgo,* which attempted to limit the acquisition of realty by religious Orders.—Cf. Gomez del Campo, *El Despojo de los Bienes Eclesiásticos en Mexico: Estudio Histórico y Jurídico* (Mexico, D.F.: [no specification], 1940, p. 6.

[94] By virtue of the concordat negotiated in 1737, the properties of all *manos muertas* became subject to the same imposts and taxes as all other realty.—Cf. *Colección de Leyes, Decretos, Reglamentos, Circulares, Ordenes, Acuerdos y Estudios Relativos a la Desamortización y Nacionalización de los Bienes de Corporaciones,* formada por el Lic. G. Labastida, con autorización de la Secretaría de Estado y del Despacho de Hacienda y Crédito Público (Mexico, D.F.: Palacio Nacional, 1893), p. 4.

[95] Zamacois, *Historia de Mejico* (19 vols., Mexico, D.F.: J. F. Parres y Comp., 1877-1882), V, 335.

[96] Alamán, *Historia de México* (5 vols., Mexico: Editorial Jus, 1942), I, 70. The Spanish Cortes, by decree of September 27, 1820, abolished all kinds of entails, and provided as follows: "Art. 15. Churches, monasteries, convents, and all ecclesiastical communities, as well secular as religious, hospitals, charitable institutions, houses of charity and instruction, *cofradías,* brotherhoods, *encomiendas,* and all other permanent establishments, whether lay or ecclesiastical, known by the appellation of mortmain, cannot for the future acquire any real or immovable property in any province of the monarchy, either by donation, sale, exchange, confiscation, emphiteutic rent, abjudication as pledge (*prenda pretoria*), or in payment of money due, nor by any other title, whether lucrative or onerous. Art. 16. Nor can, for the future, mortmain impose or acquire, by any title, capital or rent of any kind imposed on real estate, nor impose nor acquire tributes, nor other species of encumbrance on such property, whether it consist in the granting

In the present discussion, it is important to distinguish the succession of events. It is, of course, taken for granted that, when Spain took possession of a given region, the Crown claimed and exercised full dominion thereon. There were, naturally, no churches, no monasteries, in that region. But as the mechanism of colonization was set in motion within that region, one of the first things attended to was the work of evangelization, which sooner or later postulated a church building, a convent, and lands. For that, as well as for maintaining the work of evangelization, the Crown provided as it saw fit and as it was able:

> In New Mexico, the burden of holding the colony and converting the Indians . . . devolved completely on the Crown. Friars, soldiers, and settlers alike looked to the government for everything . . . There was the cost of supporting the friars, their clothing, supplies, provisions, church equipment—in short, everything—to say nothing of the cost of travel from Mexico to Santa Fe and the transport of supplies over a distance of about 1,200 miles . . . From the time [the friars] left Mexico City till their return (and many spent a lifetime in the distant colony) the Crown paid for their every need, in so far as it could be provided.[97]

From the beginning, the Order of Friars Minor has been incapable of holding or transferring property under its own name. What it has possessed, and possesses, has been and is held in trust by the Order, but ownership and legal title to such possessions has always resided in the Holy See as a corporation sole. This is clearly evidenced by Article 266 of the Franciscan Rule and Constitutions:

> § 1. Ordo noster, super altissimam paupertatem fundatus, neque in particulari neque in communi ullam proprietatem habere potest, sed omnes res temporales in Ordinis usum legitime datae ad S. Sedem pertinent eidemque in posterum acquiruntur, salva, quoad dominii attributionem alteri personae, contraria benefactorum voluntate.

---

of the sum of money, or certain portions of the fruits, or of some service in favor of the mortmain, nor in any other species of annual income."—*Legislación Mexicana*, I, p. 528, n. 230. [Translation by Schmidt, p. 331.]

[97] Hammond-Rey, "The Crown's Participation in the Founding of New Mexico," *N.M.H.R.*, XXXII (1957), 306.

§ 2. Quapropter sive singuli religiosi sive Ordo, sive pro-
vinciae sive domus, prohibentur omni juridico actu quoad
proprietatem et usum rerum temporalium . . .[98]

And as a natural and logical consequence, it follows, too, that
any alienation of property held in trust by the Franciscans must
be done in the name of the Holy See through its syndic [99] for the
respective province (or custody):

Art. 267, § 1. Quoties rationabiles temporum et locorum
circumstantiae exigant ut bona mobilia vel immobilia al-
ienentur, id fieri nequit nisi de legitima Superiorum licentia
et per syndicum apostolicum . . .[100]

The law, traditions, and spirit of the Order in regard to the
ownership and tenure of property are perhaps best epitomized
in Article 4, entitled, "The Church's Proprietorship of Things
Allowed the Friars," of the Constitution *Exiit qui seminat*, issued by Pope Nicholas III on August 14, 1279:

§ 1. The Friars can acquire nothing for themselves either
individually or for their Order, also in common. Yet, when
anything is offered, granted or donated to the Friars for
the love of God, it is presumed, unless otherwise specified, to
be the likely intention of the person so offering, granting or
donating the thing to make a complete offering, grant or
donation thereof, abdicating the right thereto and desiring
to transfer the right to some one else for the love of God.
There is, however, nobody to whom in God's stead the
ownership of such a thing can be more fittingly transferred
than to the Holy See or the person of the Roman Pontiff,
the Vicar of Christ, who is the father of all the faithful indeed, but in a special manner the father of the Friars Minor.
Now, as the ownership of such things should not be left
in doubt; and as, each in his fashion, a son acquires for his
father, a bondman for his master, and a monk for his monastery whatever is offered, granted, or donated to him: We

[98] *Regula et Constitutiones Generales Ordinis Fratrum Minorum*
(Romae: Curia Generalis Ordinis, 1953), cap. VI, tit. 1, p. 94.

[99] The apostolic syndic is an agent of the Holy See acting for it in matters temporal. Nowadays the syndic is a Franciscan, but during the mission period he was a layman. The syndic's counterpart at Anglo-American law would be the attorney in fact executing general agencies.

[100] *Loc. cit.*

of our Apostolic authority take over for ourself and the Roman Church the property right and ownership of all the utensils, books and other movables present and future which, or the use of which (use of fact, of course), the Order or the Friars may lawfully have—just as our predecessor Pope Innocent IV of happy memory is known to have done—and with this Constitution, to be perpetual in effect, We do decree that said right pertains wholly and without reserve to us and to said Church.

§ 2.   Moreover, places bought with the various alms, or offered or granted to the Friars under whatever formality, we do likewise with the same authority take over as the right, property and domain of ourself and said Church from the persons possessing said places in whole or sharing them in part, provided said possessors in whole or in part have not in such offering or cession reserved anything thereof to themselves.   The Friars, however, are cautioned in any such transactions not to use terms that are incompatible with their status.

§ 3.   On the other hand, if the Friars at the pleasure of the benefactor are dwelling in places or houses still to be granted or also offered by an individual or a group to the Friars as their place of abode, the Friars may live there only for the duration of the benefactor's pleasure.   Should the benefactor change his mind and signify as much to the Friars, let them without demur relinquish said places, except the church, oratories meant for church purposes, and the cemetery. These latter we do likewise take in like manner and with like authority, both present and future, as the right and property of ourself and said Roman Church.

In the ownership, however, and the proprietary rights of said places themselves we do retain nothing whatever for ourself or said Roman Church unless they are accepted with the explicit consent of ourself or said Roman Church. Whenever the benefactor in extending his favor has reserved the ownership of such places to himself, such ownership shall not pass over into the right of said oft-mentioned Church by reason of the Friars' residing therein, but rather it shall remain fully and without reserve with the benefactor.[101]

---

[101] Translation from *The Constitutions of Pope Nicholas II, Clement V, and Innocent XI Clarifying the Rule of the Friars Minor,* translation authorized and distributed by the Very Reverend Ministers Provincial O.F.M. in the United States (Chicago: Franciscan Herald Press, [no date]), p. 17.   The Latin version of this Constitution may be found in *Bullarium Franciscanum Romanorum Pontificum . . . ,* notis illustratum

The obvious question now arises: did the Holy See have dominion over Franciscan-held churches, convents, and lands, or did legal title thereto reside in the Crown, with the Church, through the Franciscans enjoying a mere usufruct thereof? From the preceding observations, as well as on the force of further arguments to be adduced hereinbelow, it is the considered opinion of the writer that, in general, legal title to the Franciscan-held properties in New Mexico resided in the Crown until such a time as the latter formally ceded its ownership thereof to the Holy See through the Franciscans. The foregoing represents a general principle; what was ceded when is a question of fact.

In attempting to determine such questions of fact, numerous and varying circumstances must be examined. Some would claim, for example, that there existed in fact a complete divorcement between the provisions of the Code of the Indies and the *de facto* extant situation in the colonies.[102] Others assert that some of the sovereigns of Spain—notably Charles III (1759-1788) and Charles IV (1788-1808)—were of the opinion that ownership of ecclesiastical property in the American colonies had always resided in the Crown.[103]

The American courts have ruled that the power and authority to issue grants of land in the Spanish colonies was vested in the viceroys,[104] governors,[105] and captains-general,[106] and that the

---

studio et labore Fr. Joannis Hyacinthi Sbaraleae (3 vols., Romae: Typis Sacrae Congregationis de Propaganda Fide, 1759-1765), III, 404.

[102] Moreno, *Influencia de la Legislación de Indias en el Derecho Agrario Mexicano* (Mexico: Universidad Nacional Autónoma de Mexico, 1950), cap. III, p. 15.

[103] Hall, p. 226, § 769. It should be observed that the properties belonging to the Inquisition of the Holy Office in the colonies were confiscated and made part of the public domain by decree of the Spanish Cortes issued on February 22, 1813.—Cf. *Legislación Mexicana*, I, p. 401, n. 111. And by disposition of the Spanish Cortes on August 17, 1820, the goods belonging to the Society of Jesus were likewise confiscated and applied to the public credit.—Cf. *Legislación Mexicana*, I, p. 522, n. 223, 10°.

[104] De Armas v. City of New Orleans, 5 La. 132 (1833).

[105] United States v. Acosta, 42 U.S. (1 How.) 24, 11 L.Ed. 33 (1843).

[106] Jones v. Muisbach, 26 Tex. 235 (1862).

presumption is in favor of the power of Spanish officers who made grants of land.[107] The term "grant" is understood to mean any warrant, concession, order, or commission, to survey, possess, or settle, evinced by writing or parol, or presumed from possession.[108] However, no title passed from the Spanish sovereign by a mere order of survey or requête and permission to settle. This only conferred an equitable right to demand a title, and until a complete grant was made, the title remained in the sovereign, and all inchoate grants within his discretion.[109] Nonetheless, when part of the public domain was separated from the rest by metes and bounds, and possession put in, and this possession continued a number of years, this title was valid.[110]

Two cases at Anglo-American law warrant particular attention in this period, not because mission property in New Mexico was involved—one case is from Texas, the other from California— but because, besides delineating Anglo-American jurisprudence concerning tenure and ownership of mission property in those areas, the courts' *dicta* afford some interesting surprises in regard to their concept of the nature of Church-State relations during the Spanish period. In the Texas case, Blair v. Odin,[111] the court found that to sustain an action for property as a dedication to religious uses, plaintiff must show a legal title, or a possession of the use and a deprivation thereof. The opinion of the court continues:

[107] United States v. Peralta, 60 U.S. (19 How.) 343, 15 L.Ed. 678 (1856).

[108] Strother v. Lucas, 37 U.S. (12 Pet.) 410, 9 L.Ed. 1137 (1838).

[109] Gonsonlin's Heirs v. Brashear, 5 Mart. (La., N.S.) 33 (1826); Lobdell v. Clark, 4 La. Ann. 99 (1849).

[110] Sanchez v. Gonzales, 11 Mart. (La., O.S.) 207 (1822); Le Blanc v. Victor, 3 La. 44 (1831); Landry v. Martin, 15 La. 1 (1840).

[111] 3 Tex. 288 (1848). This suit was brought by Bishop Odin, as head of the Roman Catholic Church in Texas, to recover a lot or square of ground in the town of Victoria. The town of Victoria was laid out and surveyed in 1832; the lot in controversy was designated on the map of the town as the church square; and it was admitted that at that time it was designed for a church, curate's dwelling, and other ecclesiastical offices; that it had never been occupied or used for any other purpose, prior to the Texan revolution, nor down to the time it was occupied by defendant. Plaintiff was suited, and defendant appeals.

In consequence of those grants [of Alexander VI and Julius II], the Spanish monarchs became, *in effect, the heads of the Catholic Church,* in their American possessions . . . If the right of church property, in other Catholic countries, was in the Pope, as head of the church, the same right was in the Crown of Spain, in Spanish America, as the head of both temporal and spiritual jurisdiction. The right of property in fee being in the King, as long as his dominion was acknowledged in America, after the revolution, was in the Mexican government, as successor to the former sovereign power; the clergy being permitted only to the enjoyment of the use . . .

It is doubtful whether the church, as an institution, could have held real estate by fee simple, or perfect title, even before the abolition of mortmain, because from the constitution of the church in the King of Spain's American dominions, the temporal sovereign was essentially the head of the church . . .

The result of our examination, so far as our very limited means afforded us the opportunity, is that the church, at the period of our revolution, held no real estate by perfect title; that it only enjoyed and held the usufruct interest in such land as it possessed.[112]

The judgment was reversed, and cause dismissed.

In the California case, Nobili v. Redman,[113] appellee's counsel argued that:

1. The Church was originally incapable of acquiring, holding or conveying landed property.

2. Subsequently, when this power to acquire and hold (not to alienate) worldly goods, so variant from the divine purposes of its establishment, was conferred upon the church, it was under great restrictions, and could never be lawfully exercised without the express sanction of the sovereign power of the State to each acquisition.

3. The members of the religious orders, called the regular

---

[112] Blair v. Odin, at 295-297.

[113] 5 Cal. 325 (1856). Father John Nobili, pastor of the Mission and Church of Santa Clara, brought suit in ejectment to recover a lot of land which formerly constituted a part of the cultivated lands pertaining to the Mission of that name. He exhibited no grant, conveyance, or other paper title and pretended to no other right to recover except the fact that the land in question had always been occupied and cultivated by the Mission. On this state of facts, plaintiff was non-suited, and appeals.

clergy, who alone were employed as missionaries in the Indies, are considered in law as civilly dead ("dead to the world"), and incapable of acquiring and holding property by any title.[114]

Appellant argued that, though it were held that the title to mission property remained in the king of Spain, and the use only was vested in the Church, it was a complete dedication; that the title would have passed to Mexico and then to the United States, subject to the use; and that the dedication could not be revoked.[115]

The opinion of the court follows:

According to all the Spanish and Mexican authorities, the missions were political establishments, and in no manner connected with the Church. The fact that monks or priests were at the head of these institutions, proves nothing in favor of the claim of the Church to universal ownership of the property. It is here unnecessary to determine in what manner, or by what form of conveyance, the Church, as a political or corporate body, could validly acquire title. It is sufficient that there must have been some mode, so as to take the right out of the Government, or individual, and vest it in the Church, and certainly nothing of the kind is here shown to have existed.

If it is to be relied on that a priest or monk had government and control of the mission, the answer is simply that they were the civil governors; and although they combined with the power of civil government the functions of spiritual fathers, this was only the more effectively to carry out one of the objects of those establishments, which was, to convert and Christianize the Indians. And it appears fully, from all the investigations made into the Spanish and Mexican polity in reference to missions, that neither the missions, nor the priests of the missions, were incorporated into the general body of the Church, nor were, in any respect, under the control or direction of its diocesan ecclesiastics, whose rule was absolute over all their inferiors. On the contrary, the mission establishments arose directly from the action and authority of the government of the country; laws and regu-

---

[114] Hawes, *The Missions in California and the Rights of the Catholic Church to the Property Pertaining to Them,* argument before the Supreme Court of California (San Francisco: Daily Evening News Office, 1856), pp. 4-5.

[115] Nobili v. Redman, at 331.

lations were made for them by its legislative authority, without referring to, or consulting the authority of the Church; the lands settled by them were not conveyed to anyone, neither to priest or neophyte, but remained the property of the governments; and there is not a word in all the decrees and acts of the government, which would even show that the church building, devoted to worship alone, ever became the property of the church corporate, until the decree of secularization of 1833.[116]

The judgment of the court below was affirmed.

On April 25, 1521, Pope Leo X had confirmed a previous apostolic grant to the Order of Friars Minor as missionaries in the Americas whereby they were vested with the faculty and power to accept places and houses in which to live in any of the cities and villages of the colonies, as well as power to sell any such already accepted, and to exchange or transfer title thereto under whatever formality of donation. This Bull, entitled *Alias felicis*, reads in part:

> ... Quique [Nicholaus IV, Ioannes XX, Urbanus V et Eugenius IV necnon alii Romani Pontifices] eisdem Fratribus [Ordinis Minoris] auctoritate apostolica concesserunt, ut in civitatibus, castris, villis seu locis quibuscumque, ad habitandum domos et loca quaecumque recipere, seu hactenus recepta mutare, aut ea venditionis, permutationis, aut cuiusvis donationis titulo in alios transferre valerent . . . [Nos praedictam facultatem] concedimus et indulgemus.[117]

Since nothing to the contrary is specified, it must be presumed that the grant in question allowed the friars to accept property in trust in the name of the Holy See without need of recourse for each particular case, but did not derogate from the Franciscan Rule and Constitutions and earlier papal constitutions by the provisions of which the Order was rendered incapable of acquiring or transferring property in its own name.

It seems clear that the Franciscans in New Mexico adopted the same attitude that the American courts, as cited *supra*, have sustained in regard to the tenure and ownership of Franciscan-held property during the Spanish era, viz., that their occupation constituted a mere tenancy at will which, however, created an

[116] Nobili v. Redman, at 342.

[117] The complete text of *Alias felicis* may be found in Hernaez, I, 377.

equity entitled to confirmation. This is patently evidenced by documents such as the following:

To: Governor and Captain-General.

From: Fray Joaquin de Hinajosa, of the Regular Observance of St. Francis, Missionary Father, President
in capite, Ecclesiastical Judge Ordinary, and by
apostolic authority Judge Delegate of His Holiness
for this kingdom of New Mexico and its environs.

. . . The Reverend Father Fray Francisco de Vargas, former Custodian of this Custody, presented to Your Excellency a petition in which he asks and begs Your Excellency
that he be given [the official act of] possession for the convents and churches which have been built by the Reverend
missionary Fathers of this Custody in the last twelve years
. . ., and for the recently started mission among the Sumas
under the title of San Diego, in accordance with the favorable concession and privilege granted by His Holiness,
Pope Leo X, of happy memory, by virtue of which religious
missionaries laboring among the infidels . . . may build
churches . . . and convents, for the maintaining of which
some lands on which grain can be cultivated are necessary,
as well as for the support of the missionaries. . . .

Wherefore, I respectfully ask and entreat that on the occasion of your next official visit Your Excellency vest me or
the Reverend missionary Fathers President with the afore-
mentioned [official act of royal] possession for the churches,
convents, and lands, in order that on the part of His Majesty (whom God keep) the missionaries of these missions
may be legally considered by royal wish to be vested with
possession thereof, and so that by such solicitude the religious of this Holy Custody may feel the necessary security
toward the Royal Patronage which His Majesty enjoys in
these parts. . . .

. . . I swear *in verbo sacerdotis* that this my petition is
not made with malice, and in accordance with the law which
supports [it] I hope to receive a favorable reply. . . .

—P. Joachin de Inajosa [*rubric*][118]

The above petition is followed by an attestation, also made by Hinajosa, to the fact that the governor and captain-general had sent him the official instrument of possession sought.

Another document, dated 1697, again bears out that the Crown, through its colonial officials, made grants of property to the Franciscans in New Mexico:

[118] *Santa Fe*, [1692] Mission 1. [Translation by the writer.]

In the Villa of Santa Fe, Headquarters-Capital of this Kingdom and Provinces of New Mexico, on the 20th day of August, 1697, before me the Captain Don Alonso Rael de Aguilar, secretary of government and war of this said Kingdom, there appeared the Señor Don Pedro Rodriguez Cubero, Governor and Captain-General of it and Castellán of its forces and garrisons for His Majesty, for whom I vouch. . . . He declares before me, said secretary of government and war, and the witnesses who should be present, that said Lord Governor and Captain-General was making and did make gift and donation of [the] convent freely, purely, clearly, and irrevocably, according to what law calls *inter vivos*, to the Very Reverend Father Preacher, Fray Juan Alvarez, most worthy Custos of this holy Custody of the Conversion of Saint Paul, as head that he is of it, so that in the name of his sacred Order he might accept this said donation which said Señor makes according and as it now stands . . ., and he shall place said Very Reverend Father Custos, Fray Juan Alvarez, in Royal Possession in order that he may accept it in the name of his sacred Order, that they possess and keep it freely and frankly and without any impediment, and that if some person or persons should place one, said Señor shall answer to the charge since he is mak- and building said convent with his own resources and funds; and with regard to the ground on which it stands [he declares], as Governor and Captain-General that he is of said Kingdom, that none of its inhabitants have right or share to it by reason of its being on royal lands won with the arms of His Majesty; for which cause, in his royal name, he made and has made grant of said ground together with all the rest of the land which should be needed both for building the church as well as [that needed] if said Reverend Father Custos should wish to extend said convent further, and likewise a piece of land for a garden which is situated and extends along the east side and reaches up to said old church. And if any of the settlers of this said Villa had a grant made [here], said Señor annuls them from now on and declares them null and void and of no validity or effect. . . .

—Pedro Rodriguez Cubero [*rubric*]

Before me:

—Alonso Rael de Aguilar [*rubric*]
Secr. of gov.ment and war.[119]

[119] *Santa Fe,* 1697 Mission 1 [13]. [Translation by Chavez, in "Santa Fe Church and Convent Sites in the Seventeenth and Eighteenth Centuries," *N.M.H.R.*, XXIV (1949), 85.]

On the margin of this document there is noted the official act of royal possession to the properties in question.[120]

One last document is worthy of brief attention at this point in order to note how property owned by the Holy See and held in trust by the Franciscans was conveyed [121] in New Mexico:

> In the Villa Nueva de Santa Cruz de la Cañada on the 21st day of April, 1777, before me, the alcalde mayor and war captain of the jurisdiction and district of said villa, Don Salvador Garcia de Noriega, there appeared Don Clemente Gutierrez, citizen of the post of Pajarito and syndic of these interior missions of St. Francis, party of the first part, at the request and opinion of the Reverend Father Fray Francisco Atanasio Dominguez, Custos of this Custody of the Conversion of St. Paul of New Mexico, and in the name of the Apostolic See, and Juan Bautista Vigil, party of the second part. And they said that they are agreed and in accord to make, as they did make, a mutual exchange of two pieces of land in this way:
>
> Don Clemente Gutierrez said that inasmuch as the land belonging to the convent of the said Villa of La Cañada is near the old church and at a distance from the new one, and therefore inconvenient for the mission father of the said villa to be able to harvest some grain on it, in accordance with the request and opinion of said Reverend Father Cus-

120 " . . . It may be said that in the bestowal of grants in Spanish and Mexican possessions there was similarity to the English livery of seisin, known to the common law. The English method was for the sovereign or his representative actually to go upon the land and exert dominion over it, by breaking a twig from a tree, or throwing earth into the air, thus vesting title in the grantee. The Spaniards, and later the Mexicans, had a similar idea, possession being delivered personally, by a representative of the ruling power, with ceremony, accompanied at the same time or later by delivery of a written document explaining in detail the method of delivery of the grant, its boundaries, and the reasons prompting the generosity of the ruling power. The thought behind the so-called English livery of seisin and the delivery of possession of land customary to Spanish and Mexican rulers was that there could be no valid vesting of title to real estate unless there was a personal, manual delivery and investiture."— Keleher, "Law of the New Mexico Land Grant," *N.M.H.R.,* IV (1929), 353.

121 For a treatise on modes of conveyance in early New Mexico history, cf. Warner, "Conveyance of Property, the Spanish and Mexican Way," *N.M.H.R.,* VI (1931), 334 ff.

tos, in the name of the Apostolic See as syndic, administrator of eccleciastical property, and administrator of all temporalities pertaining to said missions and to the use of their religion, he exchanged and did exchange the said land for another piece which is next to the new church of said villa on the west and northwest with its owner and legitimate possessor, Don Juan Bautista Vigil, giving him in the name of His Holiness the Roman Pontiff full and incontestable ownership and free possession of the said land pertaining to the said convent . . ., in such a way that right to, possession, or use of the said land may never be nor can be alleged on behalf of the said convent. And in the same way he received and did receive the other land mentioned near the new church, receiving right to and possession of it in the name of His Holiness.

Don Juan Bautista Vigil said that he willingly accepted and did accept the exchange, receiving for himself and his heirs the said land pertaining to the convent, and that he gave and did give the aforesaid land for it, with full legal ownership, usufruct, and possession, free of ground rent, mortgage, or any other lien, to said Don Clemente Gutierrez as such syndic, administrator of ecclesiastical property, and administrator for the Holy See, in such a way that neither he nor his heirs may ever allege any right to the said land in or out of court.

. . . And in order that it may be of record whenever and wherever necessary, they signed [this] with me, the said alcalde mayor, and corroborating witnesses with whom I am acting as the court for lack of a notary, because there is no notary of any kind in this kingdom, on the said day, month, and year. Salvador Garcia de Noriega, *juez receptor.* Juan Bautista Vigil. Clemente Gutierrez, syndic. Francisco Valdes y Bustos, witness. Juan Ignacio de Mestas, witness.[122]

---

[122] *Santa Fe,* 1776 Mission 5, 6. [Translation by Adams-Chavez, in *The Missions of New Mexico, 1776: A Description by Fray Francisco Atanasio Dominguez with other Contempopary Documents,* translated and annotated by Eleanor B. Adams and Fray Angelico Chavez (Albuquerque: University of New Mexico Press, 1956), pp. 319-320. At 320, footnote 3, Adams-Chavez observe that "the *juez receptor* was a notary commissioned to preside over and record certain legal proceedings, and in this case Garcia de Noriega was acting as such for lack of a notary. Under these circumstances, he was required by law to have two *testigos de asistencia,* or corroborating witnesses, to act with him."]

Section 2.   During the Mexican Period: 1821 to 1846

The Republic of Mexico, after the revolution of 1821,[123] adopted the Spanish laws for its government.   There was, therefore, but slight difference between the Spanish and Mexican laws.[124]   Basically, then, the character of Mexican jurisprudence did not differ from that of Old Spain.

By decree of August 7, 1823, the Mexican Congress confirmed the abolition of entails, and revoked the provisions prohibiting ecclesiastical corporations from acquiring property, which had been enacted by the Spanish Cortes on September 27, 1820:

> Art. 1.   All property which at any time has been entailed (*vinculado*) ceases to be so from the 27th September, 1820, by virtue of the law of that date, and shall continue to be absolutely free, and no one is in future permitted to entail either such or any other property.
> Art. 14.   The articles of the law of the 27th September, 1820, relative to ecclesiastical curacies, pious works, and mortmain, are hereby abolished, and the ancient laws in relation to the acquisition of real estate by ecclesiastical institutions (*amortización*) shall remain in force.[125]

In 1828, "the Spaniards were expelled from the territory [of New Mexico], pursuant to the law of proscription enacted against them, the year before, by the Congress of Mexico. . . . As regards the Church, the same law deprived her of almost all the Spanish missionaries." [126]   And in 1833-1834, all the missions of the Republic were secularized in accordance with provisions such as the following contained in the decree of April 16, 1834:

> Art. 1.   All the Missions of the Republic shall be secularized.
> Art. 2.   The Missions shall be converted into curacies

[123] Actually, the Mexican government started, not as a republican government, but rather as an imperial government with Iturbide as emperor. The Empire lasted until 1824, at which time it became a Republic.

[124] Cf. Blackmar, p. 62.

[125] *Legislación Mexicana*, I, p. 662, n. 347.   [Translation by Schmidt, pp. 309, 319.]

[126] Salpointe, p. 164.

and the Governors of the States where said Missions exist shall define boundaries.

Art. 3.   This decree shall have its full effect within four months from the day of its promulgation.[127]

By the provisions of the decree of secularization, the Franciscan-held properties in New Mexico became subject to the bishop of Durango, under whom the various administrators of the divers canonical corporations held the properties thereof in trust, in accordance with Spanish and Mexican jurisprudence. The Mexican government did not attempt to divest the Church of title to its churches.   On the contrary, that government maintained the Roman Catholic religion as the state religion; it continued the church establishment in existence as it was under the former sovereignty.

The American courts have held that a church building on mission land became the property of the church corporate with the decree of secularization,[128] that a grant to a church is good at common law and vests the title in the parson and his successors,[129] and that the priest of a mission, having charge of the church property, or at least some portion of it, coupled with an interest, may, in his character as priest, maintain in his own name an action to recover the possession of the mission lands reserved under the Mexican government for religious purposes.[130]

What the Mexican government did do, however, was to curtail the extent of church property possessed by the missions. Thus, the *fincas* and land estates became part of the public domain; the authorities empowered to grant lands dealt with them as with any other portion of the public domain,[131] and a grant of mission lands after their secularization was valid.[132]   It is

[127] *Legislación Mexicana*, II, p. 689, n. 1395.   [Translation by Schmidt, p. 185.]

[128] Nobili v. Redman, 6 Cal. 325 (1856).

[129] Town of Pawlet v. Clark, 13 U.S. (9 Cra.) 292, 3 L.Ed. 735 (1815).

[130] Santillan v. Moses, 1 Cal. 92 (1850).

[131] United States v. Ritchie, 58 U.S. (17 How.) 525, 15 L.Ed. 236 (1854).

[132] United States v. Cervantes, 59 U.S. (18 How.) 553, 15 L.Ed. 484 (1855).   It is interesting to note that the political chief of the province of New Mexico, under the government of Mexico, after the separation

difficult to ascertain precisely what was declared part of the public domain; probably the land immediately adjacent to the churches was not so declared.[133] Be that as it may, the decree of secularization did not affect New Mexico as it did California in particular, for the simple reason that the Franciscans in New Mexico had not been possessed with mission estates of the type and extent in which the Mexican government was interested for purposes of colonization. In this respect, "the New Mexican missions were radically different from the California establishments." [134]

One final observation is in order here by way of a parenthesis. There are few, if any, subjects more complex in the history of the New Mexico bar and bench than land grant litigation. Perhaps for the reasons hereinbefore suggested, there have not been any major suits in which the Church was a party; however, abstracts of titles not seldom are points of departure for field trips in legal archeology. Numerous indeed are the factors which make the venture extremely tortuous, among which may be noted that under Mexican law transfers of real estate could be made by parol contract.[135] The statute of frauds was unknown to the civil laws of Spain and Mexico; thus, prior to 1848 real estate could be sold in the same manner as personalty.

Section 3.   During the American Period: 1846 to 1912

On September 22, 1846, the Kearney Code of Laws was promulgated to govern the territory of New Mexico. It was not until the treaty of Guadalupe Hidalgo was ratified at Queretaro on May 30, 1848, however, that New Mexico was formally ceded to the United States. On December 30, 1853, by a treaty called the Gadsden Purchase, by which the United States acquired certain lands south of the Gila River, disputes over land growing out of the treaty of Guadalupe Hidalgo were finally adjusted.

---

from Spain, had no power, without express authority from the Mexican government, to grant away any part of the public domain.—Pino v. Hatch, 1 N.M. 125 (1855).

133 Cf. Blackmar, p. 326.

134 Bancroft, XVII, *History of Arizona and New Mexico,* p. 270.

135 Grant v. Jaramillo, 6 N.M. 313, 28 P. 508 (1892).

And "when the common law followed the American arms into that vast section of the continent that was ceded to the United States by the treaty of Guadalupe Hidalgo in 1848 it encountered two divisions of the civil law of Mexico which did not yield to its superior force. These two divisions of law were the Community Property Law and the conception of Waterrights by Appropriation, as opposed to the English system of Tenure by the Entirety and Riparian Rights in Water." [136]

In regard to land claims, the Kearney Code provided as follows:

Sec. 5. Every person claiming lands in this territory, by virtue of any Spanish or Mexican grant, may deliver to the register of lands a notice in writing stating the nature and extent of his claim, and shall also, at the same time deliver to the register of lands, for the purpose of being recorded, the grant, order of survey, deed of conveyance, or other written evidence of his claims, and the same shall be recorded by the register. . . .

Sec. 6. When there is no written evidence of the claim the claimant may take evidence in writing, before some officer having authority to administer oaths showing the nature and extent of his claim, how much of the land claimed has been actually cultivated and inhabited by himself, and those under whom he claims, and for what length of time; and also as to any grant, deed or conveyance relating to said land having ever existed, or any record thereof having ever been made, and as to the loss or destruction of the same, and how and when such loss and destruction happened. If any person shall neglect to deliver such evidence and notice of his claim as prescribed in this and the preceding section, within five years from the first day of next January, such claim shall be void.[137]

The following provisions of the Treaty of Guadalupe Hidalgo are worthy of note, inasmuch as title to church property in New

[136] Tittmann, "The First Irrigation Lawsuit," *N.M.H.R.*, II (1927), 363.

[137] Kearney Code of Laws, under "Register of Lands," as reported in *New Mexico Statutes 1953, Annotated*, edited by John W. Tranberg and Arie Poldervaart (12 vols. and Pocket Supplements through 1957, Indianapolis: The Allen Smith Co., 1954-1957), I, 349. [This source reference shall hereinafter be cited as 1953 N.M. Comp. Laws.] Sections 5 and 6, *supra*, of the Kearney Code were repudiated by Act of July 14, 1851.

Mexico was, at the time, held by the ecclesiastical administrators under the bishop of Durango:

> Art. VIII. . . . In the [territories previously belonging to Mexico, and which remain for the future within the limits of the United States,] property of every kind, now belonging to Mexicans not established there, shall be inviolably respected. The present owners, the heirs of these, and all Mexicans who may hereafter acquire said property by contract, shall enjoy with respect to it guaranties equally ample as if the same belonged to citizens of the United States.[138]

As a complement thereto, Article V of the Gadsden Treaty provided that

> All the provisions of the 8th . . . article . . . of the Treaty of Guadalupe Hidalgo, shall apply to the territory ceded by the Mexican republic in the first article of the present treaty, and to all the rights of persons and property, both civil and ecclesiastical, within the same, as fully and as effectually as if the said article [was] herein again recited and set forth.[139]

The American government, then, honored and respected the rights to properties previously recognized under the laws of the Republic of Mexico. And the American courts have found accordingly in numerous cases. Thus, for example, it has been held that a grant of land made by a duly authorized Mexican officer, in accordance with Mexican law, is protected by the law of nations, and also by the Treaty of Queretaro.[140] And where plaintiff's claim to land is based on a grant by officers of a foreign country, which was the sovereign of the soil at the time of the grant, the acts of the officers who made the grant and ordered the survey will be presumed to have been made with proper authority, and have been regularly executed.[141] There-

---

[138] Treaty of Peace between the United States and Mexico executed at the City of Guadalupe Hidalgo, February 2, 1848; Ratification exchanged at Queretaro, May 30, 1848; Proclamation made July 4, 1848; as reported in 1953 N.M. Comp. Laws, I, 362.

[139] The Gadsden Treaty between the United States and Mexico, signed December 30, 1853, as reported in 1953 N.M. Comp. Laws, I, 381.

[140] Reynolds v. West, 1 Cal. 322 (1850).

[141] De Lassus v. United States, 34 U.S. (9 Pet.) 117, 9 L.Ed. 71 (1835).

fore, by a cession of territory from one government to another, the rights of the inhabitants to their property is not impaired, and should be protected by legislative action of the recipient government, if this be necessary.[142] Accordingly, a petitioner claiming title to land under a grant from Mexico need not allege that the grant had been recognized by this government. The cession or conquest of a country does not affect the rights of property.[143]

When Bishop Lamy took possession of the Vicariate Apostolic of New Mexico in 1851, title to the church property in New Mexico passed to him in fee simple, although a trust was probably implied. In Santa Fe, the historical military chapel of Spanish days, called *La Castrense*, had been occupied by American troops after Kearney's occupation, and was now being used as the courtroom of one Judge Grafton Baker. Bishop Lamy "presented himself to Judge Baker and requested the return of the church, informing him that 'the deeds [were] in the possession of the Vicario,' and that 'there could be no doubt as to the title of the property' [Abel, *Correspondence of James S. Calhoun*, 409]. In his refusal to the Bishop's request the judge presented only the difficulties of authority and legal procedures. Among his friends . . . he made the boast that 'he would not give up the church to Bishop Lamy and Father Machebeuf, but that he would have them both hanged from the same gibbet' [Howlett, *Life of Bishop Machebeuf*, 177]." [144] Needless to say, the people of Santa Fe found something to be desired in such an attitude. And so Bishop Lamy was able to write Archbishop J. B. Purcell of Cincinnati in the following terms on September 2, 1851:

> . . . We have just recovered few days ago the finest chapel we had here. Since the time of war it was in the possession of the American troops. Having got the documents I brought them to the authorities; there was at first some difficulties, but when it was found out that I was determined to

[142] Teschemacher v. Thompson, 18 Cal. 11, 79 Am. Dec. 151 (1861).

[143] Hardy v. DeLeon, 5 Tex. 211 (1849).

[144] Sister M. Philibert, S.L., *Bishop Lamy, The Castrense, and the Court of Judge Baker* (Denver: Denver Catholic Register Press, 1955), [no pagination].

have it, and that I had in my favor not only the Mexicans, but three fourths of the Americans, and that there was danger in not giving up the church which they were using as a court house, then they surrendered the building according to all the formalities of the law, the court itself sitting in the church, myself being present, they gave me the keys. . . .[145]

In the "Constitutions of the Diocese of Santa Fe" promulgated by Bishop Lamy on March 2, 1861, following their adoption at two synods held in 1857 and 1867, it was decreed that the properties and goods of the churches were to be entered in the records as such and not as personal property of the respective pastors.[146] And in the Third Synod, in 1874, Bishop Lamy legislated as follows:

> Statute 26. In accordance with the decree of the [Second Plenary] Council of Baltimore (n. 183), "optamus maxime nullam in posterum erigi ecclesiam aut consecrari, nisi fuerit episcopo in cuius dioecesi erigenda est, in cultum divinum et utilitatem fidelium instrumento scripto adsignata." Accordingly, no church or chapel may be built without Our written permission; and Mass is not to be celebrated in said churches or chapels until the instrument of ownership is in Our hands.
> Statute 27. It is likewise necessary to have Our permission and the deed of ownership prior to the blessing of a cemetery.[147]

Meanwhile, the Legislative Assembly of the Territory of New Mexico for 1863-1864 passed an Act declaring the legal right to property under lawful title granted by the authorities, prior to the treaty of peace between the governments of the United States and the Republic of Mexico, with a view to preventing contentious litigation. Section 1 of that Act declares that

> Every person, or persons, being of the class or condition that have held, or hold, in lawful possession, under a legitimate title, derived from the authorities of Spain or Mexico, and which, according to the laws of that time, had legitimate

145 *Santa Fe*, 1851 Diocesan 14.

146 Chapt. III, Art. III, n. 5.—*Santa Fe*, 1861 Diocesan 6.

147 *Santa Fe*, 1874 Diocesan 10. [Translation from the Spanish by the writer.]

authority to grant such title to property, upon whatever lands belonging to said governments, prior to the treaty of peace by the latter with the United States, who actually find themselves in legal possession upon said lands, in quiet and peaceful possession, and without being interrupted, from the time that the Government of the United States comprised within its limits this Territory; the said persons are entitled to lawful claim of property and legal ownership, under the limits thereof, to the lands mentioned, in the same manner as those who had acquired by purchase, inheritance, or legal conveyance, be the same whatever it may, according to law, exclusively, and against any other persons whatsoever, who lay claim subsequent to that date.[148]

And the 1871-1872 Legislative Assembly passed an Act empowering foreigners to hold real estate in the territory of New Mexico:

Foreigners shall have full power and authority to acquire or hold real estate by deed, will, inheritance or otherwise, when the same may be acquired in good faith and in due form of law, and also to alienate, sell, assign and transfer the same to their heirs or other persons, whether such heirs or other persons be or not citizens of the United States; and when a foreigner having title or interest in any lands or estate dies, such lands or estate shall descend and vest in the same manner as if such foreigner were a citizen of the United States, and such circumstance shall not be an impediment to any person holding an interest in said estate, although not a citizen of the United States, for all said persons shall have the same rights and recourses and shall in all respects be treated on the same footing as native citizens of the United States with respect to the personal estate of a foreigner dying intestate and all persons interested in said estate under the laws of this Territory whether foreigners or not.[149]

ARTICLE 7. THE RECEPTION AND APPLICATION OF THE COMMON LAW OF ENGLAND IN NEW MEXICO

Reference has already been made in Section 3 of the preceding Article to the effect that the common law of England followed

---

[148] *Laws of the Territory of New Mexico Passed by the Legislative Assembly, 1863-1864* (Albuquerque: Hezekiah S. Johnson, 1864), p. 54. [Hereinafter, references to New Mexico session laws will be cited as N.M. Laws, prefixed by the year of the legislative assembly in question.]

[149] 1871-72 N.M. Laws, chapt. V, § 1.

the American occupation into New Mexico, thus supplanting the civil law.

More specifically, the Legislative Assembly for the Territory of New Mexico enacted the following statute on January 7, 1876:

> In all the courts in this Territory the common law as recognized in the United States of America shall be the rule of practice and decision.[150]

The change that was wrought in the legal life of New Mexico by this enactment was, of course, tremendous. The history alone behind English law is nothing short of spectacular, having been patient, as it was, of contributory influence from Roman, Anglo-Saxon, Scandinavian, Frankish, Norman, and Canon law.

The term *common law* (*ius commune*) was a phrase well known to canon lawyers of the middle ages, who used it to distinguish the general and ordinary law of the Universal Church from particular legislation in vogue in a given region. From the ecclesiastical the term easily passed into the secular law and courts of England,[151] where it eventually was used in contrast to statute law, signifying the unwritten rules or customs common to all parts of England, the *lex non scripta*. Thus, the unenacted part—and this was the great bulk—of the law was conceived as *consuetudo,* or custom. And the most important of all customs was the custom of the king's court. Reliance upon previous court decisions for the ascertainment of rules applicable to a given situation or case became a judicial habit, and finally a custom or rule in itself. This rule of referring to legal precedents engendered the judicial doctrine of *stare decisis.*[152]

This, then, is the system of law which supplanted the civil law in New Mexico. The legislature of New Mexico intended, by the language in the section above-cited, to adopt the common

---

150 1875-1876 N.M. Laws, ch. 2, § 2, being section 21-3-3 of 1953 N.M. Comp. Laws.

151 Cf. Pollock-Maitland, *The History of English Law* (2 vols., 2. ed., Cambridge: University Press, 1909), I, 156 (hereinafter cited Pollock-Maitland).

152 From the maxim, *"Stare decisis, et non quieta movere."*

law, or *lex non scripta*, and such British statutes of a general nature not local to that kingdom, nor in conflict with the Constitution or laws of the United States, nor of the Territory of New Mexico, which are applicable to the conditions and circumstances in New Mexico, and which were in force at the time of the American separation from the mother country.[153]

The statement, namely, that by the adoption of the common law in New Mexico the civil law was completely supplanted, must be understood in the sense that the latter was indeed supplanted by the former, but without prejudice to the incorporation of the civil law in the statutes of the Territory.[154] Accordingly, by the adoption in New Mexico of the common law as the basis of jurisprudence, there was intended indeed not the repeal of the statute laws, but the acceptance of only so much of the common law as did not conflict therewith.[155]

It follows from the foregoing that by the statute enacted on January 7, 1876, the common law is the rule of practice and decision in New Mexico, except where modified by statute.[156] Consequently, the common law as a rule of practice and decision prevails where there are no special statutory provisions in respect to a given matter.[157] One example where the common law

[153] Browning v. Browning's Estate, 3 Gild. (N.M.) 659, 3 John. (N.M.) 371, 9 P. 677 (1886); Territory ex rel. Wade v. Ashenfelter, 4 Gild. (N.M.) 93, 4 John. (N.M.) 85, 12 P. 879 (1887), appeal dismissed 154 U.S. 493, 14 S.Ct. 1141, 38 L.Ed. 1079 (1893); Gurule v. Duran, 20 N.M. 348, 149 P. 302, L.R.A. 1915F, 648 (1915); Plomteaux v. Solano, 25 N.M. 24, 176 P. 77 (1918); Blake v. Hoover Motor Co., 28 N.M. 371, 212 P. 738 (1923); Yeo v. Tweedy, 34 N.M. 611, 286 P. 970 (1930).

[154] Eals v. Ares, 25 N.M. 459, 185 P 780 (1919), overruling Barnett v. Barnett, 9 N.M. 205, 50 P. 337 (1897); Field v. Otero, 35 N.M. 68, 290 P. 1015 (1930).

[155] Bent v. Thompson, 5 N.M. 408, 23 P. 234 (1890), affirmed 138 U.S. 114, 11 S.Ct. 238, 34 L.Ed. 902 (1891).

[156] Sandoval v. Albright, 14 N.M. 345, 93 P. 717 (1908), affirmed, Albright v. Sandoval, 216 U.S. 331, 30 S.Ct. 318, 54 L.Ed. 502 (1910); State v. De Armijo, 18 N.M. 646, 140 P. 1123 (1914); Dye v. Crary, 12 N.M. 460, 78 P. 533 (1904), affirmed 208 U.S. 515, 28 S.Ct. 360, 52 L.Ed. 595 (1908).

[157] Walker v. N. M. & S. P. R. Co., 165 U.S. 593, 17 S.Ct. 421, 41 L.Ed. 837 (1897); affirming 7 N.M. 282, 34 P. 43 (1893).

does not prevail as a rule of practice and decision in New Mexico is in the matter of community property. Since the civil law of Spain and Mexico served as the model for the statutory law of New Mexico concerning the property rights of husband and wife, that law will be looked to as the basis for interpretation and definition.[158]

[158] McDonald v. Senn, 53 N.M. 198, 204 P.2nd 990, 10 A.L.R.2d 966 (1949).

CHAPTER III

THE FICTION THEORY AT ANGLO–AMERICAN CORPORATION LAW AND THE ATTITUDE OF INNOCENT IV CONCERNING THE ELEMENT OF FICTION IN JURISTIC PERSONALITIES

ARTICLE 1. INTRODUCTION

Besides physical persons, civilized peoples have for a long time recognized the existence of moral persons as well. These juristic personalities, these corporations, have long been regarded as subjects of rights. That much should provoke a universal plea of nolo contendere. Unanimity, however, ceases therewith. Much has been written concerning the metaphysical nature of these juristic personalities. It would indeed be an exaggeration to suggest that there are, in this matter, *tot sententiae quot homines;* but it can be said that much controversy and many theories have arisen.

The legal entities which enjoy and exercise certain transcendent rights are generally called juristic persons or corporations, although the Code of Canon Law refers to them as moral persons, the usual expression employed in the immediate past centuries to indicate the metaphysical element involved. However, in this same frame of reference the Code of Canon Law also employs the terms *persona iuridica* [1] and *ens iuridicum.*[2] This legal entity, a juridical person, may be described as one distinct from a physical person, but which nonetheless is considered as such, having capacity at law, being a subject of legal rights and duties. But the precise nature of this consideration has been the subject of much controversy among jurists. There exist sharp differences of opinion as to exactly what forms the basis of this juridical en-

[1] Cf. canon 687.

[2] Cf. canon 1409.

tity, a subject not identical with either the incorporated members in the case of a corporation, or the accumulation of property in the instance of an institution. Whether the basis for such consideration in the mind of the law is a mere fiction, or something real, or something else again, has been and still is a matter of controversy among jurists.

And among the most famous of these theories is the so-called Fiction Theory. For all practical purposes, this theory is considered orthodox at Anglo-American law. Now, many people credit Pope Innocent IV with the paternity of the Fiction Theory.[3] The primary object of this chapter, then, is to investigate the mind of this great jurist concerning the element of fiction in juristic personalities, considered in juxtaposition to a very brief summary of the Anglo-American law on a parallel basis. The writer has exhausted those cases which have been decided by the New Mexico Supreme Court and which reveal the jurisprudence of that jurisdiction on the points relevant to this study. Since the number of such cases is relatively meager, however, and since a general view of American jurisprudence is contemplated anyway, cases adjudged by the United States Supreme Court, by the federal courts, and by courts of various jurisdictions will be cited as representative of the mind of Anglo-American law in this matter.

Section 1. *Roman Juridical Personality*

Roman law gave relatively little consideration to what we call corporations as such, and the law on the subject contains not a small number of ambiguous phrases which, unfortunately, have been the source of much of the confusion concerning the nature of a juristic personality. And yet it was Roman law which evolved the intricate legal conception of a person existing only within the contemplation of the law.[4] The juristic notion of the Roman law was later absorbed by the Canon law, transfused into the body of the law of the European continent, and from

___

[3] "Pope Innocent IV has been called the father of the modern theory of corporations."—Pollock-Maitland, I, 494.

[4] Cf. Wernz-Vidal, II, 25.

there into the English common law. From this latter source it has entered American jurisprudence.[5]

The Roman corporation was designated by various ambiguous terms: *societas, ordo, sodalitas, corpus, collegium.*[6] Under the earlier Roman law, only the natural person could be *capax,* the subject of rights, within the domain of the *ius privatum;* and only the State could enjoy a similar privilege in the realm of the *ius publicum* and *ius sacrum.* Eventually, however, the Roman State came to be recognized as a person in private law in respect to the *fiscus.* And thus the theory of juristic personality came to be recognized in imperial Roman law. And this concept of juristic personality began to be expanded as Roman activity became more and more organized.

It appears that the technical expression for the idea of corporation is *universitas personarum.* Nowhere indeed is there to be found any statement or definition concerning the precise nature of a corporation. But juridical personality is inferable from situations in which these corporate bodies exercised such personal rights and privileges as the right to sue and to be sued, to contract, to own property and the like, in their own name, independently of the rights of the members by which the body was constituted: "Si quid universitati debetur, singulis non debetur; nec quod debet universitas, singuli debent" [D. (40, 3) 1.].

Before the time of Justinian (527-565), the notion of an *universitas personarum* postulated simply an organized body of physical persons. Broadly considered, there were two kinds of such bodies: the *societas* and the *collegium.* The former was an

[5] Unless otherwise noted in specific instances, the synopsis on Roman law in this section has been condensed from the treatment thereof by Brown, *The Canonical Juristic Personality with Special Reference to its Status in the United States of America,* The Catholic University of America Canon and Civil Law Studies, n. 39 (Washington, D.C.: The Catholic University of America Press, 1927), pp. 8-23 (hereinafter cited Brown) and Schulz, *Classical Roman Law* (Oxford: Clarendon Press, 1954), pp. 86-102.

[6] "[Termini] in genere ambigui, perchè adibiti anche ad usi, in cui non esprimono l'associazione, nè significano la personalità."—Bonfante, *Istituzioni di Diritto Romano* (10. ed., Torino: G. Giappichelli, 1946), p. 64, § 19.

organized body of persons with a fixed number of members, each
partner having a disposable share of the common property; when
a partner died or withdrew, the partnership was inevitably dissolved. By contrast, the *collegium* was an organized body of
persons with a variable number of members, no member having
a fixed and disposable share of the common property; thus,
when a member died or withdrew, the "corporation" was not
dissolved.

But at the time of Justinian the institution appeared, at least
in embryonic form. The institution was designated as an *universitas rerum,* a patrimony or quantity of property destined
for a charitable work or purpose, such as a hospital or an or-
phanage. It is debatable whether at this time the institution
appeared in the form of a strict foundation standing alone as an
independent personality, wherein the patrimony itself is personified and considered as a subject of rights. In any event, impetus was given to the creation of institutions by the favorable
attitude of Constantine toward Christianity which fostered charitable and religious undertakings.

By way of conclusion, it may be said that there is a recognition of the corporate conception in the sources of Roman law;
yet it is not defined anywhere, nor do Roman jurists of any age
speak of what are now called "juristic persons" by that name.

Since the Church developed under Roman law, it is not surprising that ecclesiastical jurists took the idea of juridical personality from Roman law, and adapted it to their own needs.[7]
The sources indicate that ecclesiastical organizations were given
recognition as juridical persons under Justinian law, and this
was doubtless a vital factor in the development of the notion of
juridical personality in the ecclesiastical law of the time.

*Section 2. Different Theories on the Metaphysical Nature of
Juristic Personalities*

Nowhere does the Code of Canon Law proffer a real definition
of the notion of a juristic personality. And at Anglo-American
law, lawyers and judges have merely reiterated the doctrine that
a corporation is an intangible legal entity, without body and

7 Wernz-Vidal, II, 26.

without soul, separate and distinct from the personality of the members who compose it. The jurisprudence of both Canon law and Anglo-American law, while both in their own way delineate and suggest preferences to a certain extent in this controversial matter, has not formulated a clear notion of the metaphysical nature of a juridical person. European jurists have waged war over this question; indeed, volume upon volume has been devoted to the subject.

Savigny (1779-1861), in the first half of the 19th century in Germany, began the modern scientific consideration of the subject.[8] He observed that property can belong in law to a corporation and not to any individual. His question, then, was: "Who or what is the real owner of this property?" And his answer to that query gave rise to the Fiction Theory: corporate property belongs to a fictitious being and not to any real person or entity. Savigny took as his point of departure the proposition that ownership involves the possession of a will by the owner; and he concluded that inasmuch as a corporation does not really possess a will, it must as a property-owner be a fictitious person.

The Purpose Theory, fathered by Brinz (1820-1887)[9] in Germany, taught that corporate property is not owned by a fictitious being created by the State, but by no person at all. It is not the property of a person, but of a purpose—"Zweckvermögen." This theory was primarily intended to explain the ownership of property by charitable institutions. This theory, like that of Savigny, regarded the personality of corporations as fictitious.

Meanwhile, Gierke (1841-1921)[10] in Germany founded a rival school of thought with his Realist Theory. He taught that corporations are real persons. This personality is neither fictitious, nor artificial, nor created by the State, but both real and natural, recognized but not created by the State.

[8] Savigny expounded his theory in his *System des heutigen Römischen Rechts* (Berlin, 1840).

[9] *Lehrbuch der Pandecten* (Leipzig, 1895).

[10] *Das Deutsche Genossenschaftsrecht* (4 vols., Berlin, 1868-1913).

Jhering (1818-1892) (in Germany),[11] de Vareilles-Sommières (in France),[12] and Schwabe (in Switzerland),[13] rejected all the foregoing views. Essentially, they taught that the "subject of rights" in cases of corporate ownership of property is simply the natural persons who compose the entity. They concurred with the advocates of the Fiction Theory in maintaining that the personality of a corporation, or even its existence as an entity, is a pure fiction or metaphor; but they maintained that the fictitious personality is not "created" by the State, because it does not really exist. To the proponents of this, the Symbolist Theory, a corporation is merely an abbreviated form or way of writing the names of the members several.

ARTICLE 2.   ANGLO-AMERICAN LAW AND THE ATTITUDE OF
INNOCENT IV

For all practical purposes, no English or American lawyer has philosophized about the metaphysical nature of a corporation. American jurisprudence has followed common law in accepting the Fiction Theory of Savigny,[14] who, in turn, endeavored to sustain his theory from the sources of Canon law, particularly the commentaries of Innocent IV.[15] Generally, "lawyers from the thirteenth century onwards have been wont to attribute to the corporation a 'personality' that is 'fictitious' or 'artificial' . . . [and] the theory which speaks of a corporation's personality as fictitious was borrowed by English lawyers from medieval canonists." [16]

Even Coke (1552-1634) and Blackstone (1723-1780) referred to the nature of the juridical person only incidentally. Coke spoke of a corporation as a "fiction," and then proceeded to say in an obiter dictum:

[11] *Geist des Römischen Rechts* (Leipzig, 1891).

[12] *Les Personnes Morales* (Paris, 1902).

[13] *Rechts-subject und Nutzbefugnis* (Basel, 1901).

[14] Brown, p. 59.

[15] *Ibid.*, p. 46.

[16] Pollock-Maitland, I, 488.

And it is great reason that an hospital, etc., in expectancy or intendency, or nomination, should be sufficient to support the name of an incorporation when the corporation itself is only in abstracto, and rests only in intendment and consideration of the law; for a corporation aggregate of many is invisible, immortal, and rests only in intendment and consideration of the law . . . [Corporations] cannot commit treason, nor be outlawed, nor excommunicate, for they have no souls, neither can they appear in person, but by attorney.[17]

Blackstone observed that a corporation, "as Sir Edward Coke says, is invisible, existing only in intendment and consideration of law . . . Neither can a corporation be excommunicated: for it has no soul, as is gravely observed by Sir Edward Coke." [18] Both Coke and Blackstone simply and as a matter of course accepted the Fiction Theory of Savigny. Accordingly, "all student's of the common law will recognize in [Savigny's] theory the most prominent features of the orthodox doctrine of Anglo-American law—even including its self-contradictions. The orthodox American lawyer would probably be apt to say, 'A corporation is a fictitious, artificial person, composed of natural persons, created by the State, existing only in contemplation of law, invisible, soulless, immortal.' " [19] And it is interesting to note that "our curious phrase 'corporation sole' only appears late in the day and seems to be exclusively English; but the canonists had come very near to it in their treatment of the cases in which an *ecclesia* had but one cleric connected with it; the *dignitas* or the *sedes* or the like could be personified. Here, as in the case of a 'corporation aggregate,' there is 'fictitious personality.' So the canonists' corporation is rather a personified institution than an unified group of men." [20]

[17] Sutton's Hospital Case, 10 Co. 23, 32, 77 Eng. (6 K.B.) 973 (1613).

[18] Blackstone, *Commentaries on the Laws of England,* annotated by George Sharswood (4 vols. in 2, Philadelphia: Lippincott, 1898), I, 476 (hereinafter cited Blackstone Commentaries).

[19] Machen, "Corporate Personality," *Harvard Law Review,* XXIV (1910), 255.

[20] Pollock-Maitland, I, 502.

Section 1.   Classification and Establishment of Corporations

A.   Anglo-American Law

Beginning with the common law concept of a corporation as a body politic for municipal, ecclesiastical, or eleemosynary purposes only, the use of such artificial persons at Anglo-American law has been gradually extended to profit-making enterprises until, at the present time, it is through such legal entities that a very large part of the business of the country is transacted.[21]

A corporation was defined by the United States Supreme Court at an early date in the terms following:

> A corporation is an artificial being, invisible, intangible, and existing only in contemplation of law. Being the mere creature of law, it possesses only those properties which the charter of its creation confers upon it, either expressly, or as incidental to its very existence. These are such as are supposed best calculated to effect the object for which it was created. Among the most important are immortality, and, if the expression may be allowed, individuality; properties, by which a perpetual succession of many persons are considered as the same, and may act as a single individual. They enable a corporation to manage its own affairs, and to hold property, without the perplexing intricacies, the hazardous and endless necessity, of perpetual conveyances for the purpose of transmitting it from hand to hand. It is chiefly for the purpose of clothing bodies of men, in succession, with these qualities and capacities, that corporations were invented, and are in use. By these means, a perpetual succession of individuals are capable of acting for the promotion of the particular object, like one immortal being.[22]

The foregoing definition is classical; it has been frequently cited and approved.[23]

So familiar is the word "corporation" that the term "person" prima facie, at common law and apart from any statutory enact-

---

[21] *American Jurisprudence* (58 vols. and Indices, Rochester, N.Y.: Bancroft-Whitney Co., 1935-1952), XIII, § 1, [Hereinafter cited by Volume and Section, thus: 13 Am. Jur., Corporations, § 1.]

[22] Dartmouth College v. Woodward, 17 U.S. (4 Wheat.) 518, 636, 4 L.Ed. 629 (1819).

[23] 13 Am. Jur., Corporations, § 2.

ment limiting its meaning, includes both natural and artificial persons, and therefore as a general rule includes corporations.[24] It follows that a corporation is deemed a citizen of the state, territory, or other political body wherein it is organized.[25]

At Anglo-American law, corporations are classified as corporations aggregate and sole, public and private, quasi-public, eleemosynary, *de jure* and *de facto*, foreign and domestic. A corporation aggregate is a corporation which is or may be composed of more than one member, as in the case of a joint-stock corporation or a non-stock corporation of which there are two or more members, while a corporation sole is composed of a single member and his successors in office.[26]

Corporations which are created for public purposes only, connected with the administration of government, and interests and franchises of which are the exclusive property and domain of government itself, are "public corporations," while corporations created for private as distinguished from purely public purposes are "private corporations." [27]

A quasi-public corporation may be described as a private corporation which has been given certain powers of a public nature in order to enable it to discharge its duties for the public benefit.[28] Corporations created for charitable purposes—eleemosynary corporations—are those which are constituted for the perpetual distribution of free alms to such purposes as their founders and supporters have directed.[29]

[24] McKinley v. Wheeler, 130 U.S. 630, 9 S.Ct. 638, 32 L.Ed. 1048 (1888); State ex rel. Northwestern Colonization & Improvement Co. of Chihuahua v. Huller, 23 N.M. 306, 168 P. 528, 1 A.L.R. 170 (1917), certiorari denied 246 U.S. 667, 38 S.Ct. 336, 62 L.Ed. 929 (1918), error dismissed 247 U.S. 503, 38 S.Ct. 426, 62 L.Ed. 1239 (1918).

[25] Food Machinery & Chemical Corp. v. Marquez, 139 F.Supp. 421 (D.C.N.M. 1956).

[26] *Corpus Juris Secundum* (95 vols. and Indices, Brooklyn, N.Y.: The American Law Book Co., 1936-1951), XVIII, § 15. [Hereinafter cited by Volume and Section, thus: 18 C.J.S., Corporations, § 15.]

[27] State v. Sunset Ditch Co., 48 N.M. 17, 145 P.2d 219 (1944).

[28] 13 Am. Jur., Corporations, § 18.

[29] 13 Am. Jur., Corporations, § 19.

If there has been substantial compliance with statutory requirements in the formation of a corporation, the result is a corporation *de jure*—one whose existence cannot be successfully questioned even in a direct proceeding brought by the state for that purpose. If there has not been such substantial compliance with statutory requirements, the result may be a corporation *de facto,* which is like a corporation *de jure* except that its existence may be successfully questioned by a direct proceeding brought by the state for that purpose.[30]

In general, a domestic corporation with respect to a particular state or country is one created by or existing under the laws of that state or country, while a foreign corporation is one created by or existing under the laws of some other state or country.[31]

It must also be noted that where the requirements for a corporation *de facto* have not been met—that is, where there is no valid law under which the association might have organized as a corporation, or where there has been no colorable compliance with statutory requirements, or where there has been no user of corporate powers—an association may in a particular case be treated as if it were a corporation. This doctrine is called the doctrine of corporation by estoppel, even though the usual requirements of estoppel—damage sustained in reliance upon a misrepresentation—may not be present.[32]

It is fundamental at Anglo-American law that a corporation may be created and can exist only by virtue of authority from the government.[33] Unless prohibited by constitution, a state legislature may create corporations by special statute, but nearly all corporations today are organized under a general statute.[34]

[30] 13 Am. Jur., Corporations, §§ 45-62.

[31] 18 C.J.S., Corporations, § 20.

[32] 13 Am. Jur., Corporations, §§ 63-69.

[33] 13 Am. Jur., Corporations, § 30.

[34] Such a statute usually requires that each of the persons forming a corporation prepare and sign a memorandum or certificate or articles of incorporation and acknowledge it before a notary. The incorporators must be adults, and there need not be any fixed number of incorporators unless the statute so provides. The statute usually requires that some officer issue to the incorporators a certificate of incorporation and that

B.   The Attitude of Innocent IV [35]

It is a known fact that neither the Glossators nor the Decretists could conceive of a juridical personality subsisting without the substratum of a collectivity of physical persons. For the Glossators and Decretists, every such collectivity came under the common concept of corporation (*universitas, collegium,* etc.), provided that said substratum presented itself as a subject of public or private rights. Hence, even the State and the Church were regarded by them as corporations. In addition, it is debatable whether they recognized a clear distinction between corporations on the one hand and simple associations or societies

---

this certificate be filed with the Secretary of State or some other officer either as a condition precedent to the existence of the corporation or its right to do business. Finally, the certificate must be accepted by the corporation; such acceptance is usually inferred from its election of officers and—in the case of a business corporation—its beginning business.—13 Am. Jur., Corporations, §§ 20-44.

[35] Sinibaldo dei Fieschi was born in Genoa; the exact date of his birth is not known. He pursued his juristic studies at the University of Bologna under such learned canon lawyers as Laurentius Hispanus, Vincentius Hispanus, and Ioannes Teutonicus; and under such famous Roman lawyers as Azo, Accursius, and Iacobus Balduini. After completing his studies he stayed on at the University as professor of canon law until 1226, when he was called to be an *auditor litterarum contradictarum* in the Roman Curia. In 1227 he was raised to the cardinalate. After a distinguished curial career he was elected Supreme Pontiff on June 25, 1243, taking the name of Innocent IV. During his pontificate he wrote a splendid commentary on the Decretals of Gregory IX. Innocent IV prepared this work, entitled *Commentaria in Quinque Libros Decretalium,* as a private doctor, rather than as the supreme legislator of the Church, and by using an exegetical method he set forth the canonical teaching outlined in the Decretals. He died in Naples on December 7, 1254. Innocent IV is considered by many to have been the greatest lawyer ever to sit on the Chair of Peter.—Cf. Heintschel, *The Medieval Concept of an Ecclesiastical Office,* The Catholic University of American Canon Law Studies, n. 363 (Washington, D.C.: The Catholic University of America Press, 1956), pp. 84-85; Van Hove, *Prolegomena ad Codicem Iuris Canonici,* editio altera auctior et emendatior (Mechliniae-Romae: H. Dessain, 1945), p. 477; Ruffini, *La Classificazione delle Persone Giuridiche in Sinibaldo dei Fieschi (Innocenzo IV) ed in Federico Carlo di Savigny (1898),* in *Scritti Giuridici Minori* (2 vols., Milano: A. Guiffrè, 1936), II, 5, at footnote 1 (hereinafter cited Ruffini).

on the other. In general, then, it can be said that the Glossators and Decretists were deprived of substantial and distinctive criteria with which to determine a classification of juristic persons.[36]

It was the Decretalists who sought, for the first time, to effect the semblance of a clear classification and determination of juridical personalities. And the credit for such a classification, in very large measure, must be attributed to Innocent IV.[37]

First of all, Innocent IV distinguished between *collegia realia* and *collegia personalia.* As examples of the first division he cited *civitates, burgi, ecclesiae;* as examples of the latter type he enumerated *collegia professionum, negotiationum, officiorum, religionum, scholarium.*[38] In making the foregoing distinction Innocent IV very explicitly stated that there was no basis for his division in the sources, but that, nonetheless, he had deduced the distinction by means of analogy from real and personal servitudes:

> . . . Quod autem praedicta collegia appellantur personalia et realia non habetur in iure, sed per simile dicitur munerum servitutum realium et personalium.[39]

Secondly, Innocent IV distinguished between *collegia necessaria et naturalia* and *collegia non necessaria et voluntaria.* The former class consisted of those *collegia* to which one belongs of necessity and to which one is determined by reason of origin, or domicile, or other similar reasons.[40] To the latter class belong those who so wish to by means of their own volitional act, given that "etiam illi qui sunt de eadem professione vel negotiatione, sive sint plures vel pauciores quam illi qui ita coierunt collegium, non coguntur illud intrare," [41] and from which it is possible to

[36] Cf. Ruffini, II, 10.

[37] Cf. Gillet, *La Personnalité Juridique en Droit Ecclésiastique spécialement chez les Décrétistes et les Décrétalistes et dans le Code de Droit Canonique* (Malines: W. Godenne, 1927), p. 108, § 2. [Hereinafter cited Gillet.]

[38] Innocentius IV, *Commentaria in Quinque Libros Decretalium* (Venetiis, 1570), X, v, 31, 14. [Hereinafter cited Innocent IV.]

[39] *Loc. cit.*

[40] *Loc. cit.*

[41] *Loc. cit.*

secede at will, since "qui ita intraverunt possunt inde exire." [42]

It must be noted, too, that Innocent IV drew a very clear line of separation between a simple society and a corporation, observing very succinctly:

> Societas . . . non constituit collegium . . . vel corpus . . . Societas non est collegium per se, nisi aliter constituatur per principem, vel senatusconsultum, vel alio modo.[43]

The decretal upon which Innocent IV's commentary hereinbefore considered is based was written in 1225 by Honorius III to the archdeacon of Soissons. By means of that decretal, Honorius III enjoined private persons from attempting to establish a *collegium* and to have a corporate seal without due authorization.[44]

Two elements concur in making up a moral person. There is, first of all, the material element, which is composed of the members who constitute the given moral personality. Ordinarily, two or three physical persons are postulated for the forming of a juridic personality. For an ecclesiastical *collegium* two members are sufficient.[45]

Besides the material element, there is required the formal element in the constitution of a moral personality. This amounts to the intervention of legitimate authority in the establishing of a moral person as such. Innocent IV observed that a given *corpus* or *universitas* derived its rights from this formal intervention of the legitimate superior, and that a collectivity of members not so favored by legitimate authority could not pretend to enjoy the special rights otherwise granted to a corporation:

> Intellige de illa universitate quae constituta est per superiorem sic quod sit universitas, nam si tot essent homines

---

[42] *Loc. cit.*

[43] *Loc. cit.*

[44] X, v, 31, 14: ". . . Mandamus . . . ne praesumant vel de novo fabricare sigillum, vel uti eo, si forte noviter fuerit fabricatum . . ."—Potthast, *Regesta Pontificum Romanorum inde ab anno post Christum natum MCXCVIII ad annum MCCCIV* (2 vols., Berolini, 1874-1875), n. 7845 (hereinafter cited Potthast). [Note: all citations from the *Corpus Iuris* are from the *Corpus Iuris Canonici* (ed. Lipsiensis secunda, post Aemilii Richteri curas . . . instruxit Aemilius Friedberg, 2 vols., Lipsiae, 1879-1881).]

[45] Cf. X, i, 6, 1; Innocent IV in h. c., n. 1.

simul collecti quot sunt Romae et non haberent tacitum vel expressum consensum a superiore non possent sibi constituere iudicem nec haberent alia iura et privilegia universitatis.[46]

In this same frame of reference it is noteworthy that according to the text just cited, Innocent IV expressly declared that the required formal element need not be express, that is, he noted that the consent of the superior can be either tacit or express.

Section 2.   Tortious and Delictal Capability of a Corporation

A.   Anglo-American Law

From the definition of a corporation as delineated, for example, in the Dartmouth College case, it follows that a corporation is regarded as a legal entity, separate, distinct, and apart from the members who compose it.[47]   And this doctrine applies equally to corporations aggregate and corporations sole.[48]   This doctrine is a legal theory introduced for purposes of convenience and to subserve the ends of justice.[49]   The concept cannot, therefore, be extended to a point beyond its reason and policy, and when it is invoked in support of an end subversive to this policy it will be disregarded by the courts.[50]   Accordingly, in furtherance of justice, the circumstances of a case may sometimes require a court of equity to ignore the separate entity of a corporation, and to look to the individual owners or sole owner of its capital stock as the real party in interest.[51]

Although the liability of a corporation for a tort seems to have

[46] Innocent IV, ad X, i, 31, 3.

[47] New Colonial Ice Co. v. Helvering, 292 U.S. 435, 54 S.Ct. 788, 78 L.Ed. 1348 (1933), affirming New Colonial Ice Co. v. Commissioner of Internal Revenue, 66 F.2d 480 (C.C.A.2d 1933), certiorari granted New Colonial Ice Co. v. Helvering, 290 U.S. 621, 54 S.Ct. 208, 78 L.Ed. 542 (1933); Aiello v. Crampton, 201 F. 891, 120 C.C.A. 189 (C.C.A.N.M. 1912).

[48] 18 C.J.S., Corporations, § 4.

[49] Western Battery & Supply Co. v. Hazelett Storage Battery Co., 61 F.2d 220 (C.C.A. 8th 1932), certiorari denied 288 U.S. 608, 53 S.Ct. 399, 77 L.Ed. 982 (1933).

[50] 13 Am. Jur., Corporations, § 7.

[51] State v. Trust & Savings Bank v. Hermosa Land & Cattle Co., 30 N.M. 566, 240 P. 469 (1925); Kutz Canon Oil & Gas Co. v. Harr, 56 N.M. 358, 244 P.2d 522 (1952).

been denied under the early common law, the old idea that inasmuch as a corporation is an artificial creature which has no "soul" it can not commit a tort may now be regarded as obsolete.[52] At the present time it is universally recognized that ordinary private corporations may commit almost every kind of a tort and be held liable therefor, and this liability may be enforced in the same manner as if the wrong had been committed by a natural person.[53] Therefore, a corporation is civilly liable for torts committed by its servants or agents [54] within the scope of their express, implied, or apparent authority, or in the course of their employment as such.[55] This is true even though the tortious act may not have been authorized in the first place or subsequently ratified,[56] or may have been committed in excess [57] or in disobedience [58] of instructions, or even wantonly and recklessly.[59] Thus, the rule of respondeat superior within its proper scope is applicable to corporations, and the doctrine of ultra vires, as formerly understood and applied, no longer has any application in such cases.[60]

[52] 13 Am. Jur., Corporations, § 1118.

[53] Van Zandt v. Bergen County, N.J., 79 F.2d 506 (C.C.A.N.J. 1935); Byrd v. Blue Ridge Rural Electric Co-op., 215 F.2d 542 (C.C.A.S.C. 1954), certiorari denied 348 U.S. 915, 75 S.Ct. 295, 99 L.Ed. 717 (1955).

[54] De Ronde v. Gaytime Shops, Inc., 239 F.2d 735 (C.A.N.Y. 1956).

[55] Egan v. United States, 137 F.2d 369 (C.C.A.Mo. 1943), certiorari denied 320 U.S. 788, 64 S.Ct. 195, 88 L.Ed. 474 (1943); Union Electric Co. of Missouri v. United States, 137 F.2d 369 (C.C.A.Mo. 1943), certiorari denied 320 U.S. 788, 64 S.Ct. 195, 88 L.Ed. 474 (1943); Stewart v. Potter, 44 N.M. 460, 104 P.2d 736 (1940).

[56] Epperson v. First National Bank, 209 Ala. 12, 95 So. 343 (1923), Jones v. Sherwood Distilling Co., 150 Md. 24, 132 Atl. 278 (1926).

[57] Barret v. Minneapolis, etc., R. Co., 106 Minn. 51, 117 N.W. 1047, 130 Am.S.R. 585, 18 L.R.A.(N.S.) 416 (1908).

[58] J. J. Newberry Co. v. Judd, 259 Ky. 309, 82 S.W.2d 359 (1935); Rickman v. Safeway Stores, 124 Mont. 431, 227 P.2d 607 (1951).

[59] Dickerson v. Atlantic Refining Co., 201 N.C. 90, 159 S.E. 446 (1931); Brown v. Great Atlantic & Pacific Tea Co., 89 N.Y.S.2d 247, 279 App.Div. 304 (1949).

[60] Denver & R. G. R. Co. v. Harris, 3 John. (N.M.) 109, 3 Gild. (N.M.) 114, 2 P. 369 (1884), affirmed 122 U.S. 597, 7 S.Ct. 1286, 30 L.Ed. 1146 (1886).

Conversely, a corporation is not liable for the torts committed by its servants or agent outside the scope of his authority or agency, or the course of his employment,[61] except where it previously authorized the particular act,[62] or subsequently ratifies or adopts it.[63]

Indeed, the broad general rule is now well established under American criminal law, namely, that a corporation may be criminally liable for their criminal acts,[64] and the imposition of such liability is one of the significant departures from common law precedents.[65]   Except for such crimes as a corporation is held incapable of committing by reason of the fact that they involve personal malicious intent, a corporation may be subject to indictment or other criminal process,[66] although the criminal act is committed through its agents.[67]

In statutes defining crimes, the prohibition is frequently

[61] Clark v. Chesapeake & Potomac Telephone Co., 42 App.D.C. 444 (1914); Winkelman v. General Motors Corporation, 44 F.Supp. 960 (D.C. N.Y. 1942); Morrison v. Heller, 183 F.2d 38 (C.A.N.J. 1950). When one employee participates in a fraud for the benefit of a co-employee, the corporation is not charged with the knowlege of the former.—Wells, Fargo & Co. Express v. Walker, 9 N.M. 456, 54 P. 875 (1898).

[62] Colonial Stores v. Sasser, 17 Ga. App. 604, 54 S.E.2d 719 (1949); King v. Citizens Bank of De Kalb, 88 Ga. App. 40, 76 S.E.2d 86 (1953).

[63] Sandoval v. Southern California Enterprises, 98 Cal. App.2d 240, 219 P.2d 928 (1950); Gomez v. Loumat Realty Corp., 78 N.Y.S.2d 772 (1948); Lechner v. Ebenreiter, 235 Wis. 244, 292 N.W. 913 (1940).

[64] New York C. & H. R. R. Co. v. United States, 212 U.S. 481, 29 S.Ct. 304, 53 L.Ed. 613 (1908).

[65] People on Complaint of Styler v. Commonwealth Sanitation Co., 107 N.Y.S.2d 982 (1951). There are early authorities to the effect that a corporation cannot commit a crime.—State v. General Fire Extinguisher Co., 9 Ohio N.P.(N.S.) 438 (1910); United States v. Maryland State Licensed Beverage Ass'n., 138 F.Supp. 685 (D.C.Md. 1956), reversed on other grounds 240 F.2d 420 (C.A.Md. 1957).

[66] United States v. Crummer, 151 F.2d 958 (C.C.A.Kans. 1945), certiorari denied 327 U.S. 785, 66 S.Ct. 704, 90 L.Ed. 1012 (1946); Golden Guernsey Farms v. State, 223 Ind. 606, 63 N.E.2d 699 (1945).

[67] Zito v. United States, 64 F.2d 772 (C.C.A.Ill. 1933); United States v. Wilson, 59 F.2d 97 (D.C.Wash. 1932).

directed against any "person" who commits the prohibited act, and it is well established that the term is usually construed to include a corporation so as to bring it within the prohibition of the statute and subject it to punishment.[68]

It is well established, then, that a corporation may be held criminally liable for the performance or nonperformance of some act where the crime apparently involves no element of intent.[69] In addition, however, a corporation may be liable for certain crimes of which specific intent is a necessary element,[70] as where the criminal offense consists of purposely doing the things prohibited by statute.[71] However, there are certain crimes which a corporation, on account of its nature, cannot commit,[72] such as crimes so involving personal malicious intent that a corporation manifestly cannot commit them.[73] Nevertheless, even as to such crimes, the corporation may be charged criminally with the unlawful purpose and motive of its agents while acting in its behalf within the real or apparent scope of their authority.[74] The requisites for imputing an agent's criminal intent to the corporation are essentially the same as those which are postulated for imputing his malice to the corporation in civil actions,[75] in line with the cardinal principle that the intent must be shown to be

[68] 13 Am. Jur., Corporations, § 1135. Cf. also Alamo Fence Co. of Houston v. United States, 240 F.2d 179 (C.A.Tex. 1957).

[69] Commonwealth v. Weiler, 84 Pa. Super. 481 (1925).

[70] United States v. Nearing, 252 F. 223 (D.C.N.Y. 1918).

[71] *Loc. cit.*

[72] People v. Duncan, 363 Ill. 495, 2 N.E.2d 705 (1936).

[73] People v. Rochester R., etc., Co., 195 N.Y. 102, 88 N.E. 22, 133 Am. S.R. 770, 21 L.R.A.(N.S.) 998, 16 Ann. Cas. 837 (1909).

[74] Mininsohn v. United States, 101 F.2d 477 (C.C.A.N.J. 1939); People v. Canadian Fur Trappers' Corp., 248 N.Y. 159, 161 N.E. 455 (1928), reversing 226 N.Y.S. 876, 222 App. Div. 791 (1927); State v. Eastern Coal Co., 29 R.I. 254, 70 Atl. 1, 132 Am.S.R. 817, 17 Ann. Cas. 96 (1908).

[75] Old Monastery Co. v. United States, 147 F.2d 905 (C.C.A.S.C. 1945), certiorari denied 326 U.S. 734, 66 S.Ct. 44, 90 L.Ed. 437 (1945); Telegram Newspaper Co. v. Commonwealth, 172 Mass. 294, 52 N.E. 445, 70 Am.S.R. 280, 44 L.R.A. 159 (1899).

that of the corporation and not merely that of the agent.[76] In other words, a corporation may be held criminally liable for the acts of an agent within the scope of his employment.[77]

A corporation may be punished by fine,[78] but not by imprisonment;[79] hence, where the penalty prescribed for the violation of a criminal statute calls for imprisonment or death only, a corporation cannot be prosecuted therefor.[80] But where the penalty of a fine is prescribed, the corporation may be prosecuted,[81] whether or not an alternative penalty of imprisonment is prescribed.[82] However, where the statutory penalty for a crime is both fine and imprisonment, only the pecuniary penalty is operative against the corporation;[83] where such a penalty is inflicted, the fine is assessed against the corporation as a political body, and

[76] 13 Am. Jur., Corporations, §§ 1132-1145. A corporation has an existence separate and apart from those of the persons constituting its officers and agents, and corporations may be guilty of violations of law separate and apart from the guilt or innocence of its officers.—United States v. St. Louis Dairy Co., 79 F.Supp. 12 (D.C.Mo. 1948), reversed, Pevely Dairy Co. v. United States, 178 F.2d 363 (C.A.Mo. 1949), certiorari denied 339 U.S. 942, 70 S.Ct. 794, 94 L.Ed. 1358 (1950), and United States v. St. Louis Dairy Co., 339 U.S. 942, 70 S.Ct. 794, 94 L.Ed. 1358 (1950).

[77] United States v. George F. Fish, Inc., 154 F.2d 798 (C.C.A.N.Y. 1946), certiorari denied 328 U.S. 869, 66 S.Ct. 1377, 90 L.Ed. 1639 (1946). If a fire is purposely started on a corporation's premises by an officer, agent, or employee, the setting of the fire and the destruction of its property is outside the course of employment, and the corporation is not liable for his act to one whose property was destroyed by fire communicated from its premises.—Archuleta v. Floersheim Mercantile Co., 25 N.M. 632, 187 P. 272, 40 A.L.R. 199 (1920).

[78] United States v. Cotter, 60 F.2d 689 (C.C.A.N.Y. 1932), certiorari denied Cotter v. United States, 287 U.S. 666, 53 S.Ct. 291, 77 L.Ed. 575 (1932).

[79] State ex rel. Kropf v. Gilbert, 213 Wis. 196, 251 N.W. 478 (1933).

[80] Joplin Mercantile Co. v. United States, 213 F. 926, 131 C.C.A.(Mo.) 160, Ann. Cas. 1916C, 470 (1914), affirmed 236 U.S. 531, 35 S.Ct. 291, 59 L.Ed. 705 (1915).

[81] People v. Strong, 363 Ill. 602, 2 N.E.2d 942 (1936).

[82] State v. Truax, 130 Wash. 69, 226 P. 259, 33 A.L.R. 1206 (1924); State ex rel. Losey v. Willard,——Fla.——, 54 So.2d 183 (1951).

[83] People v. Duncan, 363 Ill. 495, 2 N.E.2d 705 (1936).

not against its officers.[84] It goes without saying, of course, that a corporation can sustain a "death" penalty by the forfeiture of its charter.

In some jurisdictions it is held, on the ground that the criminal law of the particular jurisdiction is entirely statutory in its origin, that a corporation cannot be indicted for a crime except as specifically provided by statute.[85] And in at least one jurisdiction, under a code provision expressly so providing, a corporation cannot commit any crime in its corporate capacity.[86]

That contradictions abound in the Fiction Theory as employed at Anglo-American corporation law is patently evident. On the one hand, a corporation is a fictitious, artificial, invisible, intangible being existing only in intendment and contemplation of law, and yet that same fictitious entity can, and does, sustain criminal prosecution. Indeed, there are contradictions within contradictions, working havoc with the consistency of inconsistencies. Thus, for example, a corporation cannot be indicted or convicted of a felony or criminal offense involving imprisonment or death because of its artificial nature,[87] and yet the guilty intent of corporate officers to commit a crime may be imputed to the corporation to prove the corporation's guilt.[88] Thus, where a corporation is guilty of a crime, it is because of a corporate act and a corporate intent, and the fact that a corporation can act only by human agents is immaterial, since a corporation may be found guilty of a crime the essential element of which is a specific criminal intent.[89]

[84] State v. Barksdale, 5 Humphr. (Tenn.) 154 (1844).

[85] State v. Terre Haute Brewing Co., 186 Ind. 248, 115 N.E. 722 (1917).

[86] Music Box v. Mills, 10 La. App. 665, 121 So. 196 (1929).

[87] People v. McArdle, 295 Ill. App. 149, 14 N.E.2d 683 (1939), error dismissed 370 Ill. 513, 19 N.E.2d 328 (1939).

[88] Mininsohn v. United States, 101 F.2d 477 (C.C.A.N.J. 1939).

[89] American Medical Association v. United States, 76 U.S.App.D.C. 70, 130 F.2d 233 (1942), certiorari granted in part 317 U.S. 613, 63 S.Ct. 44, 87 L.Ed. 434 (1943); Medical Society of the District of Columbia v. United States, 76 U.S.App.D.C. 70, 130 F.2d 233 (1942), certiorari granted in part 317 U.S. 613, 63 S.Ct. 44, 87 L.Ed. 497 (1942), affirmed 317 U.S. 519, 63 S.Ct. 326, 87 L.Ed. 434 (1943).

The *punctum dolens* involved is precisely this: how can criminal intent be predicated of a fictitious, artificial entity when voluntariness is contingent upon an entity's possession of a free will which, in turn, postulates a rational intellect? Has the legal axiom, *actus non est reus, nisi mens sit rea,* become a meaningless and empty *vox et praeterea nihil?* [90] McGrath observes that "the doctrine of *mens rea* is to be found in much of the jurisprudence of the Anglo-American law. In more recent times the doctrine has been watered down until there is little left but the words. There is not even agreement on what, if anything, the doctrine means in American criminal jurisprudence." [91] But, at the same time, there are consistencies. Thus, a corporation whose operations are conducted over a large territory by various agents may commit offenses at the same time in different places or at the same place at different times.[92]

B.   The Attitude of Innocent IV

It is within the frame of reference of the delictal capability of a corporation that the doctrine of Innocent IV regarding the nature of a juristic personality becomes specific. This concept proves to be most important—invaluable, actually—in evaluating Innocent's views on the subject, given that this concept represents one of his most noteworthy vehicles in transmitting his doctrine on the matter.

Above all, it must be remembered that Innocent IV—like most canonists of the middle ages—was primarily interested in solving concrete problems with which the Church was faced; consequently, interest and attention were less focused on the essence, structure, and theory of a corporation than on the practical

---

[90] For a scholarly disquisition on the problem of *mens rea,* cf. McGrath, *Comparative Study of Crime and Its Imputability in Ecclesiastical Criminal Law, and in American Criminal Law,* The Catholic University of America Canon Law Studies, n. 385 (Washington, D.C.: The Catholic University of America Press, 1957), pp. 37-41.

[91] *Ibid.,* p. 20.

[92] Baltimore & Ohio R. Co. v. United States, 220 U.S. 94, 31 S.Ct. 368, 55 L.Ed. 384 (1911).

question of whether sanctions against a corporation were permissible.

> [The canonists] were determined that in these questions of corporation structure their doctrines should be genuinely responsive to the needs of the time, that they should provide effective guidance in the circumstances actually encountered in practice. The ultimate sanction of their principles is to be found, not in contemporary philosophy nor even in Roman law, but in the application of those principles to the concrete problems of diocesan administration. The maintenance of orderly life in the Church—nothing less—was the real task that the canonists faced in dealing with the flood of litigation, usually petty in itself, concerning the authority of ecclesiastical corporations and the rights of their various members. It was a considerable intellectual achievement that they both solved the immediate problems and, in the process, evolved a subtle and harmonious theory of corporation structure. They themselves were not usually aware of the wider implications that their doctrines would acquire in later theories of Church government, but, when one considers the growth of such theories, it is important to bear in mind that the fundamental assumptions on which they rested were not abstract formulas, derived from external sources and imposed on the Church by doctrinaire reformers. They were rather principles of ecclesiastical authority that had grown up within the Church itself, engendered by the daily exigencies of medieval life.[93]

In this matter of the delictal capability of a corporation, the primary concern is the famous text of Innocent IV from his *Commentaria*. This text, in turn, constitutes Innocent IV's commentary on his own earlier decree [94] concerning the excommunication of a corporation. After a brief analysis of the decree itself, the commentary thereon can be examined.

To begin with, the actual wording of the decree, which forms part of the Bull *Romana Ecclesia*, promulgated by Innocent IV on March 17, 1246, must be noted:

[93] Tierney, *Foundations of the Conciliar Theory: The Contribution of the Medieval Canonists from Gratian to the Great Schism* (Cambridge: University Press, 1955), pp. 104, 105. [Hereinafter cited Tierney.]

[94] VI°, v, 11, 5.

In universitatem, vel collegium proferri excommunicationis
sententiam penitus prohibemus, volentes animarum pericu-
lum evitare, quod exinde sequi potest, cum nonnunquam con-
tingeret innoxios etiam huiusmodi sententia irretiri, sed in
illos dumtaxat de collegio, vel universitate, quos culpabiles
esse constiterit, promulgetur.[95]

The first thing that must be observed is that the practice of
excommunicating corporations, which Innocent IV condemned,
was apparently a normal and recognized practice until then.
"We must remember that the punishment of communities in
various ways was a familiar feature of medieval politics, and
anyone who declared it to be impossible would have been laughed
at as an academic theorist who took no account of everyday
facts." [96] As a matter of actual fact, there is a decretal of Gregory II, written between 1227 and 1234, which recognized this
practice. This letter,[97] sent to the abbot of the monastery of
the Holy Saviour at Paris and to the prior at Vercelli, was incorporated in the official collection, known as *Decretales Gregorii Papae IX*, promulgated in 1234. This decretal was elicited
upon a question of procedure arising out of the excommunication of a chapter, but the excommunication itself was not im-
pugned by anyone—perhaps because *ab assuetis non fit passio*.

Bearing the foregoing in mind, let us return to the actual
wording of Innocent IV's decree. It is extremely important to

[95] Mansi, XXIII, 673. One could easily be led to believe that the Bull
Romana Ecclesia was promulgated in 1245 in the Council of Lyons. Actually, it was published some eight months after the dissolution of the
Council. And yet the decree quoted *supra* carries the inscription *Idem*
[Innocentius IV] *in eodem* [concilio Lugd.]. But "Innocent IV sent the
constitution *Romana Ecclesia* to the University of Paris on April 21, 1246.
Soon afterwards he sent to the same university the decrees that in 1245
he had promulgated in the Council of Lyons. To these decrees he added
the constitution *Romana Ecclesia* which he had divided into ten chapters.
In this way arose the common but erroneous belief in later times that the
constitution *Romana Ecclesia* was published in 1245 in the Council of
Lyons."—Schroeder, *Disciplinary Decrees of the General Councils* (St.
Louis: B. Herder Book Co., 1937), p. 317, at footnote 17.

[96] Smith, *The Law of Associations, Corporate and Incorporate* (Oxford:
Clarendon Press, 1914), p. 152.

[97] X, ii, 25, 11; Potthast, n. 9613.

take cognizance of the fact that Innocent IV did not declare the punishment of a corporation to be impossible. Nor yet did he forbid all kinds of punishment. What he did say was that *universitates* and *collegia* were no longer to be excommunicated. As might be expected, the reason which he gave for his prohibition is not theoretical and abstract, but strictly practical. He forbade the excommunication of corporations, not because they were legal fictions, but because such a sentence would involve the innocent along with the guilty, thus jeopardizing the spiritual welfare of the former. Accordingly, he decreed that a sentence of excommunication was to be leveled only against those individual members of a corporation who were personally culpable.

As noted above, Innocent IV was not primarily concerned with a theoretical question as such in this matter. Indeed, a closer examination reveals that as a matter of actual fact no theoretical question was involved, since a sentence of excommunication upon an *universitas* or a *collegium* could hardly be regarded by anyone as a sentence upon a corporate body, but merely as a summary method of excommunicating all the individual members who composed the corporate body. For, obviously, no one can be excommunicated if he is not in communion, and no one can be in communion if he has not been baptized. And equally patent is the stubborn fact that baptism is, *natura sua*, restricted to natural persons as individuals. As a later decretalist puts it, "excommunicatio requirit verum corpus et animam baptizatam." [98]

So much for the decree of Innocent IV. We are now in a position to go a step farther. Sinibaldo dei Fieschi was not only a legislator, but a consummate lawyer as well; and shortly after the Council of Lyons he published his *Commentaria*. In this he elaborated his views upon the subject of the delictal capability of a corporation. Hear him now at length:

> Universitas non potest excommunicari; quia impossibile est, quod universitas delinquat; quia universitas sicut est capitulum, populus, gens, et huiusmodi, nomina sunt iuris, et non personarum; ideo non cadit in causa excommunicatio.

[98] Panormitanus (Nicholaus de Tudeschis), *Commentaria in Quinque Libros Decretalium* (5 vols. in 7, Venetiis, 1588), ad X, iii, 49, 7.

Item in universitate sunt et pueri unius diei. Item eadem est universitas, quae est tempore delicti, et quae futuro tempore, quo nullo modo delinquunt; esset autem multum iniquum, quod huiusmodi, qui nullo modo delinquunt, excommunicarentur. Item universitas nihil potest facere dolo. Fatemur tamen, quod si rectores alicuius universitatis, vel alii aliquod maleficium faciunt de mandato universitatis totius, vel tantae partis quod invitis aliis maleficium fecerint, vel etiam sine mandato fecerint, sed postea universitas quod suo nomine erat factum, ratum habet, quod universitas punietur speciali poena suspensionis et interdicti. Et etiam temporali, puta pecuniaria. Item poena capitali vel mortis vel relegationis punietur universitas, si contra eam agatur civiliter . . ., sed poena capitis mutabitur in pecuniariam. Quidam tamen dicunt, et forte non male, quod etsi possit contra universitatem agi civiliter vi bo. rap. et lege Aquil. et iniuriarum, et aliis huiusmodi, quibus irrogatur poena pecuniaria, non tamen potest contra eam agi criminaliter. Sententia autem contra universitatem mandabitur executioni in bonis universitatis, si habet alia communia; et si nihil habet, commune privabitur privilegio universitatis, ut ulterius non sit universitas, et sic patietur capitis diminutionem. Item dicunt quidam, quod fiet collecta pro solvendis huiusmodi poenis per libram, et solidum, et ab ista collecta erunt immunes illi qui contradixerunt maleficio, pueri, et alii qui omnino sunt sine culpa. Alii tamen dicunt nullum ab hoc eximi.[99]

From this important and famous text there can be no doubt, upon a prima facie impression, that Innocent's words at least suggest that he held a "fiction theory": he insisted that corporate bodies were incapable of doing wrong (*delinquere*), since they reflected *"nomina iuris, et non personarum."* The reason why such corporations as chapters and groups of people should not be excommunicated was that it would involve the condemnation of innocent individuals, "pueri unius diei," and others who could not possibly be guilty in any moral sense of the word, along with the condemnation of the criminals themselves. Consequently, as a canon lawyer he declined to admit excommunication as a legitimate sanction against a corporation. He went farther. The consequences of such a criminal condemnation

[99] Innocent IV, ad X, v, 39, 53 (= VI°, v, 11, 5).

would affect also those who would be born long after the commission of the crime. He was, of course, most logical; for how could such individuals ever consent to the delictal action? The underlying legal motive for such reasoning was that a corporation was the same after the commission of a crime that it was at the time of the given delict; it lived on: "eadem est universitas, quae est tempore delicti, et quae futuro tempore, quae nullo modo delinquunt; esset autem multum iniquum, quod huiusmodi, qui nullo modo delinquunt, excommunicarentur." It would be supremely unfair.[100]

It must be borne in mind that the foregoing is said with reference to the penalty of excommunication alone, to this qualified criminal condemnation of a corporation. This certainly does not preclude the possibility of a corporation committing a crime. Or so at least it seems. Actually, it is rather difficult to excuse Innocent IV from what seems to be a contradiction. First of all, he categorically stated that "universitas nihil potest facere dolo." But then he proceeded to consider the possibility of a *maleficium* committed by the officials of a corporation upon the explicit mandate of the corporate body, or without a mandate but with later corporate ratification. In such cases the corporation could be punished with the special penalties of suspension and interdict, and/or with a pecuniary fine. It seems that *dolus* was not necessarily excluded in such a case, and it further seems that Innocent did not necessarily consider such a case to be outside the ambit of a criminal action.[101]

Be that as it may, Innocent IV did contend that "poena capi-

---

[100] Gratian himself, commenting on the problem of excommunicating a whole family on the grounds of the sins committed by one member of the family, stated in a *rubrica* of the Decree: "Non ergo pro alicuius peccato tota familia excommunicanda est."—C, xxiv, 3, 1 (rubric).

[101] The writer disagrees with Professor Ullmann in his unqualified contention that "Innocent envisaged as *civil* sanctions the interdict and suspension which could be inflicted only on ecclesiastical bodies" [emphasis supplied].—"The Delictal Responsibility of Medieval Corporations," *Law Quarterly Review*, LXIV (1948), 82. It is unthinkable that a jurist of Innocent IV's caliber would have denied that a *maleficium* could sustain a criminal action, with or without an accompanying action in tort.

tali vel mortis vel relegationis punietur universitas, si contra eam agatur criminaliter . . . sed poena capitis mutabitur in pecuniariam." Here he explicitly acknowledged that criminal proceedings could be instituted against a corporation, and he advised that the capital punishment be commuted into a pecuniary fine. It seems quite clear, therefore, that Innocent did not preclude the possibility of a corporation's committing a crime. The immediate and logical question and problem which now arises is the matter of reconciling a criminal action against a corporation with the fact that "impossibile est, quod universitas delinquat."

It seems that Innocent contradicted himself. Granted that in his incision concerning a *maleficium* committed by a corporation he was treating—indeed in all likelihood—*primarily* of civil actions in tort, it must be assumed that as a canon lawyer Innocent IV would demand something, at least, in the nature of a corporate *mens rea* both for a crime as well as for a tort. And yet, *"impossible est, quod universitas delinquat."* Walter Ullmann suggests that "the apparent contradiction . . . can be solved . . . by the adequate evaluation of the term *'delinquere,'* which he reserved for those offenses which entailed canonical punishment, that is, excommunication." [102]   It is true that Innocent was at that stage concerned with outlawing the excommunication of corporations. But Innocent's immediate legal motive therefor cannot be overlooked: "quia universitas, sicut est capitulum, populus, gens, et huiusmodi, *nomina sunt iuris, et non personarum"* [emphasis supplied].   Now, this places Innocent between the Scylla of contending that a corporation participates of the element of fiction to the extent of doing away with the requirement of a *mens rea* with reference to corporate crimes and torts, both of which Innocent allowed, and the Charybdis of having contradicted himself. The second alternative is the more appealing one. Actually this indictment is somewhat softened by the fact that Innocent immediately proceeded to suggest that he was not sure of his legal motives. For he immediately observed that "quidam tamen dicunt, *et forte non*

[102] *Ibid.,* p. 83.

male, quod etsi possit contra universitatem agi civiliter . . . non tamen potest contra eam agi criminaliter" [emphasis supplied].

Innocent IV apparently felt no difficulty about making a corporation liable *"civiliter,"* or, as we would say, in tort.[103] The remedy against a corporation in such an instance consisted in levying execution upon its property, *"si habet aliqua communia"*; and if the corporation proves to be insolvent, then *"privabitur privilegio universitatis,"* just as a corporation at Anglo-American law would be dissolved under similar conditions.

Indeed, Innocent IV was concerned with finding a reasonable solution for certain practical difficulties, and not with the construction of a purely theoretical theory in this matter. He was forced to condemn an existing usage, not because it violated an abstract formula of the philosophy of law, but because it was found in practice to produce unjust and unreasonable results. Indeed, one may go farther: the *"non potest delinquere"* seems to envisage not delictual responsibility in general, which might or might not involve *dolus,* but simply that *delictum* which was (theologically) truly a *reatus*—a positive act of the will, a *peccatum voluntarium.* But in cases where no injustice was occasioned to individuals, Innocent IV found no more difficulty than we do in enforcing the liability of corporations. He most assuredly held that a corporation could in certain circumstances be made liable in tort. With regard to the criminal prosecution of a corporation, one could indeed contend that in the text under consideration Innocent IV—while being aware of the opinion of some who maintained that this was impossible—nevertheless made allowance for such prosecution, and that this indeed postulated his admission of something in the nature of a

---

103 A plausible explanation for this concession on Innocent's part has been offered, and it merits consideration: "Era infatti così diffusa nella legislazione e nella pratica la possibilità d'un delitto d'una corporazione che il principio astratto [viz., 'impossibile est, quod universitas delinquat'] doveva apparire una stranezza. Ed Innocenzo IV è costretto a venire a delle concessioni, ed appoggiandosi ad un'illecita estensione del concetto di rappresentanza, soggiunge: 'fatemur tamen, quod si rectores alicuius universitatis vel alii quod maleficium faciant de mandato universitatis . . . universitas punitur.' "—Ferrara, *Teoria delle Persone Giuridiche* (2. ed. riveduta, Napoli: Eugenio Marghieri, 1923), p. 79.

corporate *mens rea*. So much can be said for this famous text and its implications.

Innocent IV's commentary on a decretal of Innocent III to Hubert, archbishop of Canterbury, dated 1201, merits attention at this point. This decretal is of great moment to the purpose at hand, since it furnished occasion for Innocent IV to solidify, so to speak, his thoughts on the matter of the criminal prosecution of a corporation. The decretal instructed the archbishop of Canterbury on the method and extent of punishment to be meted to those in a monastery wherein, during an episcopal visitation, he discovered simoniacal practices.[104] The important thing to note in this decretal is that, even in the case where a regular trial was conducted by way of a criminal prosecution of the crime of simony within a monastery or any other such place, only the accused individuals within the corporation were to be tried and punished. The corporation as such was to be left unpunished in any event. So Innocent III had provided.

Innocent IV in his commentary on the decretal in question was most explicit in drafting a categorical norm and clear-cut distinction:

> Nos dicimus quod universitas non potest accusari vel puniri, sed delinquentes tantum; civiliter autem conveniri et pecuniariter [puniri] potest ex delicto rectorum.[105]

His words leave no room for discussion. Very simply, a corporation cannot be prosecuted on a criminal charge, but it can be cited as defendant in a civil suit in tort. If found liable, the punishment to be executed upon it is a fine. This, of course, represents a very determined jurist in contrast to the vacillating Innocent IV as previously considered. Here, truly, *"impossibile est, quod universitas delinquat,"* with reference to crime.

The only general conclusion which can be drawn suggests that a corporation cannot commit a delictual act; that only those members who are *delinquentes* may be criminally prosecuted and punished; and that a corporation is liable in tort.

[104] X, v, 3, 30; Potthast, n. 1403.

[105] Innocent IV, ad X, v, 3, 30.

Section 3. Agents of the Juridic Personality

A. Anglo-American Law

After the subject of the criminal and tortious liability of a corporation, there is perhaps no area of Anglo-American corporation law which so effectively and simply serves as a vehicle in transmitting the doctrine of fictitious personality as the jurisprudence surrounding agency.

All corporations must and can, out of absolute necessity, act and contract only by and through individuals, be they officers or duly appointed agents thereof.[106] So absolute is that rule that it can suffer not one exception, not by way of thought,[107] word,[108] or deed.[109] Consequently, a corporation is deemed to act in person and on an equal footing with a natural person when, in the performance of a corporate act, it uses the officers and agents as a vehicle and conduit and does not go outside its own corporate machinery.[110] So merged are the identities of the corporation and its agent that one may not be an accessory of the other,[111] and even the knowledge of its officers and agents is generally imputed to the corporation.[112]

Without prejudice to such limitations or restrictions which may be imposed by special charter, by-laws, or statutory pro-

[106] Sanchez v. Securities Acceptance Corp., 57 N.M. 512, 260 P.2d 703 (1953); J. Berkman Iron & Metal Co. v. Striano, 111 F.Supp. 221 (D.C. Minn. 1953); United States v. E. Brooke Matlack, Inc., 149 F.Supp. 814 (D.C.Md. 1957).

[107] Steelco Stainless Steel v. Federal Trade Commission, 187 F.2d 693 (C.A. 7th 1951).

[108] Sparks v. Rudy Fick, Inc.,——Mo. App.——, 309 S.W.2d 687 (1958).

[109] Mandel Brothers, Inc. v. Federal Trade Commission, 254 F.2d 18 (C.A. 7th 1958); Tallman v. Southern Motor Exchange, Inc.,——Ga. App.——, 103 S.E.2d 640 (1958).

[110] Sellent-Repent Corporation v. Queens Borough Gas & Electric Co., 290 N.Y.S. 887, 160 Misc. 920 (1936).

[111] Haverty Furniture Co. v. Foust,——Tenn.——, 124 S.W.2d 694 (1939).

[112] Knox v. First Sec. Bank of Utah, N.A., 206 F.2d 823 (C.A.Utah 1953).

visions,[113] the same general principles of law which govern the relations of agency for a natural person govern the officer or agent of a corporation in regard to his power to act for the corporation.[114] The authority of such officer or agent may be actual, that is, express or implied, or it may be an authority which is variously described as apparent, ostensible, or by estoppel; and such authority, of course, must necessarily depend, as that of the agent of a natural person, on the terms and scope of his appointment.[115] The agent of a corporation stands in place of the corporation itself in the line of his assigned duties,[116] and acts within his authorized employment are the acts of the corporation.[117] Thus, too, directors are the chosen representatives of the corporation and constitute for all purposes of dealing with others the corporation, and what they do within the scope of the objects and purposes of the corporation, the corporation does.[118]

Because it is an artificial and fictitious entity created by law, a corporation as such can neither practice law nor appear or act in court in person; in matters in court it can act only through licensed attorneys.[119] And given its nature, a corporation naturally can, and must, testify through its officers.[120]

[113] Prudential Insurance Co. of America v. Saxe, 134 F.2d 16, 77 U.S. App.D.C. 144 (1943), certiorari denied 319 U.S. 745, 63 S.Ct. 1033, 87 L.Ed. 1701 (1943).

[114] Merrion v. Scorup-Somerville Cattle Co., 134 F.2d 473 (C.C.A.Utah 1943), certiorari denied 319 U.S. 760, 63 S.Ct. 1317, 87 L.Ed. 1712 (1943); United States v. United Shoe Machinery Corp., 87 F.Supp. 349 (D.C.Mass. 1950).

[115] 13 Am. Jur., Corporations, § 889.

[116] Hoff v. Peninsula Drainage Dist. No. 2, 172 Ore. 630, 143 P.2d 471 (1943).

[117] Nelson Radio & Supply Co. v. Motorola, Inc., 200 F.2d 911 (C.A.Ala. 1952), certiorari denied 345 U.S. 925, 73 S.Ct. 783, 97 L.Ed. 1356 (1953).

[118] Signal Oil & Gas Co. v. Ashland Oil & Refining Co.,——Cal.——, 322 P.2d 1 (1958).

[119] Paradise v. Nowlin, 86 Cal. App.2d 897, 195 P.2d 867 (1948).

[120] U. S. Tire Co. v. Keystone Tire Sales Co., 153 S.C. 56, 150 S.E. 347, 60 A.L.R. 1264 (1929).

Briefly, then, and in summation, a corporation is an artificial and fictitious entity which lacks animation to function except through the activities of its officers, directors, agents, and servants.[121]

B. The Attitude of Innocent IV

The two principal organs of the collegiate church—the moral personality with which the Decretalists in general are most concerned—are the prelate and the chapter.[122]   In addition, there is the cleric *praebendarius* who represents the interests of his prebend.   The concern in this section, then, is with the attitude of Innocent IV in regard to these agents as representatives of their respective moral personalities.   Two texts will be considered: the first concerning the bishop and his chapter, the second dealing with the cleric and his prebend.

The first text from Innocent's *Commentaria* under consideration is based on a decretal of 1208 of Innocent III to a Praemonstratentian abbot and community regarding the abbot's power of agency.[123]   The decretal provides that such abbots are bound, *ex officio*, to represent the interests of their congregations unless their own interests and those of their congregations are entirely distinct.   Thus the abbot would, with the foregoing proviso, represent his congregation in an action at law.

In commenting upon this decretal, Innocent IV stated:

> Si negotium sit commune inter episcopum et capitulum, simul debent dare syndicum vel actorem; si vero sit omnino divisum, canonici cum suo praeposito vel decano possunt suum facere syndicum et episcopus faciat suum.[124]

As is at once apparent, Innocent IV merely transferred the principle enunciated by Innocent III to an analogous situation involving the bishop and his chapter.   He was here concerned with the respective competence of these two organs of the collegiate church.   He provided that affairs affecting the whole

[121] Templeton v. Scudder, 16 N.J.Super. 576, 85 Atl.2d 292 (1951).

[122] Cf. Gillet, p. 129.

[123] X, i, 3, 21; Potthast, n. 3305.

[124] Innocent IV, ad X, i, 3, 21.

collegiate church shall be represented by one agent appointed by the bishop and chapter together; when, on the other hand, the interest in question was proper only to the bishop or the chapter, the affair was left to the decision of whatever organ was affected: the bishop appointed his own agent, and the chapter likewise chose its own representative.

The second text under consideration here deals with the juridic personification of the prebend. The basis for this text is a decretal written sometime between 1181 and 1185 by Lucius III to a bishop concerning a lawsuit between the bishop and his archdeacon. The point in litigation was the determination of the boundaries of two villas owned, respectively, by the bishop and the archdeacon.[125]

Innocent IV, while commenting on this particular decretal, had this to say: "Nota clericos pro praebendis suis posse agere et conveniri." [126] We have here, clearly, an extension of the juridic personification accorded the two moral personalities just treated. A cleric, then, can sue and can be sued on behalf of his prebend. Furthermore, our text continues:

> ... Sed dices, quomodo ageret [clericus] nomine praebendae, cum praebenda nihil habeat, vel possideat? Respondeo, immo haec praebenda potest habere iura sua et possessiones sicut episcopatus, abbatia, hospitale, vel quaecumque alia domus, vel dignitas, vel administratio.

Therefore, a cleric can truly act as agent for his prebend; and a certain personality is predicated of the latter. Indeed, Innocent IV considered the prebend as a non-collegiate moral person capable of possessing a certain amount of rights and endowments; these notions and their implications, obviously, cannot be squared with the embryonic form of the non-collegiate moral personality nurtured by Justinian.

---

125 X, ii, 19, 3; Jaffé, *Regesta Pontificum Romanorum ab condita Ecclesia ad annum post Christum MCXCVIII* (ed. 2. correctam et auctam auspiciis Gulielmi Wattenbach curaverunt S. Loewenfeld, F. Kaltenbrunner, P. Ewald, 2 vols., Lipsiae, 1885-1888), n. 13845 (hereinafter cited Jaffé).

126 Innocent IV, ad X, ii, 19, 3.

Still on the question of non-collegiate corporations, the following text must be noted:

> Et si contempti velint consentire, eligentes autem velint resilire ab electione, non possunt. . . . Sed quid si mortui sint contempti? Dicimus quod si sint tales successores, qui succedant in honore et onere, ut sunt abbates et praepositi, tales successores si quid factum est in praeiudicium dignitatis, possunt prosequi contemptum praedecessorum, quia tunc potius dicitur contempta dignitas, quam persona. . . . Finguntur enim eaedem personae cum praedecessoribus.[127]

As can be readily appreciated, the notion of a "fiction" with reference to one and the same juristic personality in the case of the succession of many agents to that same office is patently indicated by Innocent: *"finguntur enim eaedem personae cum praedecessoribus."*

It is while commenting on the role of agents that Innocent IV offered a deeper view of his attitude concerning the structure of a corporation. In this section two main texts will be treated: the first one concerning the location of jurisdiction in a corporation, the second regarding oaths taken by a corporation.

On the issue concerning the location of jurisdiction in a corporation, Innocent IV was uncompromising; and this led him to contradict himself. In this first text he commented on a decretal of Innocent III to the bishop of Trent, written in 1207, wherein the latter pontiff had instructed the bishop that once a dignity enjoyed by a church had been revoked by its chapter, that dignity could not again revive except by a contrary statute of the chapter.[128]

Innocent IV stated emphatically:

> Et est notandum, quod rectores assumpti ab universitatibus habent iurisdictionem et non ipsae universitates. . . . Aliqui tamen dicunt, quod ipsae universitates, deficientibus rectoribus, possunt exercere iurisdictionem sicut rectores, quod non credo.[129]

[127] Innocent IV, ad X, i, 6, 28.

[128] X, i, 2, 8; Potthast, n. 2996.

[129] Innocent IV, ad X, i, 2, 8.

According to Innocent IV, therefore, jurisdiction in a corporation resided in the major official of that corporate body. In the case of a diocese, then, the jurisdiction resided in its head, the bishop. But in considering particular cases, Innocent IV was forced to depart from his avowed position. He emphasized the authority and jurisdiction of the bishop over his church; he favored a strict authoritarianism. But the canon law itself provided that the chapter play a considerable part in managing the affairs of that corporation, to a point that the chapter exercised important acts of jurisdiction during a vacancy, as well as in other instances. Innocent IV necessarily accepted these doctrines, but in so doing he contradicted himself. So, for instance, we have his *"episcopo enim mortuo, potestas iurisdictionis transfertur in capitulum."* [130] Also to be noted is his explicit, ". . . In magnis negotiis capituli consensus requiritur. Item in alienationibus voluntariis semper est necessarius consensus episcopi et capituli." [131] The foregoing "concessions" were, of course, in opposition to his avowed principle that "aliqui tamen dicunt quod universitates, deficientibus rectoribus, possunt exercere iurisdictionem sicut rectores, *quod non credo"* [emphasis supplied].

As one eminent scholar observes, "Innocent's picture of a corporation was simplicity itself; but it happened not to correspond either with the facts of ecclesiastical life or with the recent decretals that had sought to regulate that life." [132]

We come now to what is perhaps the most important text by which Innocent IV betrayed his attitude concerning the element of fiction in a juristic personality. The text itself is very famous in this connection, finding a place as it does in practically every serious discussion of this question. There is, naturally enough, divergence of opinion in its interpretation and meaning. The basis for the commentary of Innocent IV is itself important, and thus it must be considered first. [133] The decretal in

130 Innocent IV, ad X, i, 33, 11.

131 Innocent IV, ad X, i, 2, 8.

132 Tierney, p. 108.

133 Innocent IV commented on the instant decretal in his *Commentaria,* ad X, ii, 20, 57. But as a matter of actual fact, the *Corpus Iuris* contains

question was written in 1239 by Gregory IX to the Archbishop of Rouen. Innocent IV then incorporated this decree in his own Bull, *Romana Ecclesia,* which he promulgated on March 17, 1246. The actual wording of the decretal follows:

> Praesentium auctoritate mandamus, quatenus in causa, quae inter abbatem et conventum S. Nicholai Andegavensis ex una parte, et priorem et conventum de Paldigen. Lyconensis dioecesis ex altera super eo, quod iidem abbas et conventus se ab ipsis priore et conventu de Paldigen. possessione subiectionis eiusdem prioratus asserunt spoliatos, et super irritanda quadam compositione olim inita inter partes, et rebus aliis vertitur, ab eisdem abbate et priore nomine suo, et in animas conventuum eorundem, vel maioris et sanioris partis ipsorum, recepto iuramento de veritate dicenda, iniungas dictis abbati et priori, ut tam ponendo quam respondendo dicant veritatem, quam super positionibus tibi sub bulla nostra transmissis ipsi sciunt, et per illos intelligunt, in quorum animas iuraverunt. . . .[134]

The decretal, then, dealt with a lawsuit involving two monasteries over a situation concerning corporate property. Gregory IX prescribed that, among other things, the two superiors involved in the lawsuit be sworn in with the traditional oath *de veritate dicenda* on their own behalf and on behalf of the other members of the respective corporation.

Innocent IV commented upon this in the following words:

> Hodie licitum est omnibus collegiis per alium iurare, et ideo est quia cum collegium in causa universitatis fingatur una persona dignum est quod per unum iuret, licet per se iurare possint si velint. C. de iura. calum. l. 2. §. hoc etiam. et etiam propter facilitatem ponendi et respondendi.[135]

The discussion on this important text will be limited to a brief consideration of two interpretations thereon. The first in-

---

only 56 chapters under title 20 of the second book of the Decretals. What Innocent IV treated in his 57th chapter is actually found in the *Liber Sextus.* According to Ioannes Andreae, "ista decretalis (et sequens) fuerant Gregorii et deberent esse in antiqua complatione ultimae in h. t."— 2 Friedberg 1002, at footnote ad tit. X, cap. 1.

[134] Mansi, XXIII, 657.

[135] Innocent IV, ad X, ii, 20, 57 (= VI°, ii, 10, 2).

terpretation is given by Vermeersch, the second by Feenstra. The *punctum dolens* involved is, of course, the incision, *"fingatur una persona."*

Vermeersch (1858-1936)[136] contended that Innocent IV was talking about a physical person, not a fictitious entity. His reasoning was that Innocent stressed the *number* ('una'), not the word *persona;* that Innocent asked how the Pontiff could permit an agent to take an oath on behalf of the abbot and the community, and then answered that this was possible "quia collegium fingitur *una.*"[137]

Vermeersch further added, "Conventus autem non est fictitium quodpiam ens. Singuli enim monachi dicuntur eius partes; plerique monachi omnes omnem faciunt conventum, nisi velis partes non per se sed per formam a se distinctam efficere totum."[138]

Professor Feenstra[139] opines as follows. Vermeersch rightly suggests that Innocent IV stressed the word *una.* But Vermeersch neglects to observe that the term *una persona* is borrowed by Innocent IV from the Roman law text which he cited immediately after using the phrase in question. In C. (2, 58) (2, 5) we read, regarding *iuramentum calumniae:*

> Hoc etiam huic legi addendum esse sancimus, ut, si quis pro alio litem movere voluerit nullo mandato prolato, sed per fideiussionem ratam rem dominum habiturum suam personam firmaverit, ne vel ex hac machinatione lex circumscribi videatur, sancimus si quid tale in posterum emerserit, sive pro *una persona* quis litem movere voluerit sive pro aliquo corpore vel vico vel alia universitate, fideiussionem quidem solitam praestare, litem autem ulterius minime procedere, nisi intra a iudice statuendum tempus faciat personas principales sacramentum subire, vel praesente adver-

[136] "De communi monasterii possessione," *De Religiosis et Missionariis Supplementa et Monumenta Periodica,* V (1913), (20)-(23).

[137] *Ibid.,* p. (22).

[138] *Loc. cit.*

[139] "L'Histoire des Fondations," *Tijdschrift voor Rechtsgeschiedenis-Revue d'Histoire du Droit,* XXIV (1956), 415 ff.

sario, si hoc maluerit, vel alio pro eo agente, vel penitus altera parte cessante inter acta apud defensorem locorum huiusmodi sacramentum vel ab ipso pro quo agitur vel plurima parte vel idonea universitatis procedat.[140]

Professor Feenstra proceeds to observe that in this provision of the Code of Justinian—which has a direct *rapport* with the question treated by Innocent IV in his *Commentaria*—the term *una persona* is completely opposed to *corpus* and *vicus* and *alia universitas*. It is evident, consequently, that the word *persona* is employed to indicate a physical persona: *una persona* is opposed to *universitas*, which is made up of many *personae*. Therefore, the "fiction" of Innocent IV consists precisely in considering *collegium* as one single physical person.

For Innocent IV, so Feenstra continues, the difficulty was that an ordinary procurator could not take an oath *"in animam alterius."* In the decretal in question the matter under consideration was the case of an abbot and a prior who were to take an oath *"in animas conventuum."* The "fiction" proposed by Innocent IV consisted in its considering the *collegium,* the corporation, as one single person in such a way that if one of its members took an oath—which ordinarily he could do only *"in animam suam"*—he automatically did so *"in animas"* of the other members as well.

Professor Feenstra concludes:

> La provenance du terme *una persona* et le motif pour lequel Innocent emploie la "fiction" donnent évidemment a ce texte un sens très spécial et très limité, qui n'autorise pas les conclusions de Gierke; mais il n'en reste pas moins qu'on trouve ici—sous une forme encore assez rudimentaire, il est vrai—un première construction de la personne juridique à l'aide des mots *fingere* et *persona*.[141]

Feenstra's point is well taken. However, it seems that he is somewhat—unduly, perhaps—conservative in his conclusion. While completely agreeing with him that Innocent IV was primarily interested in the practical solutions to concrete problems

---

[140] As quoted by Feenstra, *ibid.,* p. 416.

[141] *Ibid.,* p. 417.

and difficulties, the writer feels, nonetheless, that Innocent's *fingatur una persona* affords much more in the way of a fiction theory than just the alleged "forme assez rudimentaire" therefor.[142]

ARTICLE 3.   NATURE OF A CORPORATION: A SUMMATION

Section 1.   Anglo-American Law

The doctrine that a corporation is a wholly artificial creation,[143] a legal entity existing separate and apart from the persons composing it, is a mere fiction introduced for purposes of convenience and in subservience to the ends of justice, and said fiction cannot be urged to an extent and purpose not within its reason and policy.[144] Accordingly, the fiction of separate existence may be disregarded, and acts of the individual members treated as acts of the corporation where circumstances warrant it; [145] in such instances, the courts will pierce the corporate veil and look behind the corporate fiction.[146]

[142] While Duff denies that the phrase in question makes Innocent IV a Savignian, he does concede that the incision is, technically at least, patient of a more elastic interpretation: "It may be granted that the Fiction Theory takes its name from the words of Innocent: 'cum collegium in causa universitatis fingatur una persona.' This could no doubt mean 'is a fictitious person,' in Savigny's sense; but it can equally well mean 'is treated as an inividual,' as one person, not as a number of persons." —Duff, *Personality in Roman Private Law* (Cambridge: University Press, 1938), p. 222. Note that in saying that Innocent's *fingatur una persona* affords not a small impetus to a fiction theory, the writer means exactly that—a fiction theory—but not *the* Fiction Theory in the modern sense. Actually, any divergence which may seem to exist between the views of Vermeersch (and Duff) and those of Feenstra on this point are, in the end, reducible to a *lis de verbis*. Be that as it may, it remains true that Innocent IV did not mean to say that a corporation has no legal existence except by fiction.

[143] Cohen v. Beneficial Industrial Loan Corp., 337 U.S. 541, 69 S.Ct. 1221, 93 L.Ed. 1528 (1948).

[144] E. O. Bailey & Co. v. Union Planters Title Guaranty Co., 33 Tenn. App. 439, 232 S.W.2d. 309 (1949).

[145] Fitzgerald v. Central Bank & Trust Co., 257 F.2d 118 (1958).

[146] Smith v. Feigin, 77 N.Y.S.2d 229, 273 App. Div. 277 (1948), affirmed 298 N.Y. 534, 80 N.E.2d 668 (1948).

Only in exceptional instances, however, may the separate corporate identity be disregarded.[147]   The rule of piercing the fiction of the corporate entity is to be applied with great caution,[148] and the courts will avoid one extreme as diligently as the other. On the one hand, the fiction of a corporate entity will not be allowed to bring about unjust results;[149] but at the same time, before a court may disregard the fiction of separate corporate existence, it must appear that the observance of this fiction would sanction a fraud or promote injustice, and accordingly bad faith in one form or another must be shown.[150]

The present Anglo-American jurisprudence is well epitomized by Federal Judge Arraj in the terms following:

> Although a corporation is ordinarily regarded as a legal entity separate and distinct from its members, there is today no doubt that this fiction of separate existence may be disregarded and the acts of members treated as acts of the corporation where circumstances warrant it. . . .
>
> This doctrine is particularly applicable when the facts demonstrate that the corporation is merely the alter ego or business conduit of its governing or dominating personality. In such cases, the courts in many jurisdictions have not been hesitant to pierce the corporate veil and look to the ultimate person in order to regard them as one for the purpose of preventing an injustice. However, the facts on which it will be determined that the corporation is the alter ego of a person, and the reasons that will justify a decision that an injustice has been committed, are too varied to enumerate; each case presents its own peculiar problems. . . .
>
> The effect of applying the alter ego doctrine, of course, is that the corporation and the person who dominates it are treated as one person, so that any act committed by one is attributed to both, and if either is bound, by contract, judgment, or otherwise, both are equally bound. It should be

---

[147] Gardner v. The Calvert, 253 F.2d 395 (C.A.N.J. 1958).

[148] Plant v. Cameron Feed Mills, Inc., —— Ark. ——, 309 S.W.2d 312 (1958).

[149] Wolfe v. National Lead Co., 156 F.Supp. 883 (1958); Satler v. Rice, —— Pa. Super. ——, 135 Atl.2d 775 (1958).

[150] In re Zipco, Inc., 157 F.Supp. 675 (1958).

noted, however, that this is done only for the purpose of adjudging the rights and liabilities of the parties in the case.[151]

Section 2.   The Attitude of Innocent IV

As previously noted, the Fiction Theory supposes that a corporation, a subject of rights, is a fictitious person created by the will of the legislator.   It does not seem that Innocent IV espoused the principles of such a theory, for he considered the ensemble of physical members to be the real subject of corporate rights.

Nevertheless, Innocent IV really came very close to formulating such a theory.   In the opinion of the writer, Innocent IV could have been called the Father of the Fiction Theory had he followed his natural instinct to authoritarianism.   He could indeed be very categorical; had he lived a few years later, he most likely would have held a theory of pure fiction.   The basis for such a theory is certainly there; this basis is reflected in somewhat of a rudimentary form, perhaps, but still it is there.   In the matter of the delictal capability of a corporation, for instance, Innocent started out with the general principle that a corporation cannot commit a wrong because it is a *"nomen iuris,"* albeit with physical members as real subjects. Had he not had as much opposition in legislative tradition as he did, he would not have felt constrained to water down his general principle to the point of apparent contradiction.

It is again to be recalled that Innocent IV was not so much interested in formulating abstract theories as in proffering solutions to concrete problems that circumstances conditioned.   Perhaps he could have afforded to be more of a jurist than a legislator had he lived a few years later.

In the absence of one's agreement with Ferrara's ultimate and unqualified conclusion—he proceeds too far—one may nevertheless not disregard his logical premises:

> Si noti intanto che *persona* nel concetto teologico-cristiano vuol dire uomo, ente ragionevole—'est rei rationabilis indi-

[151] Shamrock Oil & Gas Co. v. Ethridge, 159 F.Supp. 693, 696, 697 (D.C.Colo. 1958).

vidua substantia'—perciò l'applicazione di tal concetto alla corporazione non poteva esser fatta che o in via di metafora o per finzione. Ed infatti Innocenzo IV osserva che 'collegium in causa universitatis *fingatur* una persona.' Si trata dunque d'una finzione di personalità: così s'inaugura il dogma che doveva essere poi per tanti secoli dominante.[152]

Consideration is also to be given to the fact that Innocent IV was not fundamentally opposed, on principle, to the idea of a legal fiction, even where physical persons were concerned. As indicative proof of this the following can be adduced:

> Nos dicimus quod si episcopus interest capitulo, non tanquam episcopus, sed quodam iure segregato tamquam canonicus, puta quia papa de gratia sibi reservavit canonicatum, vel etiam episcopatus habet speciale privilegium quod quicunque est episcopus sit canonicus, ita fingitur gerere duas personas.[153]

Certainly, it can be said that Innocent IV contributed the decisive step toward the "marche vers la personnification"; [154] that under different circumstances of time he would have held a strict theory of fiction; that perhaps he would have said that "pour la science du droit, la notion de personne est et doit rester une notion purement juridique. Le mot signifie simplement un sujet de droit, un être capable d'avoir des droits subjectifs lui appartenant en propre,—rien de plus, rien de moins." [155]

[152] Ferrara, p. 77.

[153] Innocent IV, ad X, i, 31, 13.

[154] Feenstra, "art. cit.," *Tijdschrift voor Rechtsgeschiedenis–Revue d'Histoire du Droit,* XXIV (1956), 411.

[155] Michoud, *La Théorie de la Personnalité Morale en son Application au Droit Français* (3. ed., míse au courant par Louis Trotabas, 2 vols., Paris: Librairie Générale de Droit et de Jurisprudence, 1932), I, 7.

CHAPTER IV

GENERAL PROVISIONS OF NEW MEXICO LAW
AND OF CANON LAW CONCERNING
NON-PROFIT CORPORATIONS

ARTICLE 1. FORMATION OF CORPORATIONS

By divine institution, both the Church and the State are juridically perfect societies, each sovereign in its respective domain.
For reasons which do not interest us here, the Church in the United
States of America, however, finds its sovereignty very effectively
challenged, especially in the field of corporation law. Thus, in
the United States, all corporations must be created by the authority of the State. Anglo-American law does not recognize
the right of the Church to establish a juridical person as a corporate entity capable of exercising corporate civil rights. Substantially, the Church must go through the same procedure as
any business or lay association to incorporate. And should this
not be done, "the law will recognize an organization whose rights
are the aggregate rights of the totality of the members exercised by duly appointed representatives, but it will not acknowledge corporate existence." [1] This view is, of course, shared by
the individual States, New Mexico not excepted.

But at internationl law, the Holy See is recognized as a sovereign power.[2] And it was the acknowledgement by the United
States of this sovereignty enjoyed by the Church at international
law that motivated this country to recognize by the Treaty of
Paris in 1898 the juridical personality of the Holy See in those
territorial acquisitions—notably in Puerto Rico and in the Phil-
ippine Islands—which were originally under Spanish dominion.[3]

---

[1] Brown, p. 133.

[2] Moore, *Digest of International Law* (8 vols., Washington, D.C.: Government Printing Office, 1906), I, 39.

[3] Cf. Ponce v. Roman Catholic and Apostolic Church in Puerto Rico,
210 U.S. 296, 28 S.Ct. 737, 52 L.Ed. 1068 (1908); Santos v. Holy Roman
Catholic and Apostolic Church, 212 U.S. 463, 29 S.Ct. 338, 53 L.Ed. 599
(1909).

Section 1. New Mexico Law

A. Historical Development

Prior to 1867, there was no general incorporation law in New Mexico. As a consequence, the formation of a body corporate for whatever purpose postulated special individual enactment by the territorial legislative assembly. The first corporation under Anglo-American law to come into existence in New Mexico was the Corporation of the City of Santa Fe, created by special act of the first legislative assembly in 1851.[4]

Following that enactment, successive legislative assemblies incorporated the Santa Fe Artesian Well Company in 1853,[5] the Masons in the same year,[6] the Albuquerque Academy in 1856,[7] the Taos County Cemetery Associations and the Pious Fraternity of the County of Taos in 1860,[8] the College of Christian Brothers in Santa Fe and the Academy of the Sisters of Loretto in Santa Fe in 1873.[9]

In 1866 the legislative assembly had passed "An Act to provide for the incorporation of debating, literary, and other societies," [10] followed by "An Act to create a general incorporation act, permitting persons to associate themselves together as bodies corporate for mining, manufacturing and other industrial pursuits." [11] The latter Act was amended in 1875 to include colleges, seminaries, churches, libraries, or any benevolent, charitable, or scientific associations.[12]

A very interesting parenthesis in the history of New Mexico

---

[4] 1851-1852 N.M. Laws, p. 112.

[5] 1853-1854 N.M. Laws, ch. 15.

[6] *Ibid.*, ch. 23.

[7] 1856-1857 N.M. Laws, ch. 14.

[8] 1860-1867 N.M. Laws, p. 40, and p. 74, respectively.

[9] 1873-1874 N.M. Laws, ch. 41 and ch. 42, respectively.

[10] 1866-1867 N.M. Laws, ch. 12.

[11] 1867-1868 N.M. Laws, ch. 3. [Repealed by 1905 N.M. Laws, ch. 79, § 134.]

[12] 1875-1876 N.M. Laws, ch. 37. This act was repealed by 1905 N.M. Laws, ch. 79, § 134 (q.v., *infra*).

corporations was occasioned by "An Act to incorporate the Society of the Jesuit Fathers in New Mexico," enacted and passed over Governor S. B. Axtell's veto in 1878.[13] Axtell's venomous and puerile message [14] to the Legislative Council availed naught. Attorney General Breeden's opinion [15] against such enactment

[13] 1878 N.M. Laws, ch. 22.

[14] "January 18, 1878. To the Honorable Legislative Council of the Territory of New Mexico. Gentlemen: I return to you with my objections an act entitled 'An Act to incorporate the Jesuit Fathers in New Mexico.' For the purpose of obtaining for your information the best legal advice within my reach I requested the Attorney General of the Territory, Hon. William Breeden to prepare a careful opinion upon the law of the case; that opinion I make part of my message and lay it in full before you. Attorney General Breeden says that the bill in his opinion is clearly in violation of the law of the United States. That opinion I fully endorse and if you pass that bill over Attorney General Breeden's opinion and my veto you will do so with your eyes open, in violation of your oath of office and the laws of the United States.

"There are many other objections to the bill, a few only of which I will briefly notice. It is difficult to decide whether the man [Father Gasparri, S.J.] who seeks to establish this Society or the Society which he seeks to establish is worse. Both are so bad you cannot decide between them. This Neopolitan adventurer [Father] Gasparri . . . two years ago . . . intruded himself into the lower house and remained within the bar and by the speaker's side until he forced the passage of this bill, but at that session it was defeated by an honest council. . . . Apart from the bad character of the Society and the dangerious character of its Chief, the bill is especially objectionable because it does not require that the incorporators shall be citizens of the United States, nor residents of New Mexico. . . . The provisions of the bill are contrary to public policy and in direct violation of the laws of the United States, and cannot receive my approval. —S. B. Axtell, Governor of New Mexico."—This letter is, of course, a document of public record, and is available in ms. at the office of the Secretary of State, Santa Fe, New Mexico, 1878 Council Journal 224.

[15] "January 16, 1878 . . . Governor: . . . Section 1889 of the Revised Statutes of the United States is as follows. . . . By this section the Legislative Assembly of the Territory is clearly prohibited from granting any private charter, or in other words from creating any private corporation and also from granting any special privileges. Of course the Legislative Assembly is bound by all laws of the United States and cannot pass any act in violation thereof or contrary thereto. Any legislation attempted by our Legislative Assembly prohibited by, or in violation of, any law of the United States would be invalid and of no effect. . . .

was well founded, for section 1889, United States Revised Statutes, reads as follows:

> The legislative assemblies of the several territories shall not grant private charters or special privileges, but they may, by general incorporation acts, permit persons to associate themselves as bodies corporate for mining, manufacturing, and other industrial pursuits . . . , or for colleges, seminaries, churches, libraries, or any other benevolent, charitable, or scientific association.[16]

One year later, the Congress of the United States declared the famous act of incorporation null and void:

> Be it enacted by the Senate and House of Representatives of the United States of America in Congress assembled, That an act of legislative assembly of the Territory of New Mexico, entitled "An Act to incorporate the Society of Jesuit Fathers in New Mexico," which passed both houses of said legislative assembly on or about the 18th day of January 1878, over the veto of the governor of said Territory, being in violation of section 1889 of the Revised Statutes of the United States, . . . be, and the same is hereby, disapproved and declared null and void.[17]

On February 11, 1880, the legislative assembly enacted a law whereby "any five or more persons, a majority of whom shall be citizens of the United States and residents of New Mexico, may organize a corporation for religious, benevolent, charitable, scientific or literary purposes, or for the establishment of colleges, academies, seminaries, churches or libraries." [18]   It is not sur-

---

"No matter how meritorious the purposes of the proposed corporation may be, the Legislative Assembly has no authority or power to create the corporation or to grant it any special powers or privileges. There seems to be no reason why the persons named in the bill should not incorporate for the purposes mentioned in this bill under the general incorporation act of the Territory, but they can be lawfully incorporated in no other way. . . .—William Breeden, Attorney General."—1878 N.M. Attorney General Reports, available in ms. at the office of the Attorney General, Santa Fe, New Mexico.

[16] Act of March 2, 1867; June 10, 1872; as amended by sec. 5, ch. 818, approved July 30, 1886.

[17] 20 U.S. Statutes at Large 280, ch. 41, approved February 3, 1879, sess. III, 45th Congress.

[18] 1880 N.M. Laws, ch. 2, § 1.

prising, however, that the Archdiocese of Santa Fe or any of its parishes did not incorporate under such enactment, for one of its provisions was patently irreconcilable with Canon law: "No real estate belonging to any such corporation shall be sold or mortgaged, except by consent of a Judge of the Supreme Court, which consent shall be founded on evidence showing the propriety of such sale or mortgage, and such evidence may be taken by a master or referee, if so decided by the Judges." [19]

The General Incorporation Act of 1867,[20] as amended in 1875,[21] was repealed in 1905, at which time the General Incorporation Law for other than non-profit associations was enacted.[22] The General Incorporation Law of 1905 was taken from the New Jersey law.[23]

Finally, in regard to non-profit corporations, the legislature provided a method of establishing corporations sole on March 16, 1951.[24] It was under the provisions of this enactment that the corporation sole of the Roman Catholic Church of the Archdiocese of Santa Fe was created on June 26, 1951.[25]

B. General Provisions

The Constitution of New Mexico [26] provides that the State Corporation Commission, consisting of three members,[27] is the

[19] 1880 N.M. Laws, ch. 2, § 5. This restriction was repealed by 1909 N.M. Laws, ch. 23, § 1.

[20] 1867-1868 N.M. Laws, ch. 3.

[21] 1875-1876 N.M. Laws, ch. 37.

[22] 1905 N.M. Laws, ch. 79, being, generally, sections 51-2-1 to 51-12-8 of 1953 N.M. Comp. Laws.

[23] Cf. Kanen, *Kanen's New Mexico Corporation Laws* (Albuquerque: Morning Journal Press, 1910), p. iv; cf. also State v. Bank of Magdalena, 33 N.M. 473, 270 P. 881 (1928).

[24] 1951 N.M. Laws, ch. 183, being sections 51-14-1 to 51-14-19 of 1953 N.M. Comp. Laws, repealed by 1957 N.M. Laws, ch. 112, being sections 51-14-20 to 51-14-40 of 1953 N.M. Comp. Laws, Annual Pocket Supplement through 1957.

[25] Certificate of incorporation no. 28329, vol. 7, p. 19, office of State Corporation Commission of New Mexico.

[26] N.M. Constitution, Art. XI, § 6.

[27] N.M. Constitution, Art. XI, § 1.

department of the State through which corporations are chartered or, in the case of foreign corporations, licensed, and through
which all constitutional provisions and laws made in pursuance
thereof relating to corporations are carried out.   In addition, the
Corporation Commission "shall prescribe the form of all reports
which may be required of corporations by this Constitution or
by law, and shall collect, receive, and preserve such reports, and
annually tabulate and publish them.   All fees required by law
to be paid for the filing of articles of incorporation, reports and
other documents, shall be collected by the Commission and paid
into the State Treasury." [28]

It is incumbent upon the legislature to provide for the organization or corporations by general law.[29]   Furthermore, "all laws
relating to corporations may be altered, amended, or repealed by
the legislature, at any time, when necessary for the public good
and general welfare, and all corporations, doing business in this
State, may, as to such business, be regulated, limited or restrained by laws not in conflict with the Constitution of the
United States or of this Constitution." [30]

Naturally, the charter of a corporation is a contract between
the State and the corporation, as well as law for the body corporate.   And together with the articles of incorporation, a general incorporation law is, itself, the charter.   It goes without
saying that where the general corporation law and the articles
of incorporation conflict, the latter will yield to the prevailing
force of the former.

With reference to non-profit corporations, New Mexico law
provides [31] for the establishment of corporations aggregate and
corporations sole, both of which, of course, fall within the category of private corporations.   Before proceeding to an individual consideration of corporations aggregate and corporations
sole, successively, it will be helpful to preface the discussion with

[28] N.M. Constitution, Art. XI, § 6.

[29] N.M. Constitution, Art. XI, § 13.

[30] *Loc. cit.*

[31] 1957 N.M. Laws, ch. 112, being sections 51-14-20 to 51-14-40 of 1953
N.M. Comp. Laws, repealing 1951 N.M. Laws, ch. 183, being sections 51-
14-1 to 51-14-19 of 1953 N.M. Comp. Laws.

a definition of terms [32] set out in the 1957 Act for the purposes of that act. Accordingly, the words hereinbelow defined shall have the meanings ascribed to them as follows, unless the context should rule otherwise:

1) *corporation:* a non-profit corporation formed under the 1957 Act having no capital stock;

2) *non-profit corporation:* a corporation formed for a purpose not involving pecuniary gain to its shareholders or members, paying no dividends or other pecuniary remuneration, directly or indirectly, to its shareholders or members as such, and having no capital stock;

3) *articles:* the original articles of incorporation, articles of incorporation as amended, articles of merger, or articles of consolidation and incorporation, as the case may be;

4) *by-laws:* the code adopted for the regulation or management of the internal affairs of the corporation, regardless of how designated;

5) *member:* an entity, either corporate or natural, having any membership or shareholder rights in a corporation in accordance with its articles, by-laws, or both;

6) *directors:* the persons vested with the general management of the affairs of the corporation, regardless of how they are designated.

Finally, any non-profit organization having a valid charter or corporate existence may continue under its existing charter, or may re-incorporate under the 1957 Act, with the proviso that no such change in the status of any such organization shall prejudice the obligations of any existing contract of such organization.[33]

C. Corporation Aggregate

It will be recalled from the preceding chapter that a corporation aggregate is a corporation which is or may be composed of more than two members, as in the case of a joint-stock corpora-

---

[32] As given in 1957 N.M. Laws, ch. 112, § 1, being section 51-14-20 of 1953 N.M. Comp. Laws.

[33] 1957 N.M. Laws, ch. 112, § 2, being section 51-14-21 of 1953 N.M. Comp. Laws.

tion or a non-stock corporation of which there are two or more members.[34]

Under the terms of the 1957 Act, a non-profit corporation may be formed in New Mexico for any lawful purpose such as the following: alleviation of emergencies, athletic, benevolent, charitable, civic, commercial, community welfare, education, eleemosynary, fraternal, general welfare, health, horticultural, industrial, labor, literary, patriotic, political, professional, recreational, religious, scientific, and social. The foregoing enumeration is demonstrative, not exhaustive.[35]

Three or more natural persons of full age may form a corporation under the provisions of the 1957 Act.[36]

The articles to be drawn up, signed by each of the incorporators and acknowledged by at least three of them, must state:

1) the name of the corporation;

2) the purpose of the corporation;

3) that the corporation does not afford pecuniary gain, incidentally or otherwise, to its members;

4) the period of duration of corporate existence which may not exceed 100 years;

5) the location by city, town, or other community, of its registered office in the State;

6) the name and address of each incorporator; and

7) the number of directors constituting the first board of directors, the name and address of each director, and the tenure of office of the first directors. In addition, the articles of incorporation may contain any other provision, consistent with New Mexico law, for regulating the business of the corporation or the conduct of the corporate affairs.[37]

Ordinarily, and without special procedure, the name chosen

[34] 18 C.J.S., Corporations, § 15.

[35] 1957 N.M. Laws, ch. 112, § 3, being section 51-14-22 of 1953 N.M. Comp. Laws.

[36] 1957 N.M. Laws, ch. 112, § 4, being section 51-14-23 of 1953 N.M. Comp. Laws.

[37] 1957 N.M. Laws, ch. 112, § 5, being section 51-14-24 of 1953 N.M. Comp. Laws.

for the corporation may not be the same as, or deceptively similar to, the name of any other domestic corporation, whether profit or non-profit, or of any foreign corporation authorized to do business in New Mexico. The use of a name in violation of the foregoing provisions, however, does not affect or vitiate the corporate existence. But upon the application of the State or of any corporations interested or affected, the district court may enjoin the corporations from doing business under a name assumed in violation of the provisions noted *supra*, even though a certificate of incorporation has been issued by the State Corporation Commission.[38] It should be observed, however, that, without prejudice to the provisions above-described, a corporation may do business under an assumed name or under a name differing from its true corporate name.[39]

The articles of incorporation are to be filed in the office of the State Corporation Commission. If the articles are found to be in conformity with law, and upon payment of the prescribed fees and charges, the State Corporation Commission will record the articles and issue and record a certificate of incorporation. This certificate will state the name of the corporation and the fact and date of incorporation. A copy of the articles duly certified is to be recorded in the office of the county clerk in the county where the principal office of the corporation is to be located in the State.[40]

Upon such filing, the persons named in the articles of incorporation become a body politic and corporate by the name stated in the articles, and for the term of existence therein specified.[41]

[38] 1957 N.M. Laws, ch. 112, § 6, being section 51-14-25 of 1953 N.M. Comp. Laws.

[39] Spain Management Co. v. Packs' Auto Sales, 54 N.M. 64, 213 P.2d 433 (1950).

[40] 1957 N.M. Laws, ch. 112, § 7, being section 51-14-26 of 1953 N.M. Comp. Laws. The fact that a religious corporation had not, previous to the commencement of a suit, caused the papers and certificates required by chapter 3 of 1880 N.M. Laws to be filed in the office of the Secretary of the Territory does not debar it from access to the courts in protecting its previously vested estate in the Territory.—Probst v. Trustees of Board of Domestic Missions, 3 Gild. (N.M.) 373, 3 John. (N.M.) 237, 5 P. 702 (1884), reversed, 129 U.S. 182, 9 S.Ct. 263, 32 L.Ed. 642 (1889).

[41] 1957 N.M. Laws, ch. 112, § 8, being section 51-14-27 of 1953 N.M. Comp. Laws.

D. Corporation Sole

As was observed in the preceding chapter,[42] "our curious phrase 'corporation sole' only appears late in the day and seems to be exclusively English; but the canonists had come very near to it in their treatment of the cases in which an *ecclesia* had but one cleric connected with it; the *dignitas* or the *sedes* or the like could be personified." [43]

At common law, the king was regarded as a corporation sole with the capacity of succession, in order to prevent a possible interregnum and to preserve the possessions of the Crown. Such corporations were mostly employed to hold in succession the rights and property of ecclesiastical establishments and to insure the proper devolution of them upon the successors of the first taker.[44] Chancellor Kent (1763-1847) remaked that "a bishop, dean, parson, and vicar are given in the English books as instances of sole corporations; and they and their successors in perpetuity take the corporate property and privileges." [45] But apart from statute, a Roman Catholic bishop is not recognized by Anglo-American law as a corporation sole.[46]

In New Mexico, under the 1957 Act, any person in whom shall be vested the legal title to the property of any church or religious society, in conformity with its constitution, canons, rites, or regulations, and of any scientific research institution maintained solely for pure research and without hope of pecuniary gain or profit, may make and subscribe written articles of incorporation, and acknowledge the same, and file a duplicate of such articles for record in the office of the county clerk of each county in which any real property of such corporation is situated together with an impression of the seal which it will adopt.[47]

[42] Cf. Chapt. III, Article 2, p. 65, *supra*.

[43] Pollock-Maitland, I, 502.

[44] Fletcher, *Cyclopedia of the Law of Private Corporations* (20 vols., revised and permanent edition, Chicago: Callaghan & Co., 1931), I, 183, § 52. [Hereinafter cited Fletcher's Cyclopedia on Corporations.]

[45] Kent, *Commentaries on American Law* (4 vols., edited by O. W. Holmes, 13. ed., edited by Charles M. Barnes, Boston: Little, Brown, & Co., 1884), II, 274. [Hereinafter cited Kent Commentaries.]

[46] Wright v. Morgan, 191 U.S. 55, 24 S.Ct. 6, 48 L.Ed. 89 (1903).

[47] 1957 N.M. Laws, ch. 112, § 7, being section 51-14-26 of 1953 N.M. Comp. Laws.

Such corporation sole shall continue as a corporation for the time limited in its articles of incorporation, but not to exceed 100 years, and shall vest in the successors in office to the person so complying with the provisions of the 1957 Act.[48]

Furthermore, title to all property vested in such corporation sole shall also vest in the incorporator's successors in office.[49]

Section 2.   Canon Law

The Church, like the State, is a juridically perfect society with the inherent right to exist.   Neither of them is a moral person, a corporation; neither of them is a legal fiction.   Both are more than moral personalities; they are, each of them, a society, albeit participating of the attributes of a corporation.

At Canon law, the Church, as a society of divine institution, is composed of persons who, through baptism, have become subjects of the Church.[50]   But besides physical persons, there are also in the Church persons constituted by public (ecclesiastical) authority.[51]   Now, since it is repugnant that an entity—legal or otherwise—create itself, and inasmuch as the constituting of a corporation postulates public authority, it follows that the Church is not a moral person.[52]   Accordingly, the Catholic

[48] *Loc. cit.* It is to be noted that corporations sole created under the provisions of the 1951 Act "shall be perpetual in existence."—1951 N.M. Laws, ch. 183, § 6, being section 51-14-6 of 1953 N.M. Comp. Laws (repealed).   However, an opinion of the Attorney General holds that "charitable and benevolent non-profit corporations are required to state in their articles of incorporation a term of existence not in excess of 100 years."— 1953-1954 N M. Attorney General Reports, No. 5723.

[49] 1957 N.M. Laws, ch. 112, § 7, being section 51-14-26 of 1953 N.M. Comp. Laws.

[50] Cf. canon 87.

[51] Canon 99.

[52] Cf. Brown, p. 90; *contra*: Augustine, *A Commentary on the New Code of Canon Law* (8 vols., Vol. II, 3. ed., St. Louis: B. Herder Book Co., 1919), II, 7 (hereinafter cited Augustine); Bouscaren-Ellis, *Canon Law: A Text and Commentary* (2. revised ed., Milwaukee: Bruce Publishing Co., 1951), p. 86 (hereinafter cited Bouscaren-Ellis).

Church and the Apostolic See have the stature of a moral person,[53] and this indeed by divine ordinance.[54]

That the Church and the Apostolic See are not moral personalities is, in a more positive way, patent from the wording of canon 100, § 1: "Catholica Ecclesia et Apostolica Sedes moralis personae rationem habent . . ." At the risk of laboring the point, it is to be noted that the canon in question does not state, ". . . SUNT *personae morales*," but speaks of the Church and of the Holy See as having the *ratio*, the nature, of a moral person.[55]

In regard to the juridical nature of the Holy See as such, there seems to be a difference of opinion among canon lawyers,[56] although perhaps the extant discrepancies may be considered reducible to a *lis de verbis*. Some would personify both the Church and the Holy See, by claiming that the distinction between the two is a *real* distinction, resting however on a non-coördinated basis inasmuch as the one is rather a part of the other.[57] Others simply predicate a juridical personality of the Church and the Holy See,[58] while still others regard the Pope (Apostolic See) as a corporation sole.[59]

Now, there can be no question—and there is not among canon lawyers—that the foundation and creation of the Church and of the Holy See along with their capacity to exercise rights are not contingent or in any way dependent upon human authority. Nor is there any doubt that the Church can exist only in conjunction with the Roman Pontiff, the latter being an absolutely essential constituent element of the former. Thus it follows that the distinction between the two is a real, but an unequal distinction. This, however, does not postulate that the Church and the Holy

[53] Canon 100, § 1.

[54] *Loc. cit.*

[55] The Apostolic See, in this frame of reference, does not include the various bureaus, or departments, of the Roman Curia.—Cf. canon 7.

[56] Cf. Wernz-Vidal, II, 37.

[57] Bouscaren-Ellis, p. 86.

[58] Coronata, I, 159; Abbo-Hannan, I, 145.

[59] Augustine, II, 7.

See be moral persons. That position and construction is not only not inferable from canon 100, § 1, but is, equivalently, excluded by the wording thereof. To forestall unwarranted connotations, and in the interests of precision, perhaps it were better to speak of the Church and the Holy Ste as quasi-juridical personalities.

More specifically, it is true that the Code speaks of the Roman Pontiff as being the successor to the primacy of St. Peter,[60] from which, obviously, it follows that there is a succession and a continuity in office—an essential note native to a corporation sole. True it is, too, that the Code itself personifies the Holy See in providing that *"Prima Sedes a nemine iudicatur."* [61]   But one must always revert to the inexorable logic consequent to canon 99: "In Ecclesia, . . . sunt etiam personae morales, publica auctoritate constitutae." At Canon law, therefore—as at Anglo-American jurisprudence—a parthenogenetic moral person is a legal monstrosity, a chimera: a corporation must be created by public authority or it is naught. Accordingly, the Holy See cannot be conceived as a corporation sole in the Anglo-American sense of the term. But if a corporation sole be viewed from the Roman law concept of the *princeps,* or more especially from the English common law focus wherein the king, by virtue of his sovereignty, was *ipso facto* a corporation sole, then the term can indeed be predicated of the Apostolic See.

Within this juridically perfect society, the Church, there are, besides physical persons, moral persons as well. And these fall into two classes: collegiate and non-collegiate.[62]

A. Collegiate Moral Person

A collegiate moral person is one which becomes constituted of an aggregate of several physical persons, the minimum number of such members being three.[63]   Thus, a religious order is composed of its members several, a chapter of its canons, a board of its individual members. It is to be noted that such a corporation is a distinct entity, legally independent from the physical

---

[60] Canon 218, § 1.

[61] Canon 1556.

[62] Canon 99.

[63] Canon 100, § 2.

members who compose it; consequently, the rights of the corporation are not the rights of the members, nor do the debts of the corporation constitute an encumbrance on the pesonal resources or credit of the members thereof.[64]   In short, the collegiate moral person of Canon law is the counter-part of the corporation aggregate of Anglo-American law.

B. Non-Collegiate Moral Person

A non-collegiate moral person is one made up, not of physical persons, but of property and resources which are separated from the ownership of other persons and dedicated to a religious or charitable purpose.[65]   The Code itself, in dichotomizing moral personality, proffers examples of non-collegiate persons: churches, seminaries, benefices, etc.[66] Hospitals, orphanages, and schools are further examples.

Again, the corporation—the property and resources, in this instance—becomes the subject of rights and duties.   It is obvious that a non-collegiate corporation is not supported by natural persons, although this support is essential for the corporation's existence *de facto*.[67]   A counter-part of the canonical non-collegiate moral person at Anglo-American law would be the eleemosynary corporation.

Aside from the stipulation that a collegiate moral person postulates a minimum number of three incorporators,[68] the other conditions for the existence of canonical moral persons are common to both collegiate and non-collegiate personalities.   There are two: the specified scope and the intervention of public authority.

C. Conditions Precedent: Scope and Authority

If the proper scope, or end, is not verified in a given instance, there can be no canonical corporation.   And this scope is explicitly delineated in the Code by the words, "ad finem *religiosum*

[64] Cf. Wernz-Vidal, II, 35.

[65] Cf. Bouscaren-Ellis, p. 86.

[66] Canon 99.

[67] Cf. Brown, p. 95.

[68] Canon 100, § 2.

vel *caritativum*": [69] an ecclesiastical corporation must be created, and must exist, for a religious or for a charitable purpose, for else it lacks the very basis for existence. No *tertium quid* is given.

Whereas Anglo-American law is satisfied with any legitimate scope, that of an ecclesiatical corporation must pertain directly to the love of God; for else it has no claim to existence, and any attempt to create a moral person in contravention of this requisite would be null and void. This follows from the fact that ecclesiastical corporations are subordinate to the Church. Hence, the *raison d'être* of such legal entities must be consonant with the supernatural mission of the Church.

Ecclesiastical corporations are constituted as such by ecclesiastical authority in two ways: through provision of the law itself, and by means of a formal decree.[70] The former type may be termed a corporation deriving *a iure,* the latter, a corporations deriving *ab homine.*[71] In either case, no canonical corporation can exist if it does not derive its authority from the Church.[72]

Moral persons constituted through provision of the law itself, expressly or equivalently, include the College of Cardinals (cc. 231, 241), the diocesan Curia (c. 363), the Roman Curia (c. 242), etc.[73]

A formal act of public ecclesiastical authority is required for the creation of all other canonical corporations. Accordingly, only the Holy See and those superiors who enjoy episcopal or at least quasi-episcopal jurisdiction are competent to act in these matters. Thus, corporations of pontifical status can be created only by the Holy See. This means that papal authority is required for the creation of ecclesiastical provinces, dioceses, ab-

[69] Canon 100, § 1.

[70] Canon 100, § 1.

[71] Cf. Beste, *Introductio in Codicem* (4. ed., Neapoli: M. D'Auria Pontificius Editor, 1956), p. 157.

[72] Cf. Cappello, *Summa Iuris Publici Ecclesiastici* (5. ed., Romae: Apud Aedes Universitatis Gregorianae, 1943), p. 44.

[73] Cf. Bouscaren-Ellis, p. 87.

bacies and prelacies *nullius*, vicariates and perfectures apostolic,[74] cathedral or collegiate chapters,[75] consistorial benefices,[76] Catholic universities or Catholic faculties.[77]

In his diocese, a residential bishop is competent to erect parishes,[78] hospitals and orphanages,[79] and seminaries.[80] Again, the foregoing enumeration is merely illustrative, not exclusive.

Those ecclesiastical corporations which postulate a positive act of public authority for their existence obviously do not become possessed of juridic personality and capacity until a formal decree of erection has been granted by the competent authority.[81] The canonical decree of erection, then, is the counter-part of the English and Anglo-American charter.

ARTICLE 2. CORPORATE POWERS
Section 1. New Mexico Law

By the provisions of the 1957 Act, a non-profit corporation in New Mexico has the capacity to act that is possessed by natural persons, but it has authority to perform only such acts as are necessary or proper for the accomplishing of its purposes and are not repugnant to law.[82]

Unless the articles of incorporation prescribe otheriwse, a corporation has authority to:

1) continue as a corporation for the time limited in its articles of incorporation, but not to exceed one hundred (100) years;

2) sue and be sued;

[74] Canon 215, § 1.

[75] Canon 392.

[76] Canon 1414, § 1.

[77] Canon 1376, § 1. The list presented is merely demonstrative, by no means being exhaustive.

[78] Canon 216, § 1.

[79] Canon 1489, § 1.

[80] Canon 1354.

[81] Cf. canon 100, § 1, and canon 687.

[82] 1957 N.M. Laws, ch. 112, § 11, being section 51-14-30 of 1953 N.M. Comp. Laws.

3) have, and alter at pleasure, a corporate seal, the affixing of which shall not affect the validity or enforceability of any instrument;

4) take and hold an interest in real and personal property;

5) lease, encumber, convey, or dispose of real and personal property;

6) enter into obligations or contracts and do any act incidental to the transaction of its business or expedient to the purposes stated in its articles of incorporation;

7) acquire, hold, mortgage, pledge, or dispose of shares, bonds, securities and other evidences of indebtedness of any domestic or foreign corporation, either public or private, and, if it is owner thereof, to exercise all the rights, powers, and privileges of ownership, including the right to vote;

8) receive, hold, and administer trust funds and endowments for the uses and purposes of said corporation;

9) conduct its affairs within and without the State;

10) make, amend, and repeal by-laws, not inconsistent with its articles or with law, for the administration and regulation of its affairs;

11) merge and consolidate with other non-profit corporations, domestic or foreign, organized for related purposes;

12) make loans and donations to other non-profit corporations, domestic or foreign, organized for related purposes, and to needy persons;

13) be a member of another non-profit corporation, whether foreign or domestic;

14) dissolve and wind up by majority vote of its duly accredited members in attendance at any regular meeting upon notice.[83]

As was brought out in the preceding chapter, all corporations must, from necessity, act and contract through the aid and by means of individuals; such individuals may be those holding corporate offices, agents,[84] or authorized employees.[85]   However, a

[83] 1957 N.M. Laws, ch. 112, § 11, being section 51-14-30 of 1953 N.M. Comp. Laws.

[84] 13 Am. Jur., Corporations, § 864.

[85] Sanchez v. Securities Acceptance Corp., 57 N.M. 512, 260 P.2d 703 (1953).

corporation may ratify an unauthorized agreement of another person, made in its behalf, and by such ratification become bound thereby.[86]

The fundamental principles governing the authority of an officer or agent of a corporation are substantially the same as those applicable to agents generally. Thus, the authority of an agent of a corporation must necessarily depend, as that of the agent of a physical person, on the terms and scope of his appointment. Furthermore, the authority of such agent or officer may be actual, that is, express or implied, or it may be an authority which is variously described as apparent, ostensible, or by estoppel.[87] In regard to the later type, one dealing with a corporation as such is estopped to deny its legal existence.[88]

Relative to the powers of suing enjoyed by corporations, it should be observed that the New Mexico Supreme Court has found that a corporation may maintain assumpsit.[89]

While a non-profit corporation can take and hold an interest in realty and personalty,[90] its capacity in this regard is qualified by the fact that a corporation can own such property as is necessary or proper for enabling it to carry out the objects of its creation.[91]

Section 2. Canon Law

An ecclesiastical corporation, whether collegiate or non-collegiate, is possessed of the capacity to do those things which a physical person may legitimately do, except, of course, that the former cannot place an act which is peculiar to the latter as such. Briefly, it is capable of performing those acts which are proper

[86] Lawrence Coal Co. v. Shanklin, 25 N.M. 404, 183 P. 435 (1919).

[87] 13 Am. Jur., Corporations, § 889.

[88] Palatine Insurance Co. of Manchester, England v. Santa Fe Mercantile Co., 13 N.M. 241, 82 P. 363 (1905).

[89] C. J. L. Meyer & Sons Co. v. Black, 4 Gild. (N.M.) 352, 4 John. (N.M.) 190, 16 P. 620 (1888).

[90] 1957 N.M. Laws, ch. 112, § 11, being section 51-14-30 of 1953 N.M. Comp. Laws.

[91] Church of the Holy Faith v. State Tax Commission, 39 N.M. 403, 48 P.2d 777 (1935).

to its end.[92] This follows from the axiom, *qui vult finem, vult medium:* the authority creating a corporation for a specific object must thereby endow the moral person with the capacity of performing such acts as are necessary and useful for the achieving of that end.

The Code of Canon Law declares all ecclesiastical corporations to be in the same class as minors: *"minoribus aequiparantur;"* [93] that is to say, they enjoy the same protection under the law. The reason for this provision is to preclude serious detriment to the corporation from possible negligence of its administrators or agents.[94] Thus, a corporation, like a minor, can maintain action for *restitutio in integrum*.[95]

Like a civil corporation, a canonical moral person can act only through its administrators and duly-appointed agents. And what these representatives decide upon and do within the scope of their authority, the corporation does.[96]

But a collegiate moral personality can also act in a collegiate manner. And in such cases, one of two possibilities will be verified: the matter in question may or may not affect each member of the corporation as an individual. In the latter hypothesis, unless the common law or particular statutes explicitly prescribe a different course of action, that act will enjoy the force of law which has received the approval of the absolute majority of the voters, no count being made of the votes that are void. If an absolute majority is not obtained on the first ballot, a second is taken. If even this fails, the relative majority decides in the third ballot. If the third ballot does not produce a relative majority because the votes are equally divided, the presiding officer

92 Cf. canon 691.

93 Canon 100, § 3.

94 Cf. Vermeersch-Creusen, II, 200.

95 Canon 1687, § 2. The counter-part of this prayer at Anglo-American law would be a bill in equity pleading for reinstatement in a previous condition. At Canon law, unlike Anglo-American jurisprudence, a recovery in equity may even be granted *ex officio* by a court.—Cf. canon 1688, § 2.

96 Cf. Brown, p. 99. It must be noted that action through authorized individual superiors is governed by canon 105.

must by his ballot dissolve the tie vote and thus decide the issue. But if there is question of elections to office and the presiding officer does not want to dissolve the tie, then the senior in ordination, or in first profession, or in age—in that sequence—is to be considered the one elected to office.[97]

In the event that the matter in question before the collegiate corporation affects each incorporated member as an individual, that measure must be approved by way of unanimous vote: "Quod autem omnes, uti singulos, tangit, ab omnibus probari debet." [98] The legal motive for the foregoing provision is that in every collegiate body there are not only rights which are proper to the corporation as such, but also rights which are native to each member as an individual, and which could otherwise be jeopardized or prejudiced by the deprivation of a vested right or by the imposition of an inequitable burden.[99] Examples of such issues would be: union with another moral person; the introduction of a new observance; a donation imposing a personal assessment.[100]

With reference to the modes of action on the part of non-collegiate corporations, particular statutes and the norms of the common law will control.[101] The acts of such corporations are treated principally in the third book of the Code, where provision is made for churches, benefices, schools, seminaries, hospitals, and pious foundations.

ARTICLE 3.   DURATION AND TERMINATION OF CORPORATE EXISTENCE

Section 1.   New Mexico Law

Blackstone regarded the capacity of perpetual succession or continuity as an essential attribute of a corporation.[102] At

[97] Canon 101, § 1, 1°.

[98] Canon 101, § 1, 2°. This norm is incorporated from Rule 29, R.J., in VI°. The Code adds the incision, *uti singulos.*

[99] Cf. Wernz-Vidal, II, 41.

[100] Cf. Abbo-Hannan, II, 149.

[101] Canon 101, § 2.

[102] 1 Blackstone Commentaries 475.

Anglo-American law, once a corporation, it presumptively continues, although the notion of perpetual succession is not generally construed to imply corporate immortality, but rather a continuity of existence, irrespective of that of its component members, limited in duration to the period stated in its charter or the act authorizing the granting thereof.[103]

Under present New Mexico law, a non-profit corporation may be chartered for a maximum term of one hundred years.[104] Nevertheless,

> Any corporation of this State organized not for profit may at any time prior to the expiration of the term of its existence, and within eight (8) years thereafter extend the term of its existence for a period of one hundred (100) years from and after the expiration of its term of existence in the manner following: The acting board of trustees or directors shall file in the office of the State Corporation a certificate signed and acknowledged by a majority of such board, setting forth (a) the name of such corporation, (b) the office where and the date when the original articles of incorporation were filed, (c) the date when the corporate existence expired, (d) the names and addresses of the members of the acting board of directors or trustees, and (e) the period for which the corporate existence is to be extended, and shall cause a certified copy of such certificate to be recorded in the office of the county clerk of the county wherein such corporation has been engaged in its principal activity. No publication of the certificate or of notice shall be required. Such proceedings, when so taken, shall have the effect of extending such corporation's existence for the period stated as herein limited, and such corporation shall be bound and shall exercise the same rights as though its charter had not expired.[105]

Furthermore,

> If within eight (8) years from the expiration of the term of existence of any corporation of the kind described in section 13 (51-14-32) of this act, the persons in control of such

103 1 Fletcher's Cyclopedia on Corporations 18, § 6.

104 1957 N.M. Laws, ch. 112, §§ 5, 7, being sections 51-14-24 and 51-14-26, respectively, of 1953 N.M. Comp. Laws.

105 1957 N.M. Laws, ch. 112, § 13, being section 51-14-32 of 1953 N.M. Comp. Laws.

corporation shall have formed a new corporation with the same name and for substantially the same purposes as the original corporation, by filing the articles of incorporation of such new corporation with the State Corporation Commission, the new corporation so formed shall be considered as an extension of the existence of the original corporation for the period stated in the articles of such new corporation, as fully and completely as if steps had been taken to obtain such extension before the charter of the original corporation had expired, and such extension shall relate back to and take effect as of the date of expiration of the original charter, and said corporation shall exercise its rights in the same manner as though the original charter had never expired, Provided that the new corporation so formed shall file with the State Corporation Commission its written acceptance of the provisions of this act.[106]

It follows, then, that a non-profit corporation may be revived by one of the two procedures above-described, provided that such action be taken within eight years subsequent to the expiration of corporate existence. And since no distinction or restriction is made in the law, a corporation's charter may be renewed for an indefinite number of maximum terms of one hundred years.

With reference to the termination of corporate existence, it is obvious that this result will ensue by provision of law where a corporation's charter is not renewed according to the above-cited procedures. In addition, a corporation may be dissolved by the surrender of its charter, a method which might be likened to a kind of suicide. In the case of a corporation aggregate, however, a majority vote of its duly accredited members in attendance at any regular meeting upon notice is a requisite for dissolving and winding up.[107]

At Anglo-American law, a corporation may also be dissolved by an act of the legislature.[108] However, the power of the state to destroy its corporations is not greater than its power to repeal

[106] 1957 N.M. Laws, ch. 112, § 15, being section 51-14-34 of 1953 N.M. Comp. Laws.

[107] 1957 N.M. Laws, ch. 112, § 11, being section 51-14-30 of 1953 N.M. Comp. Laws.

[108] 13 Am. Jur., Corporations, § 1287.

legislation, and the latter power is clearly subject to the constitutional guaranty against impairment of the obligation of contracts.[109]   In other words, since the grant of a corporate charter is contractual in its nature, such a grant is entitled to the protection of the provision of the Federal Constitution prohibiting any state from enacting any law impairing the obligation of contracts.[110]

Now, the Constitution of New Mexico provides that "all laws relating to corporations may be altered, amended or repealed by the legislature, at any time, when necessary for the common good and general welfare, and all corporations doing business in this State, may, as to such business, be regulated, limited, or restrained by laws not in conflict with the Constitution of the United States or of this Constitution." [111]

In a 1929 case, Judge Simms of the New Mexico Supreme Court wrote, in a unanimous opinion, in the terms following:

> In his concurring opinion in the celebrated Dartmouth College Case . . ., Mr. Justice Story took occasion to say, with regard to the power of the legislature to alter or amend the charter of a private corporation: 'If the legislature mean to claim such an authority, it must be reserved in the grant.' This pronouncement was followed by a practice which immediately sprang up, and has become well-nigh universal in the various states; that was to reserve the right and power to alter, amend or repeal the charter. This end has been reached in several ways; in some states it is incorporated in the Constitution, while in others it is a matter of statute, pursuant to which all charters are granted. The controlling question here is whether or not this State has reserved the power to amend the charter of a bank organized under a general banking law after the Constitution was adopted and in force.
>
> Appellant argues that the provisions of article 11, section 13, of our Constitution . . ., do not constitute such a reservation of power, and lays stress on the absence of the word 'charter' from the list of things named as subject to

[109] Graham v. Folsom, 200 U.S. 248, 26 S.Ct. 245, 50 L.Ed. 464 (1905).

[110] 13 Am. Jur., Corporations, § 1287.

[111] N.M. Constitution, Art. XI, § 13

amendment. We think the language used, 'all laws relating to corporations may be altered, amended or repealed,' is the broadest possible statement of the reserved power. It not only includes those laws relating to corporations which may properly be said to be a part of their charters, but any and all other laws relating to the subject which might not be treated as part of their charters.[112]

A final method of dissolution is forfeiture of a charter by abuse or neglect.[113] But, although the legislature may reserve unto itself the power to repeal the charter of a corporation for nonuser or misuser, the determination of the question whether there has been such nonuser or misuser, or as to give rise to a right to appeal, is a judicial and not a legislative function; accordingly, the legislature cannot repeal a charter under such a reservation of power without an investigation and judgment by a court, after due notice to the corporation.[114]

Section 2.   Canon Law

An ecclesiastical corporation is of its very nature perpetual; however, it becomes extinct on suppression by competent authority or through no show of active existence over a period of one hundred years.[115]

Since an ecclesiastical moral person is by its very nature perpetual, the two methods which the Code provides for the extinction of a corporation are exhaustive, not merely illustrative.[116]

Regarding the first method, who is the competent authority? First of all, it would be that authority by which it was established: "Omnis res, per quascumque causas nascitur, per easdem dissolvitur." [117]   Also competent would be the successors and superiors of that authority. However, the rule of law of Gregory

[112] Melaven v. Schmidt, 34 N.M. 443, 444, 283 P. 900 (1929).

[113] 13 Am. Jur., Corporations, § 1286.

[114] State v. Sunset Ditch Co., 48 N.M. 17, 145 P.2d 219 (1944).

[115] Canon 102, § 1.

[116] Cf. Abbo-Hannan, II, 149.

[117] Reg. 1, R.J., in X, v, 41.

IX just cited is patient of exceptions; in the present context, it must be noted that in certain cases Superiors who erected the corporation cannot suppress it.[118]

The second method by which a canonical corporation becomes *de iure* extinct is wrought by the operation of the law itself when the moral person has not reflected any active existence for a period of one hundred years in consequence of a complete lack of members for that length of time. In other words, the non-showing of active existence postulates a condition where not even one member of the aggregate survives, but even such a total absence of members will not engender an extinction *de iure* until that status has been verified for an uninterrupted term of one hundred years. The moral person may be revived from its dormant status at any time during this period, and a new decree is not necessary.

This latter method of extinction, as just presented, would obviously find application with reference to collegiate moral persons. What about non-collegiate corporations? Canon 102, § 1, reads: "Persona moralis . . . extinguitur . . . si per centum annorum spatium esse desierit." In the opinion of the writer, the words, *esse desierit,* cannot be limited to a collegiate corporation. In the first place, according to the legal axiom, *ubi lex non distinguit, nec nos distinguere debemus:* a gratuitous restriction is thus to be rejected on principle. And the canon does not make a distinction. Secondly, the words, "if it ceases to be in evidence," can be predicated without difficulty of either type of corporation without a necessary reference to membership, for either class of corporation will lack evidence of its existence when one of its constitutive elements ceases to be in evidence. No one can deny that the specified scope of a canonical corporation is one of its constitutive elements, for instance. Now, should a collegiate moral person be completely unable, for one or another reason, to realize its *raison d'être* for a period of time not exceeding one hundred years, it would certainly not thereby lose its juridical personality. The same reasoning can be applied to a non-collegiate corporation. Accordingly, should a non-

118 Cf. e.g., canons 493, 498, 1422, 1494. In these cases, the authority of the Holy See is required.

collegiate moral person cease to function for a period of time not exceeding one hundred years, such nonuser would not render the pertinent provision of canon 102, § 1, inoperative.

Finally, if at least one of the members of a collegiate corporation survives, the rights of all devolve upon him.[119]   In other words, a collegiate corporation once duly constituted can continue to exist without the full quorum of three members.

[119] Canon 102, § 2.

CHAPTER V

ACQUISITION AND TENURE OF CHURCH PROPERTY

ARTICLE 1.   RIGHT OF THE CHURCH TO ACQUIRE PROPERTY

From the very beginning of its establishment by Christ as a juridically perfect society, the Church succeeded in exercising its God-given right to acquire, hold, and administer property. And this materialized in spite of the severe opposition which the Church met, particularly in the way of persecution. While encroachments of greater or lesser extent were directed against the Church in this matter by the Roman Emperors, it is a historical fact that the first confiscation of church property as such did not take place until Diocletian came into power in the third century.

Under Roman law, both private individuals and associations (*collegia, universitates*) could acquire property. And when the Emperors attempted—and in many instances they succeeded, momentarily—to circumscribe the rights of the Church in this regard, such encroachment proceeded not from any provision of Roman law directed against the dedication of temporal goods to religious purposes, but rather out of enmity towards Christianity. The persecutions as such were primarily directed against the new religion. Roman law, after all, had for many centuries before made the institution of the inviolability of sacred things part and parcel of its jurisprudence: the *res sacrae, res religiosae,* and *res sanctae* enjoyed tremendous favor of law. Once dedicated to divine worship, realty and chattels were beyond the reach of plebe, patrician, emperor: such property belonged to the gods.[1]

The Roman provincial governors gradually saw that it was useless to deny organization and recognition to the Church. By the Edict of Milan (313) the right of the Church to acquire temporal goods was legally recognized.

[1] Bonfante, *Istituzioni di Diritto Romano,* p. 239, § 77.

126

Almost imperceptibly, however, abuses of lay encroachments upon the temporal rights of the Church soon crept in until, subtilities having been discarded, they reached a denouement in the first centuries of the Middle Ages. Proprietary churches sprang up simultaneously with the feudal system of land tenure. Under this system the king owned all the land of the country in fee together with everything, including churches, that might be found thereon. In parcelling out lands to the lay lords, the king thereby transferred dominion and control of churches. Except for the stipulation that the purpose of the proprietary church was to remain undiverted, the lay lord could sell, exchange, bestow, or otherwise alienate it; he could devise it, lease it, grant it as a fief, mortgage, or otherwise encumber it.

In England, various mortmain statutes and acts were enacted whereby the right of the Church to temporalities was gravely encumbered. Initially the movement was radicated on the premise that, since ecclesiastical corporations did not pay the taxes imposed upon natural persons, every acquisition by such a corporation was in reality a detriment to the treasury of the secular prince. Thus, church corporations came to be known as *manus mortuae*. With an ever-increasing vigor, however, further curtailing statutes were successively enacted until Henry VIII (1509-1547) began the legal policy of religious discrimination. By a series of acts, religious houses and monasteries were dissolved; churches and lands escheated to the Crown, until the king and his heirs and successors forever were vested with the seisin of all confiscated church property. Edward VI (1547-1553) crowned the discriminatory efforts of Henry VIII with his Statute of Chantries of 1547, invalidating all grants or gifts of property to the Church or religious institutions.[2]

Section 1. New Mexico Law

New Mexico constitutional and statutory law has never discriminated against the right of the Church to acquire temporalities. And there has been no court case in which that right has

[2] Goodwine, *The Right of the Church to Acquire Temporal Goods,* The Catholic University of American Canon Law Studies, n. 131 (Washington, D.C.: The Catholic University of America Press, 1941), p. 53.

had to be vindicated or defended.   Moreover, there is a total absence of actions in which the right of property acquisition by religious or charitable institutions has been directly tried.

The right of the Church in New Mexico to acquire property was not challenged or jeopardized in the transition from one sovereignty to the other.   On the contrary, ecclesiastical property rights were explicitly protected by the Treaty of Guadalupe Hidalgo [3] and the Gadsden Treaty.[4]   It goes without saying, of course, that the right of the Church to temporal possessions was not recognized thereby.   What was protected were personal rights; in this instance the fees simple of the successive bishops of Santa Fe were secured as absolute owners thereof, although a trust was probably implied.

When held as a fee simple by a natural person, New Mexico law imposes no restriction as to the amount of ecclesiastical property so held.   With regard to property owned by a body corporate, however, the expected circumscription is realized in the provision that a non-profit corporation "has the capacity to act possessed by natural persons, but it shall have authority to perform only acts that are necessary or proper to accomplish its purpose." [5]   In other words, although a non-profit corporation can take and hold an interest in real and personal property,[6] the extent of such holdings is contingent on the fact that a corporation can own only such property as is necessary or proper to enable it to carry out the objects of its creation.[7]

This restriction, however, is not peculiar to New Mexico law; for at Anglo-American law a corporation is restricted to powers explicitly contained in its charter and to implied powers whereby it can do only those things which are reasonably necessary to enable it to exercise the powers which are expressly granted and thus to accomplish its main objects.   Thus, for example, a rail-

[3] Art. VIII, q.v., *supra,* p. 52.

[4] Art. V, q.v., *supra,* p. 52.

[5] Sect. 51-14-30, 1953 N.M. Comp. Laws.

[6] *Loc. cit.*

[7] Church of the Holy Faith v. State Tax Commission, 39 N.M. 403, 48 P.2d 777 (1935).

road company may maintain restaurants along its route for the accommodation of its passengers; a mining company may operate a railroad to convey its ore to market, but not to transport passengers for hire; a manufacturing company may buy land on which to erect factories and for the purpose of erecting housing for its employees, but not for the purpose of holding for speculation.[8]

A corporation sole at New Mexico law can take and hold an interest in real and personal property.[9] This provision is favorably opportune, since a corporation sole at Anglo-American law, unless so empowered by statute, can take and hold real property only.[10] This is not surprising in view of the fact that at common law corporations aggregate could take in succession both real and personal property, but corporations sole could not take goods and chattels for the benefit of themselves and their successors. The reason given was that such movable property could likely be lost or embezzled, and this would engender a multitude of disputes between the successor and the executor, which the law was careful to avoid.[11]

Section 2. Canon Law

At Canon law, by the term *ecclesiastical goods* are understood all temporal goods, corporeal (movable and immovable) and incorporeal, real and personal, which belong either to the Universal Church, or to the Apostolic See, or to individual ecclesiastical legal persons.[12] That the Church has the right to acquire property flows quite logically from the premise that it is a juridically perfect society. As such, even though its mission is of a supernatural character, it is possessed of the capacity to acquire temporal goods. This, in turn, follows from the stubborn fact that this juridically perfect society is composed of physical persons, not spirits; that such members exist on a physical earth, not an

[8] 13 Am. Jur., Corporations, § 740.

[9] Sect. 51-14-30, 1953 N.M. Comp. Laws.

[10] 1 Fletcher's Cyclopedia on Corporations 181, § 51.

[11] 1 Blackstone Commentaries 477.

[12] Canon 1497, § 1.

ethereal entity; that, consequently, if a society is to exist under such conditions and circumstances it must have that native capacity.   Briefly, no society can exist without the right to acquire property.

It might be objected that the Church, albeit a society of men, was founded for a supernatural purpose; that its object is the spiritual welfare of men; that, therefore, it has no right to acquire temporal goods.   Admittedly, temporal goods of themselves are inadequate for the attainment of the supernatural end of the Church.   But they are necessary among men in order that men may act visibly and externally in the use of other, namely spiritual, means.[13]

The expression of this right is canonized in the Code of Canon Law in the provision that the Catholic Church and the Holy See have an inherent right freely and independently of the civil power to acquire, hold, and administer temporal goods for the prosecution of the proper ends of the Church.[14] The term "Catholic Church" is understood to mean the visible and perfect society founded by Christ; the term "Holy See" is understood in the context of canon 7, and it includes not only the Roman Pontiff, but also the Roman Curia.[15]

The Church in this matter has a *"nativum ius,"* an innate right, a right that is inherent, a right that is congenital, that is introduced by divine institution and not acquired or derived in any way from an outside source. This right native to the Church, then, debars all encroachment upon it by civil powers. The right of the state cannot be absolute, for God alone is the Supreme Lord of the universe; neither can it be unlimited, for the state has a right to temporal goods only insofar as they are necessary or useful for the prosecution of its own ends without prejudice to, or disregard for, the rights of others.   Since the ends of the Church and of the state are different, it cannot be said that the

13 Goodwine, *op. cit.,* p. 36.

14 Canon 1495, § 1.

15 Doheny, *Church Property: Modes of Acquisition,* The Catholic University of America Canon Law and Roman Law Studies, n. 41 (Washington, D.C.: The Catholic University of America Press, 1927), p. 26. [Hereinafter cited Doheny.]

claim of the Church curtails civil powers: there should be no conflict as long as these two perfect societies adhere to their proper spheres.

The Church enjoys the "free and independent" right of exercising its legitimate prerogatives as long as they are just and equitable. Materially, the object of the Church's right to temporalities consists in its capacity to acquire, hold, and administer such temporal goods; formally, in the actual acquiring, holding, and administering of them in the prosecution of the end proper to itself.[16]

Although vested with full capacity for ownership, the Church as a society actually possesses no property.[17] What is termed ecclesiastical property is owned by the Holy See as a corporation sole and by the various canonical corporations existing by the authority of the Church.

Canon 1495, § 2, rules that also individual churches and other moral persons which have been created as legal persons by means of ecclesiastical authority have the right to acquire, hold, and administer temporal goods according to the prescriptions of Canon law. And amongst these prescriptions is that, while the individual corporation which acquired the temporal goods has the dominion thereof, this dominion is under the supreme authority of the Holy See,[18] in which is vested an *altum dominium*, or right of eminent domain. It is a right of jurisdiction in virtue of which the Holy See can, for a sufficient reason, limit the property rights of ecclesiastical entities.[19]

There are as many subjects of dominion as there are canonical corporations capable of acquiring property in the Church. The amount of property that may be acquired is not determined by Canon law. With reference to parochial property, it is to be

[16] Munday, *Ecclesiastical Property in Australia and New Zealand*, The Catholic University of America Canon Law Studies, n. 387 (Washington, D.C.: The Catholic University of America Press, 1957), p. 21.

[17] Canon 1499, § 2: "Dominium bonorum, sub suprema auctoritate Sedis Apostolicae, ad eam pertinet moralem personam, quae eadem bona legitime acquisiverit."

[18] Canon 1499, § 2.

[19] Vermeersch-Creusen, II, 570.

borne in mind that the subject of dominion is the ecclesiastical corporation, personified in the parochial church,[20] and not the parochial community.[21]

In regard to the right of religious corporations, the Code rules that not only the religious organization itself, but also its provinces and individual houses, are capable of acquiring and holding temporal goods, unless such capacity is excluded or restricted by their individual rules and constitutions.[22] The Holy See acquires ownership of the property of those religious societies which by their rules and constitutions are forbidden to own temporal goods.[23]

Finally, the right of ecclesiastical corporations to the property they have legitimately acquired is protected, against those who would dare usurp it or hinder its use, by way of an excommunication incurred *ipso facto* which is in a simple manner reserved to the Holy See.[24]

ARTICLE 2.   MODES OF TENURE

At Anglo-American law, there can be no corporation which is not the creation of the civil law, and "all tenure of property likewise requires civil authority." [25]   In the early history of our country the American bishops were confronted with perhaps no

20 *Loc. cit.*

21 Wernz-Vidal, IV, Pars II, 195.

22 Canon 531.

23 Cf. canon 582, 2°. Almost every possible variety of restriction is found among religious societies. The following are illustrative instances: the Friars Minor and Capuchins are not allowed even the common ownership of property; whatever the individual or the order acquires is acquired by the Holy See. In the Society of Jesus no capacity to acquire ownership is enjoyed by the *domus professionis*. Among the Discalced Carmelites, houses which are not destined for the missions are allowed to have their own income only in special cases.—McManus, *The Administration of Temporal Goods in Religious Institutes,* The Catholic University of America Canon Law Studies, n. 109 (Washington, D.C.: The Catholic University of America Press, 1937), p. 38.

24 Canon 2346.

25 Dignan, *A History of the Legal Incorporation of Catholic Church Property in the United States* (New York: Kenedy & Sons, 1935), p. 50. [Hereinafter cited Dignan.]

problem as thorny as that relating to the tenure of church property. Numerous states enacted legislation providing for a congregational type of church organization, in which the control of the church property was vested in lay trustees or held by corporations dominated by laymen. While this system of tenure was acceptable to the belief and practice of Protestants, then in overwhelming majority, "this was particularly unfortunate from the Catholic point of view. For in the Catholic Church, all jurisdiction and rights flow from above downwards. Thus a Catholic parish derives its rights not from the lay members who compose it, but from the fact that it is an integral part of the Universal Church." [26] Nonetheless, the Church had to accommodate itself to this legal concept in order to exist at all. Thus there was inaugurated an unfortunate era of lay trusteeship. The reasons for the difficulties which ensued are not germane to this study, and it will suffice to say that this system proved completely unsatisfactory, and in some localities brought the Church perilously close to financial ruin.

Today, "the holding of church property by lay trustees has disappeared, and the situation of the Church in respect to property is at least tolerable everywhere, and in some jurisdictions very favorable." [27] In general, the method of tenure of church property in the United States falls in one of four categories:

1) The parochial or diocesan corporation;
2) The corporation sole;
3) The holding of property by the ordinary as trustee;
4) The holding of property by the ordinary in fee. [28]

Section 1. New Mexico Law

The ordinaries of the three dioceses concerned in New Mexico [29] held church property situated within the state in fee simple prior

[26] Dignan, p. 51.

[27] *Mode of Tenure: Roman Catholic Church Property in the United States,* a Survey by the Legal Department of the National Catholic Welfare Conference (Washington, D.C.: National Catholic Welfare Conference, 1941), Supplement — 1954, p. 6. [Hereinafter cited *Mode of Tenure.*]

[28] *Loc. cit.*

[29] The Archdiocese of Santa Fe, and the suffragan dioceses of El Paso and Gallup. The diocese of El Paso, Texas, was erected in 1914, and takes

to 1951.[30] However, a trust was probably implied for the purposes of the Church in accordance with its laws.[31] No case has arisen presenting this point to the New Mexico Supreme Court, but "neighboring states [notable Texas] have in analogous instances imposed a trust upon property similarly held, and it is submitted that an identical policy would prevail. The words of grant are sufficient to indicate a trust, and parol evidence of Canon law may then be admitted to explain its terms." [32]

The present non-profit corporation law allowing for the association for religious and charitable purposes seems to prove satisfactory, as American ecclesiastical incorporation laws go, for affording in the incorporation of parishes and dioceses all reasonable assurance that the canonical concept of these two institutions will not be jeopardized. This is submitted in view of the fact that "the articles of incorporation may contain any . . . provision[s], consistent with New Mexico law, for regulating the business of the corporation or the conduct of the corporate affairs," [33] and that "duly adopted or amended by-laws may con-

---

in six New Mexico counties, plus part of a seventh. The diocese of Gallup, New Mexico, was established in 1939; it extends into Arizona, but includes three New Mexico counties, plus parts of four others. Prior to 1914, the Archdiocese of Santa Fe and the state of New Mexico were, for our purposes, co-extensive.

[30] The Archbishop of Santa Fe was created a corporation sole on June 26, 1951.—Certificate of Incorporation No. 28329. The Bishop of Gallup holds, since November 20, 1951, as a corporation sole in New Mexico; property of this diocese situated in Arizona is held in trust "for the Roman Catholic Church of the Diocese of Gallup" by the Bishop and his successors in office.—Letter of Very Rev. Dunstan Schmidlin, O.F.M., J. C. L., Chancellor of the Diocese of Gallup, to the writer, dated March 11, 1959. The property of the diocese of El Paso, both in New Mexico and in Texas, is held by the Bishop and his successors in office "for the use and purposes of the Catholic Church."—Letter of Rt. Rev. Mons. Hugh G. Quinn, J.C.D., Chancellor of the Diocese of El Paso, to the writer, dated March 20, 1959. In all three dioceses, educational and charitable institutions are separately incorporated.

[31] *Mode of Tenure,* s.v. "New Mexico."

[32] *Loc. cit.*

[33] 1957 N.M. Laws, ch. 112, § 5, being section 51-14-24 of 1953 N.M. Comp. Laws.

tain any provision for the purpose of administering and regulating the affairs of the corporation not inconsistent with law or the articles of incorporation." [34]

Such a corporation could consist of as few as three persons or as many as there are Catholics in a parish or a diocese. While it is true that the incorporation of a parish has the general effect of making each individual member of the parish a member of the corporation, and that "this occurs regardless of the fact that only a few persons are specially referred to by name in the charter, and that the franchise is extended to them," [35] it is also true that *de facto* the exercise of the sovereignty of the corporation could be properly safeguarded in the articles of incorporation and in the by-laws. Whatever property the corporation aggregate would own or acquire would be vested in the body corporate. Thus, upon the incorporation of a parish or diocese as such, *de iure* the sovereignty of the corporation would be vested in the members several thereof. The directors or trustees would not hold the property in trust, nor would they hold the fee; [36] their right to manage the property would be an authority, not an estate or title. These are corporate prerogatives.

But the exercise *de facto* of the *de iure* possessed sovereignty is governed by the method used for the appointment of the directors of the corporation. Herein lies the crucial point. Depending on the provisions of the articles and by-laws, such directors could be elected by a majority of the members, or the articles and by-laws could provide stipulations which would insure ecclesiastical control of the corporation. Thus, for example, the charter could provide that the ordinary, the vicar general, and the pastor or chancellor, together with two lay members of the parish or the diocese who receive their appointment from the ecclesiastical authority, would constitute the board of directors. Further safeguards could be provided. The tenure of office of

[34] 1957 N.M. Laws, ch. 112, § 10, being section 51-14-29 of 1953 N.M. Comp. Laws.

[35] Brown, p. 137.

[36] *"Directors* means the persons vested with the general management of the affairs of the corporation, regardless of how they are designated."— 1957 N.M. Laws, ch. 112, § 1, being section 51-14-20 of 1953 N.M. Comp. Laws.

the two laymen could be restricted, and it might even be stipulated in the charter that no act or proceeding of the directors would be valid without the sanction of the ordinary or the administrator of the diocese.

It is submitted that charter provisions akin to the ones above-described would not be inconsistent with New Mexico law.

With reference to tenure by a corporation sole, a deed at common law to a bishop and his successors in office was construed to convey the fee to such bishop in his corporate capacity.[37] Hence, conveyances should run to the corporate incumbent and his successors in office, not to him and his heirs.[38] However, it has been held that a change of name of a sole corporation (a Roman Catholic bishop) "and his successors in office" by dropping the quoted words did not affect corporate succession in title.[39]

The fee, then, is held by the corporate incumbent. Actually, a corporation sole is considered obsolescent at Anglo-American law today, and for all practical purposes is used only by Roman Catholic bishops where provision therefor is made by the divers legislatures.

Because the fee is held by the sole incorporator, it follows that one of the natural characteristics of a sole corporation is that the fee is in abeyance upon the occurrence of a vacancy in the incorporator's office. This can result from the death of the sole incorporator, his resignation, or his removal from office. The practical consequences entailed will be discussed in the following section from the canonical point of view.

Under New Mexico law, "any person in whom shall be vested the legal title to the property of any church or religious society, in conformity with its constitution, canons, rites, or regulations," [40] may become a corporation sole upon complying with the statutory requirements. The question which now arises is whether the New Mexico statute would be constructed to mean

[37] Reid v. Barry, 93 Fla. 849, 112 So. 846 (1927).

[38] 1 Fletcher's Cyclopedia on Corporations 181, § 51.

[39] McCloskey v. Doherty, 97 Ky. 300, 30 S.W. 649 (1895).

[40] 1957 N.M. Laws, ch. 112, § 7, being section 51-14-26 of 1953 N.M. Comp. Laws.

that an incorporated bishop holds or does not hold to himself. In other words, would the sole corporation be found to hold the property to itself, or in trust for another?

In all fairness, it must be said that the wording of the New Mexico statute is not to be adversely criticized for being patient of ambiguities. It is submitted that a statute alone could not decide the question. For one thing, the law by which sole corporations are governed is purely statutory, and decisions interpreting these statutes are very rare or, as in the case of New Mexico jurisprudence, non-existent. Secondly, how much bearing the common law would have on the interpretation of the statute is a matter of conjecture. The matter is further aggravated by the fact that there seems to be a divergence of opinion concerning the mode of tenure by a bishop or a parson as a corporation sole at common law. The deed by which property was granted conveyed a fee simple.[41] Moreover, according to Blackstone, "at the original endowment of parish churches, the freehold of the church, the churchyard, the parsonage house, the glebe, and the tithes of the parish, were vested in the then parson by the bounty of the donor," but "as a temporal recompense to him for his spiritual care of the inhabitants, and with the intent that the same emoluments should ever afterwards continue as a recompense for the same care." [42] The deed conveyed a fee simple. The grantee was the parson. Nonetheless, the parson did not possess the fee simple to the grant; the freehold was vested in the parson, but such freehold was not inheritable, since "the law has wisely ordained that the parson, *quatenus* parson, shall never die." [43] It follows, therefore, that the parson's tenure was similar to a trust, although it was not a trust, given that the limitations thereupon were imposed by law, not by the would-be *cestuis que trustent*. Maitland (1850-1906) very logically then inquired: "Is a beneficed clergyman . . . a corporation sole, or is he merely the administrator or representative of a corporation sole?" [44] He suggested that "the parson

[41] 2 Blackstone Commentaries 108.

[42] 1 Blackstone Commentaries 470.

[43] *Loc. cit.*

[44] Maitland, "The Corporation Sole," *The Law Quarterly Review,* XVI (1900), 335.

had the fee *in jure Ecclesiae* as one is seized in fee *in jure uxoris suae,* and yet, for some purposes he is only a tenant for life." [45]

Regardless of what the theory might have been at common law, the fact remains that Anglo-American law follows Blackstone in considering the parson, the sole incorporator, as the solitary member of the corporation sole and not merely as the administrator thereof. This, however, does not resolve the question of the sole incorporator's nature of tenure. If the corporation sole were found to be a trustee, could it be forced by the *cestuis que trustent* to convey their trust to another? Were it presumed, on the other hand, that the corporation sole is not a trustee, would it be able to part with the fee without the consent of the parish or the diocese? The sole corporation has a legal title. Who would be found to be seized with the equitable title? The sole incorporator? Would it be the canonical moral person which, however, is not, *ex hypothesi,* civilly incorporated as such? Or would it be, rather, the substratum constituting such ecclesiastical corporation? The fact that there are few points of corporation law applicable to the corporation sole [46] does not render the matter any less difficult.

Leaving the matter heretofore under consideration, one may observe, in conclusion, that the word "owner" does not necessarily imply that a person should be the holder of a fee simple, since it is frequently used as equivalent to "possessor" and to designate the person in actual possession and in control of the property in question.[47] However, possession of realty will be presumed to accompany ownership until the contrary is proved.[48]

Section 2. Canon Law

The controlling law in any canonical discussion concerning the ownership and tenure of church property is presented by canon 1499, § 2: "Dominium bonorum, sub suprema auctoritate

[45] *Loc. cit.*

[46] 2 Kent Commentaries 273.

[47] Territory v. Young, 2 N.M. 93 (1881).

[48] First National Bank of Albuquerque v. Town of Tome, 23 N.M. 255, 167 P. 733 (1917).

Sedis Apostolicae, ad eam pertinet moralem personam, quae eadem bona legitime acquisiverit." Under the supreme control of the Holy See, the ownership of temporal goods vests in the juridical person that acquired such goods legitimately. The Code thus definitively settles an age-old controversy among pre-Code jurists. Some canonists and theologians held that ecclesiastical property was owned by God, or Christ, or a saint; others maintained that it was owned by the Roman Pontiff; still others claimed that the poor formed the subject of dominion.[49] Thus, "instead of declaring that the Church of St. Rose belongs to God, or to St. Rose, or to the Pope, the law declares that this church is itself a person, and holds its own property." [50]

The equitable title to church property, therefore, vests in the ecclesiastical corporation which legitimately acquired such goods. Since, however, a corporation can act only through physical persons, the Code of Canon Law provides for administrators who, in temporal matters, will govern the affairs of the respective corporation in accordance with Church law, being, furthermore, answerable for their administration to the next higher superior authority. Thus, for example, in the case of dioceses, *"episcopi . . . regunt sub auctoritate Romani Pontificis."* [51]   In the case of pastors, they are spoken of as rectors *"qui paroeciae administrandae praeficiuntur,"* [52] but this power of administration is *"sub Ordinarii loci auctoritate exercenda."* [53]

The jurisdiction which an ordinary enjoys in his diocese includes legislative, judicial, and coercive power by means of which he governs the diocese not only in spiritual, but also in temporal, matters.[54]   Hence, the object of the exercise of this threefold division of jurisdiction extends to the teaching and the

---

[49] Doheny, p. 37.

[50] Bartlett, *The Tenure of Parochial Property in the United States of America,* The Catholic University of America Canon Law Studies, n. 31 (Washington, D.C.: The Catholic University of America Press, 1926), p. 43.

[51] Canon 329, § 1.

[52] Canon 454, § 1.

[53] Canon 451, § 1.

[54] Cf. canon 335, § 1.

governing of the clergy and the laity and the administration of ecclesiastical property.[55]

It follows, then, that the bishop at Canon law is a trustee, the ecclesiastical corporation which he governs is the *cestui que trust,* and the temporal goods belonging thereto constitute the *trust res.* These terms, however, are to be understood within the context of ecclesiastical law, not against the *mise en scène* of Anglo-American applications thereof, necessarily. The Church is a hierarchical institution, not a democracy. The Anglo-American concept of a board of corporation directors must be viewed against the climate of canonical jurisprudence surrounding the institute of the cathedral chapter (board of diocesan consultors). No one owns voting stock in a diocese as such. Hence, in the matter of alienation, for instance, the rights of the *cestuis que trustent* are protected exclusively by the judgment of the ordinary subject to the provisions of law. Even the term *trust,* then, must be correctly understood, since the restrictions placed on the ordinary's administration are imposed by law, not by the *cestuis que trustent.* Nonetheless, he is vested with a sacred trust.

In the United States, the American hierarchy had wrestled with the problem of tenure by lay trustees since the beginning. The complexities incident to modes of tenure were the subject of legislation in practically all the Provincial Councils of Baltimore. The fee simple was taken out of the hands of lay trustees and vested absolutely in the hands of the ordinary. But this system proved much too weak for the interests of the Church. Conditioned in part by the famous Purcell Case,[56] the legislation of the Third Plenary Council of Baltimore (1884) sought to forestall further complexities by ruling as follows:

[55] Abbo-Hannan, I, 360.

[56] Archbishop Purcell of Cincinnati had agreed, as a private individual, to guarantee the indebtedness of his brother who had undertaken to act as a banker for Cincinnati Catholics. Creditors sought to recover about $2.5 million from Archbishop Purcell by levying on diocesan property, the fee simple of which was vested in him. The court ruled that Archbishop Purcell did not hold diocesan property as absolute owner, but in trust.— Mannix v. Purcell, 46 Ohio St. 102 (1888).

In states where civil incorporation of parishes or ecclesiastical bodies, such as accords with ecclesiastical law, does not exist, the bishop himself may be able to become a corporation sole to hold and administer the property of the whole diocese; or the property of the diocese can possibly be committed to the bishop in trust, so that he may hold it in the name of the diocese and administer it for the benefit of the diocese in accordance with the mind of the Church; or, as a last resort, the bishop may hold the temporal goods of the diocese and administer them in his own name, under that absolute title of law which in English is called a fee simple; in which case let the bishop be always mindful that, although the full ownership of ecclesiastical property is conferred upon him by the civil law, nevertheless according to the admonition of the sacred canons he is not the owner of it but only the administrator.[57]

But in a letter of July 29, 1911, to the ordinaries of the United States, the Sacred Congregation of the Council ruled as follows hereunder:

1. Among the methods which are now in use in the United States for holding and administering church property, the one known as *Parish Corporation* is preferable to the others, but with the conditions and safeguards which are now in use in the State of New York. The Bishops should immediately take steps to introduce this method for the handling of property in their dioceses, if the civil law allows it. . . .

2. Only in those places where the civil law does not recognize *Parish Corporations*, and until such recognition is obtained, the method commonly called *Corporation sole* is allowed, but with the understanding that in the administration of ecclesiastical property the Bishop is to act with the advice, and in more important matters with the consent, of those who have an interest in the premises and of the diocesan consultors, this being a conscientious obligation for the Bishop in person.

3. The method called *in fee simple* is to be entirely abandoned.[58]

[57] *Acta et Decreta Concilii Plenarii Baltimorensis Tertii, A.D. MDCCC-LXXXIV* (Baltimorae: Typis Joannis Murphy et Sociorum, 1886), tit. IX, cap. ii, n. 267. [Translation by the writer.]

[58] S.C.Conc., 29 July, 1911 (Private).—*The Canon Law Digest* (4 vols., Milwaukee: Bruce Publishing Co., Vol. I, 1934, Vol. II, 1943, Vol. III, 1954, edited by T. Lincoln Bouscaren; Vol. IV, 1958, edited by T. Lincoln Bous-

The disadvantages of the sole corporation are that it is a matter of conjecture how the New Mexico statute would be constructed with regard to the nature of tenure by the sole incorporator; and that upon a vacancy in the incorporator's office the fee is in abeyance and no one is duly qualified to transact business during the interregnum. With reference to the first disadvantage, it is submitted that a court would probably admit parol evidence of Canon law to explain the nature of tenure and ownership of church property according to ecclesiastical law, as outlined hereinbefore.

The second drawback could very easily be precluded by way of statutory amendment.[59] While it is true that during the vacancy of the see no changes are to be made [60] that would tend to jeopardize or prejudice the rights of the diocese or of the successor bishop, still and all it is not unlikely that a matter requiring legal competence at civil law might arise during the interregnum.

A bishopric becomes vacant upon the death of the bishop, upon his resignation accepted by the Roman Pontiff, upon his

---

caren and James I. O'Connor), II, 444. [Hereinafter cited Bouscaren's Digest.] Under New York law, a parish may incorporate with five trustees: the archbishop, vicar general, pastor, and two laymen who serve for specified terms. No act or proceeding of the trustees is valid without the sanction of the archbishop, or, in his absence or inability to act, of the vicar general or administrator.—Murphy, *The Laws of the State of New York Affecting Church Property*, The Catholic University of America Canon Law Studies, n. 388 (Washington, D.C.: The Catholic University of America Press, 1957), pp. 49 ff.

[59] In this regard, the provisions in the District of Columbia are ideal. The Act of Congress which created the Archbishop of Washington a corporation sole declares that "in the event that a vacancy should occur in said archbishopric and an administrator shall be elected or appointed in accordance with the discipline and government of the Roman Catholic Church, such administrator shall, until the installation of a successor archbishop, be authorized to do and perform all acts which the corporation is authorized to do and perform."—Chapter 355, 2nd Session, 80th Congress, Act of May 29, 1948 (HR 6203).

[60] "Sede vacante nihil innovetur."—Canon 436.

transfer to another see, and upon his removal from office by the Roman Pontiff, notice of which the bishop has received.[61] A diocese cannot become vacant in any other way.[62] At Canon law, the administration of the temporal and spiritual interests of the vacant diocese is placed in the hands of an administrator, who shall govern such interests *ad interim*.[63] But he can in no wise be considered the successor in office, and the see must be unequivocably deemed vacant until the successor bishop has been appointed. Indeed, even after the appointment of a successor, until he has taken canonical possession of the diocese such appointee is forbidden to intervene under any pretext, in person or by agent, directly or indirectly, in the government of the diocese to which he has been appointed.[64] As a consequence, no one would be competent under present New Mexico law to transact business for a corporation sole during such interregnum.

Aside from these difficulties, a corporation sole under New Mexico law offers a safe method of holding church property in a manner approved by the Holy See. This mode of tenure forever protects title to church property by passing it from predecessor to successor by simple operation of law. In practice, the only formality required would be presentation of proof of the fact of succession.

ARTICLE 3. MODES OF ACQUISITION

Section 1. Donations "Inter Vivos"

A. New Mexico Law

Except as to community property laws—to be considered here-inbelow—which will indeed govern and indirectly affect gifts made to natural or corporate bodies for religious or charitable purposes, the law and jurisprudence of New Mexico contain

[61] Canon 430, § 1.

[62] Abbo-Hannan, I, 430.

[63] Canon 432, § 1; canon 427.

[64] Canon 334, § 2. Canonical possession of the diocese must be taken by the appointee within four months after receipt of the Apostolic letters, but this may be done at any time within that period.—Cf. canon 333.

nothing peculiar by way of controlling provisions in this matter.[65] Actually, the amount of litigation in the matter of religious and charitable gifts as such is negligible and generally immaterial for the purpose of this study.

Very simply, since "evangelization" and "preaching the gospel" are in New Mexico valid objects of bounty [66] to adequate beneficiaries, so likewise would be a grant for the purposes of Catholicism. And in the matter of charitable gifts, any purpose is "charitable" which is within one of the types stated in the preamble to the English Statute of Charitable Uses, including relief of the aged, maintenance of the sick, etc.[67]

More specifically, a "charity" is a gift, to be applied consistently with existing laws, for the benefit of an indefinite number of persons by bringing them under the influence of education or religion, by relieving them of disease, suffering or constraint, by assisting them to establish themselves in life, or by erecting public buildings or works or otherwise lessening the burden of government.[68] Briefly, charitable grants or trusts include all gifts for educational and religious purposes in their ever-varying di-

[65] Lack of space forbids the presentation of the New Mexico law on trusts; its provisions, however, follow Anglo-American jurisprudence and may be found, with regard to charitable trusts, in sections 33-2-1 to 33-2-24, 1953 N.M. Comp. Laws.

[66] Rhodes v. Yates, 27 N.M. 489, 202 P. 698, 22 A.L.R. 692 (1921).

[67] Santa Fe Lodge No. 460, B. P. O. E. v. Employment Security Commission, 49 N.M. 149, 159 P.2d 312 (1945). The English Statute of Charitable Uses, in force in New Mexico, lists the following purposes as charitable in a demonstrative way: "The relief of the aged, impotent, and poor people; the maintenance of maimed and sick soldiers and mariners; the support of schools of learning; free schools, and scholars of universities; repair of bridges, ports, havens, causeways, churches, seabanks, and highways; education and preferment of orphans; the relief, stock, and maintenance of houses of correction; marriage of poor maids; aid and help of young tradesmen, handicraftsmen, and persons decayed; relief or redemption of prisoners and captives; aid of poor inhabitants concerning payments of fifteenths, setting out of soldiers, and other taxes."—Statute, 43 Elizabeth, c. 4 (1601).

[68] Santa Fe Lodge No. 460, B. P. O. E. v. Employment Security Commission, 49 N.M. 149, 159 P.2d 312 (1945).

versity.[69]   Moreover, a trust for the purpose of "evangelization" and "preaching the gospel" is not void for uncertainty as to the object or beneficiaries.[70]

Inasmuch as the property rights of husband and wife will indirectly govern donations *inter vivos* where the grantors are married, it has been deemed opportune to present a brief summary of the statutory law and jurisprudence in that matter. New Mexico is one of eight states [71] which have adopted the so-called *ganancial* or Spanish community system to a greater or lesser extent.

In New Mexico, husband and wife may hold property as joint tenants, tenants in common, or as community property.[72]   A joint tenancy arises where two or more persons have any subject of property jointly in which there is a unity of interest, unity of title, unity of time, and unity of possession.[73]   If any one of the first three unities is lacking, there is a tenancy in common, which requires merely unity of possession.[74]

Borrowing from the common law, Anglo-American jurisprudence provides that, where a conveyance is made to parties who at the time are husband and wife, the parties hold as tenants by the entirety unless the language clearly indicates that they are to take as joint tenants or tenants in common.   The spouses do

69 Board of Education of Albuquerque v. School District No. 5 of Bernalillo County, 21 N.M. 624, 157 P. 668 (1916).

70 Rhodes v. Yates, 27 N.M. 489, 202 P. 698, 22 A.L.R. 692 (1921).

71 The other states are Arizona, California, Idaho, Louisiana, Nevada, Texas, and Washington.—Ballinger, *A Treatise on the Property Rights of Husband and Wife, Under the Community or Ganancial System, Adapted to the Statutes and Decisions of Louisiana, Texas, California, Nevada, Washington, Idaho, Arizona, and New Mexico* (Seattle–San Francisco: Bancroft-Whitney Co., 1895), *passim*. [Hereinafter cited Ballinger on Community Property.]

72 Sect. 57-3-2, 1953 N.M. Comp. Laws.

73 Hernandez v. Becker, 54 F.2d 542 (C.C.A.N.M. 1931).

74 The chief practical difference between joint tenancy and tenancy in common is that if one joint tenant dies his interest goes to the survivor or survivors.—14 Am. Jur., Cotenancy, §§ 6-12.

not take by shares but each one is seized of the entire interest; upon the death of one the survivor takes all as in the case of joint tenancy.[75] But the English system of Tenure by the Entirety did not overthrow the Community Property laws which New Mexico had borrowed from the Spanish civil law. And since the civil law of Spain and Mexico served as the model for the statutory law of New Mexico concerning the property rights of husband and wife, that law will be looked to as the basis for interpretation and definition.[76]

The law of Spain did not recognize the general *communio bonorum*, but admitted only the *communio quaestuum*, or community of acquests and gains. The latter is constituted between husband and wife as a legal and necessary effect of their marriage, and the property of which it consists is termed *ganancial (bienes gananciales)*.[77]

As adopted in New Mexico, the *ganancial* system provides that property owned by either spouse before marriage or acquired after marriage by gift, bequest, devise or descent, together with the rents, issues, and profits thereof, is the separate property of that spouse,[78] and all other property acquired after marriage by either husband or wife, or both, is community property.[79] Property acquired by the husband during marriage belongs presumptively to the community, but this presumption is rebuttable;[80] and the earnings of the wife, although not liable for the debts of the husband,[81] are not her own separate property.[82]

[75] 26 Am. Jur., Husband and Wife, §§ 66-86.

[76] McDonald v. Senn, 53 N.M. 198, 204 P.2d 990, 10 A.L.R.2d 966 (1949).

[77] Ballinger on Community Property, 31, § 6.

[78] Sect. 57-3-4 and 57-3-5, 1953 N.M. Comp. Laws.

[79] Sect. 57-4-1, 1953 N.M. Comp. Laws; State National Bank of Artesia v. Traylor, 22 N.M. 187, 159 P. 1006 (1916); Roberts v. Roberts, 35 N.M. 593, 4 P.2d 920 (1931); McDonald v. Lambert, 43 N.M. 27, 85 P.2d 78, 120 A.L.R. 250 (1938); Hollingsworth v. Hicks, 57 N.M. 336, 258 P.2d 724 (1953).

[80] Carron v. Abounador, 28 N.M. 491, 214 P. 772 (1923).

[81] Sect. 57-3-6, 1953 N. M. Comp. Laws.

Notwithstanding the fact that the husband has the management and control of the community property,[83] he is not vested with a larger or superior interest in the property upon division,[84] nor does he have absolute power of disposition.[85] Any transfer or conveyance of the real property of the community by either husband or wife alone is null and void,[86] and it has been held that a husband's deed to community property without a joinder by the wife is void absolutely and does not even convey the portion of the community allocable to the husband.[87]

B. *Canon Law*

Anyone who is entitled by the natural and ecclesiastical law to dispose freely of his goods may relinquish them in favor of religion or of charity by direct donation *inter vivos*.[88] Moreover, the Church has the right, independently of civil authority, to demand from the faithful whatever is necessary for conducting divine worship, for the adequate support of the clerics and other ministers, and for the other purposes for which it has been established.[89] This right follows as a logical sequence from the divine

---

[82] Albright v. Albright, 21 N.M. 606, 157 P. 662, Ann. Cas. 1918E, 542 (1916); Morris v. Waring, 22 N.M. 175, 159 P. 1002 (1916). Money earned by the wife outside of the State constitutes community property where the marital domicile continues in New Mexico.—1943-1944 N.M. Attorney General Reports, No. 4478.

[83] Sect. 57-4-3, 1953 N.M. Comp. Laws.

[84] In re Miller's Estate, 44 N.M. 214, 100 P.2d 908 (1940).

[85] Baca v. Belen, 30 N.M. 541, 240 P. 803 (1925).

[86] Sect. 57-4-3, 1953 N.M. Comp. Laws.

[87] McGrail v. Fields, 53 N.M. 158, 203 P.2d 1000 (1949). The common law disability of husband and wife to convey, the one to the other, has been expressly removed by statute (Sect. 57-4-3, 1953 N.M. Comp. Laws), and the husband may convey real estate directly to the wife and the wife directly to the husband without the other joining in the conveyance.— Trigg v. Trigg, 37 N.M. 296, 22 P.2d 119 (1923). The spouses may thus dissolve the community by contract between themselves.

[88] Cf. canon 1513, § 1. The Canon law on charitable trusts will be treated in the following section, *infra*, in connection with testamentary trusts.

[89] Canon 1496.

institution of the Church. For "if one admits that Christ established the Church as a society which was to continue His work in the spiritual government and guidance of mankind by organized effort, one must also admit that Christ gave that Church all the powers and rights incident to the work He committed to her." [90]

In general, the Code of Canon Law contains provisions for exacting financial support and for regulating donations *inter vivos* according as the grant takes the form of a contribution made by the faithful or of a contribution deriving from corporations. Within each of the foregoing divisions are found several more specific forms.

Regulations concerning tithes, first-fruits, alms, and fees constitute the provisions of Canon law with regard to contributions from the faithful. Of these forms, tithes and first-fruits as such have fallen into desuetude in the United States. But, although the Code decrees that the payment of tithes (*decimae*, or "tenth part") and first-fruits shall be governed by the special laws and laudable customs in each country,[91] it does not follow therefrom that where these forms as such do not exist the faithful are absolved from the obligation of supporting the Church. Canons 1496 and 1502 allow great latitude to each region and country in the matter of church support. Fortunately, the voluntary offerings of the faithful are generally sufficient to take care of the needs of the Church in the United States, at least to the extent that strictly defined laws have been unnecessary.[92] The general precept of contributing to the support of the Church and its ministers is binding on all the faithful according to their means. While this precept binds gravely, it is difficult to hold any individual

[90] Woywod-Smith, II, 189.

[91] Canon 1502.

[92] In the Archdiocese of Santa Fe, "Pastors must instruct the faithful of their serious obligation to support the parish. A fair minimum support at this time is two and one-half (2½%) percent of their gross income."—Statute 266, *Seventh Synod of the Archdiocese of Santa Fe*, celebrated on December 2, 1958, by His Excellency, Most Reverend Edwin V. Byrne, D.D., Archbishop of Santa Fe, Saint Francis Cathedral, Santa Fe (Albuquerque: House of Moulton, 1958).

delinquent guilty of grave sin unless his neglect to contribute his just share should place the ecclesiastical ministers in dire need or impose an undue burden upon the other faithful.[93]

Private individuals, whether clerics or laymen, are forbidden to collect alms for any charitable or ecclesiastical institution or purpose without the written permission of the Holy See or of their proper ordinary and of the ordinary of the place where the collection is to be made.[94] This prohibition is directed against persons acting in a private capacity; hence, pastors are not included in this prohibition, since they act in their official capacity while exercising their rights within the limits of their own parishes.[95]

As canon 1503 directs, permission for private individuals as such to collect alms can be obtained in two ways. The first is by written permission of the Holy See, in which case the rescript is granted by the Sacred Congregation of the Council, the Sacred Congregation for the Propagation of the Faith, or the Sacred Congregation for the Oriental Church. The second method of obtaining necessary permission to solicit alms consists in obtaining a written authorization therefor from both the collector's own ordinary and from the local ordinary within whose jurisdiction such collection of alms is sought and undertaken.

In the matter of fees, without prejudice to the prescriptions of canons 1056 and 1234, it belongs to a provincial council or a meeting of the bishops of a province to specify the fees payable throughout the entire ecclesiastical province for the various acts of voluntary jurisdiction,[96] for the execution of rescripts of the Holy See, and on the occasion of the administration of the sacraments or the sacramentals;[97] but such a schedule is of no effect

[93] Doheny, p. 49.

[94] Canon 1503. The regulations of canons 621-624 regarding the collecting of alms by religious orders and congregations are not affected by this canon.

[95] Cf. canon 415, § 2, 5°; canon 630, § 4.

[96] Acts of voluntary jurisdiction comprehend the concession of dispensations and other favors.

[97] The pastor may not refuse to serve gratuitously those who are not able to make an offering for these services.—Canon 463, § 4.

unless it is previously approved by the Holy See.[98]   Canon 1056
rules that with the exception of a moderate fee to defray chancery office expenses, exacted for dispensations granted to those
who can pay it, neither local ordinaries nor their officials are permitted to demand any stipend for the granting of a dispensation,
unless they have been expressly authorized to do so by the Holy
See; and if they demand one, they are obliged to make restitution.   And in accordance with the norms of canon 1234, local
ordinaries are authorized, with the advice of the board of diocesan consultors, to fix the funeral fees.

With the immediately foregoing two exceptions, in which the
individual ordinary is competent to act,[99] the bishops of the
whole province fix the schedule of fees for that particular ecclesiastical district.   This obtains also with regard to fees payable for judicial acts,[100] as exercised, for instance, in matrimonial
trials, but this schedule of judicial fees need not be submitted to
the Holy See for approbation.[101]

With reference to contributions from corporations, the following forms of grants are included: the cathedraticum, the seminary tax, and the charitable subsidy.   Concerning the first-men-
tioned, all churches and benefices subject to the jurisdiction of a
bishop, as well as confraternities of the laity, shall as a sign of
allegiance pay annually to the bishop a cathedratic tax, that is,
a moderate tax determined in accordance with the norm of canon
1507, § 1, unless it has already been determined by ancient custom.[102]   The cathedratic tax is a token payment of deference
and submission to the episcopal see, of an identical amount, not
varying from parish to parish. [103]   The Sacred Congregation of
the Council has replied that it is not expedient to impose a cathedratic tax on parishes in proportion to the number of parishioners

[98] Canon 1507, § 1.

[99] Canon 831 places in the hands of the local ordinary also the fixing of
the diocesan manual Mass stipend.

[100] Canon 1507, § 2.

[101] Cf. canon 1909, § 1.

[102] Canon 1504.

[103] Abbo-Hannan, II, 713.

in order to meet the expenses of the chancery office.[104]   In the determining of the sum of the cathedratic tax, which simply connotes a *"signum recognitionis honoris,"* this element in its nature is not to be lost sight of.[105]

For the establishment of a seminary and the support of its students, if it lacks its own income, the bishop can: direct pastors or other rectors of even exempt churches to take up a collection for this purpose in church at given times; levy a contribution or tax in his diocese; and if these means prove inadequate, assign and attach certain simple benefices to the seminary.[106]   Liable for the seminary assessment are the bishop's benefice (*mensa episcopalis*); all benefices, including those of regulars and all rights of presentation (*ius patronatus*); all parishes and quasi-parishes, though they have no other revenue than the offerings of the faithful; hospitals erected by ecclesiastical authority; sodalities canonically erected; church buildings that have their own income; and every religious house, even though exempt, unless the religious live solely on alms or actually have in their house a college for pupils or teachers for promoting the common welfare of the Church.   All custom exempting from the payment of the seminary assessment is rejected, every contrary privilege whatsoever is abrogated, and no appeal will be entertained.[107]   This assessment must be general, and the same rate must be levied on all churches and institutes subject to the tax; it may be increased or lowered according to the needs of the seminary, but the annual tax must not exceed five (5%) percent of the taxable income, and is to be lowered as the revenue of the seminary increases.[108]   The taxable income is that which remains at the end of the year after all obligations and necessary expenditures have been paid.   In parishes, the offerings of the faithful are not taxable revenue of the parish, unless the parish

---

[104] S.C.Conc., *Resolutio,* 14 March 1920.—*A.A.S.,* XII (1920), 444; Bouscaren's Digest, I, 719.

[105] *Ibid., A.A.S.,* XII (1920), 445; Bouscaren's Digest, I, 720.

[106] Canon 1355, 1°-3°.

[107] Canon 1356, § 1.

[108] Canon 1356, § 2.

has no other revenue than the offerings of the faithful, in which case one-third of the offerings is exempt.[109]

Besides the seminary tax authorized in canons 1356-1357, or the pension that in canon 1429 is allowed to be imposed on a benefice, the local ordinary can, to meet a special pressing diocesan need, impose a moderate extraordinary tax on all incumbents of benefices, religious as well as secular.[110] This charitable subsidy is levied against the income of the beneficiaries; it is not imposed on the benefice itself. Exempt religious are not bound by this obligation.[111]

Other taxes for the benefit of the diocese, or in favor of a patron, may not be imposed by the bishop on churches, benefices, and other ecclesiastical institutions subject to him, except on the occasion of their foundation or consecration; and in no case can a tax be imposed on manual or founded Mass stipends.[112]

Section 2. Testamentary Gifts

A. New Mexico Law

The fundamental principle and point of departure for a consideration of New Mexico law on wills is that the legislature has plenary power over descent and distribution of power, except as restricted by constitution or treaty.[113] More specifically, the right to transmit property upon the owner's death is not a fundamental right, but one conferred on the owner by statute, which must be within the scope of the legislature's constitutional powers, and the state may regulate the devolution of property, even to the extent of repealing laws relating to wills, descents and distributions, and declare that property shall be applied on the owner's death to the payment of his debts and the residue appropriated for public use.[114] Hence, the right to make a will

---

[109] Canon 1356, § 3. Parishes in the United States have no income other than the offerings of the faithful.

[110] Canon 1505.

[111] Doheny, p. 59.

[112] Canon 1506.

[113] Hernandez v. Becker, 54 F.2d 542 (C.C.A.N.M. 1932).

[114] Dillard v. N. M. State Tax Commission, 53 N.M. 12, 201 P.2d 345 (1948).

is not a property right or a natural or inherent right, and is therefore not protected by constitutional provisions for the protection of property, but is purely a statutory right subject to the legislature's complete control.[115] In practice, this means that the state has plenary power over property passing by will or through statutes of descent and distribution, and it may take all or any part of testator's or intestate decedent's estate and direct the disposition thereof.[116]

Any person twenty-one years of age or older and in sound mind may dispose by will of all his property, except what is sufficient to pay his debts and what is given by law as privileged property to his wife or family.[117] It is essential to testamentary capacity that the testator 1) have knowledge of the meaning of the act of making a will; 2) have knowledge of the character and extent of his estate, and 3) have knowledge of the natural objects of his bounty.[118]

All wills by which any property—real, personal, or mixed—is devised or bequeathed, must be reduced to writing and signed by the testator, or by someone in his presence and by his direction,[119] and attested in the presence of the testator by two or

[115] *Loc. cit.*

[116] *Loc. cit.*

[117] Sect. 30-1-1, 1953 N.M. Comp. Laws; In re McMillen's Estate, 12 N.M. 31, 71 P. 1083 (1903). Upon the death of the wife, the entire community property, without administration, belongs to the surviving husband, except such portion thereof as may have been set apart in her favor by a judicial decree for her support and maintenance, which portion is subject to her testamentary disposition, and in the absence of such disposition goes to her descendants, or heirs, exclusive of her husband.— Sect. 29-1-8, 1953 N.M. Comp. Laws. Upon the death of the husband, one-half of the community property goes to the surviving wife; the other half is subject to the testamentary disposition of the husband, and in the absence of such disposition goes one-fourth to the surviving wife and the remainder in equal shares to the children of decedent and further as provided by law.—Sect. 29-1-9, 1953 N.M. Comp. Laws.

[118] In re Armijo's Will, 57 N.M. 649, 261 P.2d 833 (1953); Calloway v. Miller, 58 N.M. 124, 266 P.2d 365 (1954).

[119] Any person capable of making a will may empower and authorize any other intelligent and well qualified person to make his last will and testament, and to dispose of this property, but in granting said power, the

more creditable witnesses.[120]   Persons becoming heirs, and those receiving benefits or legacies, by will, can not be witnesses to the will in which they are interested.[121]   The witnesses to a written will must be present, must see the testator sign the will, or someone sign it for him at his request as and for his last will and testament, and must sign as witnesses at his request in his presence and in the presence of each other.[122]

All wills, then, must be in writing,[123] since nuncupative wills are not recognized; [124] and since subscribing witnesses are essential, holographic wills are ruled out.

---

same qualifications required for the validity of a will and the grant of the relevant power shall be inserted therein.—Sect. 30-1-2, 1953 N.M. Comp. Laws.

120 Sect. 30-1-4, 1953 N.M. Comp. Laws.

121 While there are no New Mexico cases ruling this aspect of the law, it is interesting to note that a member of a parish is not disqualified by interest from being a subscribing witness to a will containing a gift to the parish.—Haven v. Hilliard, 23 Pick. (Mass.) 10, 53 A.L.R. 213 (1838); Loring v. Park, 7 Gray (Mass.) 42, 53 A.L.R. 213 (1838). In a Minnesota case, the testatrix was a member of the Order of St. Benedict, a religious order incorporated under the laws of the state. Decedent had made a will devising her property to this corporation, and the subscribing witnesses to the will were two members of the corporation. It was contended that they were incompetent. The court said: "The interest that will disqualify such a witness must be present, certain, and vested . . . This was a corporation for charitable purposes, not for pecuniary profit to its members . . . [Therefore] the witnesses could not have any present, certain, or vested pecuniary interest in property devised by this will to the corporation, and were competent witnesses.—Will v. Sisters of Order of St. Benedict, 67 Minn. 335, 337, 69 N.W. 1090, 53 A.L.R. 213 (1897).

122 Sect. 30-1-6, 1953 N.M. Comp. Laws.

123 At that time, oral wills were permitted, but a statutory amendment of 1889 decreed that "no devise or bequest to a charitable use shall be valid unless embraced in a written will duly executed."—1889 N.M. Laws, ch. 90, § 20.

124 New Mexico seems to be one of five states that do not permit a nuncupative will under any circumstances. The others: Colorado, Connecticut, Louisiana, and Wyoming.—Hannan, *The Canon Law of Wills*, The Catholic University of American Canon Law Studies, n. 86 (Washington, D.C.: The Catholic University of America Press, 1934), p. 227. [Hereinafter cited Hannan.]

Revocability is an essential element of a will,[125] and any will may be revoked by the testator by means of a written instrument, or by the making of a subsequent valid will disposing of the same property covered by the first will.[126] The two methods of revocation laid out in the statute are not exclusive, however, and wills may be revoked by operation of law.[127] Thus, for example, a will is impliedly revoked, and the property adeemed from its operation and effect, where the testator, subsequent to its execution, voluntarily conveys such estate by an absolute deed of conveyance, not because the will is invalid, but because there is no estate upon which it can operate or to which it can pass.[128] Furthermore, the marriage of a testator, whether or not it is followed by the birth of a child, revokes an antenuptial will.[129]

A will stands or falls as an entirety,[130] and the cancellation of wills is not exercised by courts of equity.[131] The right to contest a will is not a common law right, but a right conferred solely by statute, which must be strictly construed.[132] In order to contest a will, the contestant must be pecuniarily interested,[133] and proponent has the burden of proving the mental capacity of testator when it is challenged by evidence, although mental capacity is presumable when not questioned.[134] A will contest is, of course, a civil action.

The wishes and directions of testator, as expressed in his will,

[125] McDonald v. Polansky, 48 N.M. 518, 153 P.2d 670 (1945).

[126] Sect. 30-1-8, 1953 N.M. Comp. Laws.

[127] In re Teopfer's Estate, 12 N.M. 372, 78 P.53, 67 L.R.A. 315 (1904).

[128] Brown v. Heller, 30 N.M. 1, 227 P. 594 (1924).

[129] In re Lewis' Will, 41 N.M. 522, 71 P.2d 1032 (1937).

[130] In re Morrow's Will, 41 N.M. 723, 73 P.2d 1360 (1937).

[131] *Loc. cit.*

[132] In re Martinez' Will, 47 N.M. 6, 132 P.2d 422 (1943); Stitt v. Cox, 52 N.M. 24, 190 P.2d 434 (1948).

[133] In re Richter's Will, 42 N.M. 593, 82 P.2d 916 (1938).

[134] In re Chavez' Will, 39 N.M. 304, 46 P.2d 665 (1935).

must be followed.[135]   And with reference to charitable testamentary trusts, the fact that the beneficiaries are not designated as individuals or as a distinct class does not change the character of such a trust.[136]   In fact, it is not necessary that a charitable trust be confined solely to the indigent, since the modern definition of "charity" in its legal sense extends to the improvement and promotion of the happiness of man.[137]   The primary duty of the court construing a testamentary charitable trust is to ascertain the desire of testator as he has expressed it, and to carry it to fulfillment unless public policy or the general rules of law impose a prohibition.[138]   These provisions follow, to that extent, the English and Anglo-American doctrine of *cy pres* whereby, if it becomes impossible or highly difficult to carry out the original charitable intent on the part of the settlor, the property will be devoted to a similar charity, less the grant lapse.[139]

Moreover, the court will not presume in advance that the trustees of a charitable trust will violate their trust or will refuse to perform their duties.[140]   It should also be noted that a testamentary condition, which may be performed at the time or after, as well as before, the vesting of the estate devised, or which was evidently intended to be performed by devisee after taking possession of the estate, is generally held to be a condition subsequent, performance of which is excused if it was impossible when the condition was created or afterwards becomes so by an act of God or testator, in which case the estate vests in the devisee discharged from the condition.[141]

B.   *Canon Law*

Anyone who is entitled by the natural and ecclesiastical law to dispose freely of his goods may relinquish them in favor of re-

135 Sylvanus v. Pruett, 36 N.M. 112, 9 P.2d 142 (1932).

136 In re Mills' Will, 57 N.M. 577, 260 P.2d 1111 (1953).

137 *Loc. cit.*

138 *Loc. cit.*

139 10 Am. Jur., Charities, §§ 4-11; 54 Am. Jur., Trusts, §§ 136-146.

140 In re Mills' Will, 57 N.M. 577, 260 P.2d 1111 (1953).

141 Torres v. Abeyta, 42 N.M. 665, 84 P.2d 592 (1938).

ligion or of charity by direct donation as well as by testamentary disposition.[142] In last wills favoring the Church the formalities of the civil law should, if possible, be complied with; if they were omitted, the heirs should be admonished to fulfill the wish of the testator.[143] This injunction to carry out the intention of the testator is preceptive in the event that a last will made in favor of religion or of charity proves to be invalid in the civil forum.[144] The obligation thus created is binding in the internal forum of conscience.

The wishes of the faithful contributing or leaving a share of their goods to religion or charity, whether by an act of donation *inter vivos* or by testamentary disposition, are to be most faithfully executed, even with reference to the manner of administration and the distribution of the property,[145] subject to the following provisions:

1) Ordinaries are the executors of all grants to religion and charity made *mortis causa* or during the lifetime of the grantor.[146]

2) In virtue of this right, ordinaries can and must exercise vigilance even to the extent of visitation in order that the wishes of the donor or testator may be executed; other delegated executors must, upon completion of their office, render an account to them.[147]

3) Clauses inserted in last wills contrary to the foregoing rights of ordinaries are to be considered as non-existent.[148] This provision originated in the time of Justinian,[149] and has been retained and observed in canonical legislation since.[150]

[142] Cf. canon 1513, § 1.

[143] Canon 1513, § 2.

[144] Code Commission, 17 Feb. 1930.—*A.A.S.*, XXII (1930), 196; Bouscaren's Digest, I, 725.

[145] Canon 1514.

[146] Canon 1515, § 1.

[147] Canon 1515, § 2.

[148] Canon 1515, § 3.

[149] C. (1, 3) 45.

[150] Hannan, pp. 421 ff.

In accepting trusts, the Church assumes a sacred obligation, and devisors have a right to expect that their wishes will be executed according to their intent to the extent that such is possible. So inviolable is a religious or charitable intent of a settlor that Canon law empowers ordinaries to coerce, even by censure, those who, as grantees, legatees, or trustees, neglect the execution of grants *inter vivos* or of testamentary bequests.[151]

A cleric or religious who has, either by way of a grant *inter vivos* or by testamentary disposition, received property in trust for religion or charity, must notify the ordinary of the trusteeship and provide him with an inventory of the chattels and realty involved, describing the obligations attached to the trust; and if the grantor has expressly and absolutely forbidden all reference to the ordinary in this regard the trusteeship shall not be accepted.[152] The ordinary must demand that the *trust res* be safely invested, and is to supervise the execution of the religious or charitable intent, as provided in canon 1515.[153] If a religious is the trustee of property left in favor of a church of the place or of the diocese for the benefit of the people or pious causes, the ordinary in the foregoing frame of reference is the local ordinary; else, the proper ordinary of the religious is meant.[154]

Although the Code implies that a religious may act as a trustee, the constitutions of the different organizations must be consulted for the ascertainment of whether a particular order or congregation forbids it, as is the case in the Order of Friars Minor.[155]

The reduction, mitigation, and commutation of testamentary bequests, which can be effected only when justifying necessity permits, is reserved to the Holy See, unless the devisor has ex-

---

[151] Canon 2348.

[152] Canon 1516, § 1.

[153] Canon 1516, § 2. The grantor or devisor may appoint executors to act under the authority of the ordinary.

[154] Canon 1516, § 3. Cf. canons 535, § 3, 2°; 630, §§ 3-4; 631, § 3; 1425; 1525; 1550.

[155] Woywod-Smith, II, 201.

pressly granted this authority also to the local ordinary.[156] But if, through no fault of the executors, the fulfillment of the imposed obligations has become impossible because of diminished returns or some other reason, the ordinary may, after hearing the interested parties and adhering insofar as possible to the intent of the devisor, reduce the obligations according to the rules of equity; the reduction of Mass burdens, however, is always reserved exclusively to the Holy See.[157] Nevertheless, if the document or some article of the foundation expressly gives him the right, the ordinary can reduce Mass obligations.[158]

As can be readily appreciated, the Church is extremely cautious in the matter of the execution of a devisor's bequest and obligations attached thereto. Canon law holds a trust intent as inviolable, and while the equivalent of the Anglo-American doctrine of *cy pres* is indeed, within the limits above-described, found in the Code, its extent and application are very jealously guarded.

The natural right, canonized by the Code, of a person to dispose freely of personal goods is reflected in divers manners on all ecclesiastical levels. The Church is at least as eager as the State, for instance, to forestall undue influence in the testamentary disposition of such properties. In the Archdiocese of Santa Fe, for example, a synodal statute provides that "Priests shall exercise the greatest prudence in giving counsel to a lay person concerning the disposition of an estate by gift or Will, avoiding even the appearance of undue influence." [159]

Section 3. Adverse Possession

A. New Mexico Law

At Anglo-American law, title by adverse possession may be acquired by a religious corporation or by the trustees of a re-

---

[156] Canon 1517, § 1. Reduction curtails the number of acts; mitigation, the proportions of the plan; commutation substitutes acts, plans, or beneficiaries.—Abbo-Hannan, II, 722.

[157] Canon 1517, § 2.

[158] Code Commission, 14 July 1922, XI—*A.A.S.*, XIV (1922), 529; Bouscaren's Digest, I, 726.

[159] Statute 22, § 2, *Seventh Synod of the Archdiocese of Santa Fe.*

ligious society,[160] as well as by a natural person.[161] A title acquired by adverse possession is a title in fee simple,[162] and is as perfect a title as one by deed from the original owner.[163] It is defined as an actual and visible appropriation of land, commenced and continued in good faith under a color of title and claim of right inconsistent with and hostile to the claim of another.[164] In New Mexico, such adverse possession must continue for a period of ten years in the case of lands, tenements, or hereditaments before title will ripen.[165]

Although the scope of this study demands that the present discussion be confined to adverse possession of realty, it is essential to understand the notions of prescription and limitation of actions as well, since these three institutes are contained in the canonical *praescriptio* which, according to canon 1508, is to be regulated in ecclesiastical tribunals of New Mexico by the civil law of that state except for the points expressly excepted in the Code of Canon Law.

Adverse possession is distinguished from prescription in that the former is a means of acquiring title to corporeal hereditaments only and is usually the direct result of the statute of limitations, while prescription is the outgrowth of common law principles with but little aid from statute, and has to do with the acquisition of incorporeal hereditaments only.[166] In New Mexico, the statute of limitations became the law of limitations in 1876, abrogating the Mexican law of prescription.[167]

[160] 2 C.J.S., Adverse Possession, § 6.

[161] Turner v. Sanchez, 50 N.M. 15, 168 P.2d 96, 164 A.L.R. 1280 (1946).

[162] Sect. 23-1-22, 1953 N.M. Comp. Laws.

[163] 1 Am. Jur., Adverse Possession, § 2.

[164] Sect. 23-1-22, 1953 N.M. Comp. Laws.

[165] *Loc. cit.*

[166] Hester v. Sawyers, 41 N.M. 497, 71 P.2d 646, 112 A.L.R. 536 (1937).

[167] Sect. 21-3-3, 1953 N.M. Comp. Laws; Browning v. Browning's Estate, 3 Gild. (N.M.) 659, 3 John. (N.M.) 371, 9 P. 677 (1886); Musgrave v. McManus, 27 N.M. 227, 173 P. 196, L.R.A. 1918F, 348 (1918). Under the Spanish and Mexican law, ordinary prescription for realty required for its

The doctrine of adverse possession is to be strictly construed,[168] and the burden of proving title thereby rests on him who asserts it, and all presumptions are in favor of the holder of the title.[169] Thus, an adverse claimant has only an inchoate right which, if pursued and protected, may ripen into title.[170] Where this is done for a period of ten years, the adverse claimant is entitled to possession until ousted by someone showing better title,[171] since adverse possession of land for the period of time prescribed by the statute of limitations not only bars the remedy, but practically extinguishes the right of the party having the true paper title.[172]

To ripen into title, adverse possession must be under color of title,[173] which exists whenever there is a reasonable doubt regarding the validity of an apparent title, whether such doubt arises from the circumstances under which the land is held, the identity of the land conveyed, or the construction of the instrument under which the party in possession claims title.[174] Hence, some writing which purports to give title to the premises is essential to give title to an adverse occupant, and actual possession or oral transactions, however effective these may be as between parties, do not contribute color of title.[175]

---

operation good faith, just title, and continued and uninterrupted possession for ten years.—Hayes v. United States, 170 U.S. 637, 18 S.Ct. 735, 42 L.Ed. 1174 (1898).

[168] Montoya v. Catron, 22 N.M. 570, 166 P. 909 (1917).

[169] Ward v. Rodriguez, 43 N.M. 191, 88 P.2d 277 (1939), certiorari denied Rodriguez v. Ward, 307 U.S. 627, 59 S.Ct. 837, 83 L.Ed. 1511 (1939).

[170] Turner v. Sanchez, 50 N.M. 15, 168 P.2d 96, 164 A.L.R. 1280 (1946).

[171] Hallmark v. Baca, 61 N.M. 420, 301 P.2d 527 (1956).

[172] Maxwell Land Grant Co. v. Dawson, 151 U.S. 586, 14 S.Ct. 458, 38 L.Ed. 279 (1894), reversing 7 N.M. 133, 34 P. 191 (1893).

[173] Green v. Trumball, 37 N.M. 604, 26 P.2d 1079 (1933); Murray Hotel Co. v. Golding, 54 N.M. 149, 216 P.2d 364 (1950).

[174] Third National Exchange Bank of Sandusky, Ohio, v. Smith, 20 N.M. 264, 148 P. 512 (1915), affirmed 244 U.S. 184, 37 S.Ct. 516, 61 L.Ed. 1071 (1917).

[175] Sandoval v. Perez, 26 N.M. 280, 191 P. 467 (1920).

Good faith in the creation or acquisition of color of title is freedom from a design to defraud the person having the better title, but the knowledge of an adverse claim to, or lien upon, property does not, of itself, indicate bad faith in a purchaser, and is not even evidence of it unless accompanied by some improper means to defeat such claim or lien.[176] Moreover, good faith does not require ignorance of adverse claims or defects in the title.[177]

To constitute adverse possession, the occupancy of one so claiming must be 1) actual, 2) visible, 3) exclusive, 4) hostile, and 5) continuous.[178] If any of these elements is lacking, no title by adverse possession can ripen,[179] but an occupancy so endowed constitutes prima facie evidence of title in the person so possessed.[180]

The adverse possession must be actual, that is, a possession subjecting the land to the will and dominion of the occupant, not one which is constructive or established by inference.[181]

All that the law requires is that the possession, or acts of dominion, by which it is sought to be proved, shall be of a character as may be reasonably expected to inform the true owner of the fact of possession and an adverse claim of title.[182] In other words, fences, buildings, or other improvements are not necessary in order to constitute a visible possession of land.[183]

The possession must be exclusive, to the extent that the possession of all but a relatively insignificant part of a large area

[176] Thurmond v. Espalin, 50 N.M. 109, 171 P.2d 325 (1946).

[177] Witherspoon v. Brummett, 50 N.M. 303, 176 P.2d 187 (1947).

[178] Jenkins v. Maxwell Land Grant Co., 15 N.M. 281, 107 P. 739 (1910), affirmed 235 U.S. 691, 35 S.Ct. 205, 59 L.Ed. 427 (1914).

[179] City of Roswell v. Mountain States Tel. & Tel. Co., 78 F.2d 379 (C.C. A.N.M. 1935).

[180] Bell v. Skillicorn, 6 N.M. 399, 28 P. 768 (1892).

[181] Montoya v. Catron, 22 N.M. 570, 166 P. 909 (1917).

[182] Baker v. De Armijo, 17 N.M. 383, 128 P. 73 (1912).

[183] G. O. S. Cattle Co. v. Bragaw's Heirs, 38 N.M. 105, 28 P.2d 529 (1933).

of a given tract was found to be constructive and ineffectual against its true owner.[184]

In regard to the element of hostility, the possession at its inception must be hostile or adverse to that of the true owner,[185] or, although not hostile at its commencement, such acts must be done as will make it hostile.[186] Consequently, where a claimant seeks to establish his ownership of land by adverse possession, he thereby disclaims holding as a tenant or licensee, the two positions being inconsistent and not maintainable at the same time.[187] It must be borne in mind that possession is presumed to be in subordination to the title of the owner, although such presumption is not conclusive.[188]

Finally, in order to perfect title by adverse possession, such possession must be continuous for the entire period prescribed by the statute of limitations.[189] Any break or interruption of the continuity of the possession will be fatal to the claim of the party setting up title by adverse possession, but temporary vacancies in the occupation, caused by the substitution of one tenant for another, which vacancies are not longer than is reasonable in view of the character of the land, do not constitute interruptions of possession such as would destroy the running of the statute.[190] But where a person in possession of disputed

[184] Jenkins v. Maxwell Land Grant Co., 15 N.M. 281, 107 P. 739 (1910), affirmed 235 U.S. 691, 35 S.Ct. 205, 59 L.Ed. 427 (1914).

[185] Lummus v. Brakin, 59 N.M. 216, 281 P.2d 928 (1955).

[186] Apodaca v. Hernandez, 61 N.M. 449, 302 P.2d 177 (1956).

[187] Chaves v. Torlina, 15 N.M. 53, 99 P. 690 (1909); Jackson v. Gallegos, 38 N.M. 211, 30 P.2d 719 (1934).

[188] United States v. Board of National Missions of Presbyterian Church in U.S.A., 37 F.2d 272 (C.C.A.N.M. 1929). Where the evidence shows that defendant in ejectment has been in adverse possession under claim of title for the statutory period, an instruction that, "unless he had a right to the possession of such lands when he took possession of them, he has no right now; time never makes a wrong right," is erroneous.—Probst v. Trustees of Board of Domestic Missions, 129 U.S. 182, 9 S.Ct. 263, 32 L.Ed. 642 (1889), reversing 3 Gild. (N.M.) 373, 3 John. (N.M.) 237, 5 P. 702 (1884).

[189] Pratt v. Parker, 57 N.M. 103, 255 P.2d 311 (1953).

[190] Johnston v. City of Albuquerque, 12 N.M. 20, 72 P. 9 (1903).

territory concedes that the true title is in another and offers to purchase it from him, the continuity of adverse possession is broken.[191]

B. Canon Law

The method of acquiring goods and rights and of freeing oneself from obligations by prescription as found in the civil law of the individual countries is adopted by the Church in connection with ecclesiastical goods, but without prejudice to the provisions of canons 1509-1512.[192] Thus, prescription at Canon law can be acquisitive or liberative, and includes the three Anglo-American institutes of adverse possession, prescription, and limitation of actions.

The following goods and rights are not subject to prescription:

1) a right of divine law, whether natural or positive; [193]

2) that which can be obtained only by Apostolic privilege; [194]

3) those spiritual rights which lay persons are incapable of acquiring, if there is question of prescription in favor of lay persons; [195]

4) the certain and undisputed boundary lines of ecclesiastical provinces, dioceses, parishes, vicariates and prefectures Apostolic, abbacies and prelacies *nullius;* [196]

5) stipends for and obligations of Masses; [197]

6) an ecclesiastical benefice in the absence of title; [198]

[191] Chambers v. Bessent, 17 N.M. 487, 134 P. 237 (1913).

[192] Canon 1508.

[193] Canon 1509, 1°. E.g., the primacy of the Roman Pontiff, a right given by the positive divine law.

[194] Canon 1509, 2°. However, possession for one hundred years is equivalent to an Apostolic privilege.—Cf. canon 63, § 2.

[195] Canon 1509, 3°. E.g., the holding and exercise of ecclesiastical jurisdiction.—Cf. canon 118.

[196] Canon 1509, 4°. If the boundaries are uncertain or disputed, prescription is admitted.

[197] Canon 1509, 5°.

[198] Canon 1509, 6°. Prescription is operative if color of title exists.—Canon 1446.

7) the right of visitation and obedience, if this would entail that the subjects would be liberated from visitation by any prelate and from the obligation of obedience to any prelate; [199]

8) payment of the cathedratic tax.[200]

Sacred objects owned by natural persons can be acquired by natural persons through the agency of prescription, but the latter cannot relegate them to uses that are not sacred; but if these objects have lost their consecration or blessing, they may be acquired even for such purposes without restriction, but not for sordid uses.[201] Sacred objects that are not owned by natural persons cannot through the agency of prescription be acquired by a natural person, but they may be acquired by one ecclesiastical corporation from another.[202]

A period of one hundred years is required for the operation of prescription against the immovable property of the Holy See, precious movable property belonging to it, as well as against rights and claims at law, whether personal or real, pertaining thereto.[203] A period of thirty years is required in the case of other ecclesiastical corporations.[204] The period of time required in all other instances is controlled by canon 1508; thus, in New Mexico the prescription would have to run for ten years with reference to realty.[205]

---

[199] Canon 1509, 7°.

[200] Canon 1509, 8°.

[201] Canon 1510, § 1.

[202] Canon 1510, § 2.

[203] Canon 1511, § 1. A personal action reflects a *ius in rem;* a real action, a *ius in re.*

[204] Canon 1511, § 2.

[205] In New Mexico, adverse possession for personalty must run for 4 years. Limitations on some actions follow: specialties: 6 yrs. (on municipal bonds, 10 yrs.); written contracts and unsealed promissory notes: 6 yrs.; parol contracts, accounts, fraud and deceit, and trespass: 4 yrs.; nonfeasance and malfeasance: 3 yrs.; personal injury: 1 yr.; judgments: 7 yrs. (courts not of record, 6 yrs.).—Martin, *Adverse Possession, Prescription and Limitations of Actions. The Canonical "Praescriptio,"* The Catholic University of America Canon Law Studies, n. 202 (Washington, D.C.: The Catholic University of America Press, 1944), p. 141. [Hereinafter cited Martin.]

At Canon law, the time runs from the moment that the action could first be presented legally in contentious cases; in criminal cases from the day the delictal act was perpetrated.[206] With reference to the running of time in contentious cases, Canon law takes into consideration the questions of plaintiff and defendant in being, fulfillment of conditions precedent, as well as that of accrual of the cause of action.[207] Thus, the time is benignly intermittent (*tempus utile*) [208] antecedently to the actual prosecution by plaintiff, but once the time has begun to run it ordinarily becomes rigorously continuous (*tempus continuum*).[209]

Prescription will not avail unless it is radicated on good faith, which must be verified not only at the moment of entering into possession but also during the whole period of possession required for prescription.[210] Good faith (*bona fides*) at Canon law may be described as a judgment by which a person prudently decides that the thing which he possesses is his own, or at least that it does not belong to anyone else.[211] In the case of corporations, this good faith must be verified in the majority of the members of a collegiate moral person, and in the responsible administrator where a non-collegiate moral personality is involved. And since corporations always retain the same identity, the good faith of subsequent members or administrators does not counteract the bad faith of their predecessors.[212]

The requirement of good faith is thus essential in Anglo-American law and at Canon law. But there is a vast difference in practice between the provisions of the two systems of law.

[206] Canon 1705, § 1.

[207] Martin, p. 95.

[208] The term *tempus utile* means that the time for the exercise or prosecution of one's rights does not lapse if one be ignorant of his rights or be unable to act at that time.—Canon 35.

[209] Martin, p. 95. The term *tempus continuum* means that the time in its lapse and duration is not patient of any delay or suspension by reason of one's ignorance or inability to act during that interval.—Canon 35.

[210] Canon 1512.

[211] Martin, p. 31.

[212] Abbo-Hannan, II, 720.

At Anglo-American law good faith can be considered a negative requirement, in the sense that it is viewed as freedom from a design to defraud.[213]   Consequently, the question of good faith cannot be considered of paramount importance in New Mexico law as it is at Canon law, particularly because of its very nature: good faith is, after all, essentially a matter of the internal forum.

At Anglo-American law, if bad faith cannot be shown, good faith will be presumed.   But for Canon law, there is a far greater problem, "one which becomes almost insurmountable unless one keeps clearly in mind the distinction between Canon Law and Moral Theology, realizing that Canon Law as applied by an ecclesiastical court is bound to the limitations of what can be made to appear from the acts and proofs, wherefore it must at times be content with a presumption of good faith when bad faith is not proved, whereas Moral Theology, treating of the state of man's conscience and reaching that conscience in the internal forum of the tribunal of Penance, rightly is concerned with the actual state of that conscience, and can proceed to judge it when it is manifested."[214]

[213] Thurmond v. Espalin, 50 N.M. 109, 171 P.2d 325 (1946).

[214] Martin, p. 38.

CHAPTER VI

ADMINISTRATION OF CHURCH PROPERTY

ARTICLE 1. ADMINISTRATION IN GENERAL

Section 1. New Mexico Law

As in Anglo-American law in general, a distinction must be drawn at New Mexico law with reference to the administration of property for charitable or for religious purposes, in line with the way in which such goods are held. If the property is held by an unincorporated persons or persons, it must first be ascertained whether there is an implied or express trust, or whether the property is held by that person as absolute owner of the fee simple. In the former instance, and if the trust is merely implied, the canonical administrator would be competent to act and administer the property as absolute owner, but the courts would probably admit parol evidence of Canon law to explain the nature of his tenure according to Canon law; if the trust is express, the laws on trust will find application. If the property is held by an ecclesiastical administrator as absolute owner of the fee simple, and the words of grant do not imply a trust, the holder of the fee would be ruled as to his powers only by the general laws affecting property rights of private individuals. If, on the other hand, the property is held by a corporation, the laws relating to the powers of corporations aggregate or sole, as the case may be, will obtain.

The charter of a religious corporation constitutes its supreme law, to which everything else is subordinate. Its charter, however, is not intended to be the only law by which the corporation's affairs are governed. New Mexico law grants corporations aggregate the power to make by-laws consistent with law and with the articles of incorporation.[1] On the other hand, the powers of a corporation are circumscribed in various ways. Its

---

[1] Sect. 51-14-29, 1953 N.M. Comp. Laws.

power to acquire real property is limited to the quantum that is necessary or proper to enable it to carry out the objects of its creation,[2] and its administrative power in matters contractual as to the outside world is limited to such relations as are necessary or proper for accomplishing the objects of its creation.[3]

In its relation to the state, a religious corporation is a mere private corporation. And it is important to keep in mind that in its relation to the Church it is not a spiritual agency with spiritual powers to preach the gospel and administer the sacraments, "but a humble secular handmaid whose functions are confined to the creation and enforcement of contracts and the acquisition, management and disposition of property. The corporation thus has neither public nor ecclesiastical functions, being a mere business agent with strictly private secular powers." [4]

Without prejudice to such limitations or restrictions which may be imposed by charter, by-laws, or statutory provisions,[5] the same general principles of law which govern the relation of agency for a natural person govern the officer or agent of a corporation in regard to his power to act for the corporation.[6] Since a corporation must necessarily act through its officers and agents, and inasmuch as so many acts of administration are performed by agents even where the ecclesiastical corporation is not incorporated civilly, a brief inquiry into New Mexico jurisprudence on agency must be instituted.[7]

[2] Church of the Holy Faith, Inc. v. State Tax Commission, 39 N.M. 403, 48 P.2d 777 (1935).

[3] Sect. 51-14-30, 1953 N.M. Comp. Laws.

[4] Zollmann, *American Civil Church Law,* Columbia University Studies in History, Economics and Public Law, Vol. 77 (New York: Columbia University and Longmans, Green & Co., 1917), p. 79.

[5] Prudential Insurance Co. of America v. Saxe, 134 F.2d 16, 77 U.S.App. D.C. 144 (1943), certiorari denied 319 U.S. 745, 63 S.Ct. 1033, 87 L.Ed. 1701 (1943).

[6] Merrion v. Scorup-Somerville Cattle Co., 134 F.2d 473 (C.C.A. Utah 1943), certiorari denied 319 U.S. 760, 63 S.Ct. 1317, 87 L.Ed. 1712 (1943).

[7] The instant summary is intended as a supplement to the treatment on Anglo-American law on agency, presented in Chapter III hereinbefore.

A principal may limit an agent's authority,[8] in which case the latter cannot bind the former beyond the limits of authority as to those having knowledge of said limitations.[9]

The apparent authority of an agent must be determined from the nature of the business entrusted to him, the words, acts, and conduct of the principal, and not from the unqualified declarations or acts of the agent.[10]   Thus, while agency may be established by circumstantial evidence,[11] one dealing with an agent is required to know the agent's authority.[12]   But in the event that agency be admitted by words or acts, the agent's real authority is immaterial, and the principal is bound by such apparent authority as his words or acts would indicate, to a reasonably prudent man, that the agent possessed.[13]   And the secret or private instructions to an agent, however binding they may be as between the principal and his agent, can have no effect on a third person who deals with the agent in ignorance of the instructions, and in reliance on the apparent authority with which the principal has clothed him.[14]

Ordinarily, a principal is liable for the acts of his agent when dealing within the scope of his authority,[15] and where a part of the acts of an agent are within, and a part without, his authority, the former are valid.[16]   But the principal is responsible for the unauthorized acts of the agent where the conduct of the prin-

[8] Bloodgood v. Woman's Benevolent Ass'n., 36 N.M. 228, 13 P.2d 412 (1932).

[9] *Loc. cit.*

[10] Douglass v. Mutual Benevolent Health & Accident Ass'n., 42 N.M. 190, 76 P.2d 453 (1938).

[11] State v. Kelly, 27 N.M. 412, 202 P.2d 524, 21 A.L.R. 156 (1921).

[12] Douglass v. Mutual Benevolent Health & Accident Ass'n., 42 N.M. 190, 76 P.2d 453 (1938).

[13] *Loc. cit.*

[14] New Mexico-Colorado Coal & Mining Co. v. Baker, 21 N.M. 531, 157 P. 167 (1916).

[15] Stewart v. Potter, 44 N.M. 460, 104 P.2d 736 (1940).

[16] Jasper v. Wilson, 14 N.M. 482, 94 P. 951, 23 L.R.A.(N.S.) 982 (1908).

cipal justifies the party dealing with the agent in believing that such agent was acting within, and not in excess of, the authority conferred upon him.[17]   In other words, a principal is bound not only by the acts of his agent, general or special, within the authority given the latter by the former, but also by the agent's acts within the apparent authority which the principal knowingly permits the agent to assume or holds him out to the public as possessing.[18]

Section 2.   Canon Law

A.   The Roman Pontiff as Administrator of Church Property

The Roman Pontiff is the supreme administrator and dispenser of all ecclesiastical property.[19]   Since, however, the dominion over church property is vested in the ecclesiastical corporation which legitimately acquired such temporal goods,[20] the Roman Pontiff does not have direct dominion over all ecclesiastical property, although this dominion is under the supreme authority of the Holy See.[21]   This amounts to an enjoyment on the part of the Holy See of an *altum dominium*,[22] a right of eminent domain.

In practice the Roman Pontiff directly administers only the possessions of the Holy See, and even this administration is exercised through the agency of the Cardinal Camerlengo.[23]   In practice the Roman Pontiff administers the possessions of all other ecclesiastical corporations only indirectly, through the agency of subordinate administrators who, however, must follow the general or special norms promulgated therefor by him.   Thus, the Roman Pontiff reserves to himself only the more important matters concerning property administration.

[17] Smith v. New York Life Insurance Co., 26 N.M. 408, 193 P. 67 (1920).

[18] Raulie v. Jackson-Horne Grocery, 48 N.M. 556, 154 P.2d 231 (1945).

[19] Canon 1518.

[20] Canon 1499, § 2.

[21] *Loc. cit.*

[22] Vermeersch-Creusen, II, 570.

[23] Cf. canon 262.

B. The Local Ordinary and the Administration of
Church Property

The local ordinary has the duty to watch carefully within his territory over the administration of all ecclesiastical property which has not been withdrawn from his jurisdiction, without prejudice to more extensive rights which he may enjoy through lawful prescription.[24]   Within the limits of the common law and with due regard for vested rights, legitimate customs, and circumstances, the ordinaries are to issue opportune instructions for the regulation of the entire matter of the administration of church property [25] within their respective jurisdictions.

The Code of Canon Law describes the Roman Pontiff as the supreme administrator of all ecclesiastical property, while it implicitly restricts the power of the local ordinary to that of supervision, unless other titles give him direct administrative rights.[26] The supervisory right of the local ordinary may be considered tripartite, since his power extends over secular, religious, and non-parochial—non-religious property.

The supervisory power of the local ordinary over secular property extends to 1) the property of all parish churches,[27] even to those which are parochial churches in parishes united *pleno iure* to a religious house,[28] unless a parochial church is owned by the religious community with strict property rights,[29] and 2) the property of all parishes which is distinct from the property of the parochial church, such as alms for the school or other build-

[24] Canon 1519, § 1.

[25] Canon 1519, § 2.

[26] Vermeersch-Creusen, II, 587; Coronata, II, 484; Abbo-Hannan, II, 725; Comyns, *Papal and Episcopal Administration of Church Property*, The Catholic University of America Canon Law Studies, n. 147 (Washington, D.C.: The Catholic University of America Press, 1942), pp. 68 ff. (hereinafter cited Comyns).

[27] Canon 1525, § 1.

[28] Code Comm., 25 July 1926, IV—*A.A.S.*, XVIII (1926), 393; Bouscaren's Digest, I, 699.

[29] Comyns, p. 72.

ings which together with the church make up the property of the parish.[30]

The supervisory rights and obligations of the local ordinary over property possessed by religious extends to 1) income from funds or property where the grantee or devisee is a house of a religious congregation, and the grant, devise, or bequest stipulates that the property is to be invested and the revenue used for the purpose of divine worship or for a charitable use within the territory of the local ordinary; [31] 2) money donated to an individual religious or to a religious house in view of the parish or mission, as well as money given directly to the parish or mission; [32] 3) the administration of the dowry in all institutes of women religious; [33] 4) the administration of all property of diocesan-right institutes of men and women,[34] provided that the administration is conducted by a superior who resides within the territory of the ordinary,[35] and 5) all property administration exercised by nuns.[36]

Besides his supervisory rights over property which is parochial or which, if not parochial, is possessed by religious, the local ordinary must exercise vigilance over the administration of property which does not come under the above-mentioned two classi-

---

[30] *Loc. cit.*

[31] Canon 533, § 1, 3°.

[32] Canon 533, § 1, 4°.

[33] Canons 550; 535, § 2. Under Anglo-American law, it does not appear that any technical trust is created in the establishment of a dowry with a religious community.—Cf. Byrne, *Investment of Church Funds: A Study in Administrative Law,* The Catholic University of America Canon Law Studies, n. 309 (Washington, D.C.: The Catholic University of America Press, 1951), p. 79.

[34] Canon 535, § 3, 1°.

[35] Comyns, 74.

[36] Canon 535, § 1, 1°-2°. *Nuns* are women who have taken solemn religious vows, or who belong to an institute which requires that its members take solemn vows, even though some of the members actually take simple vows pursuant to a directive of the Holy See; *Sisters* are women who have taken simple religious vows.—Canon 488, 7°.

fications. This further supervision extends to 1) wills in favor of religion or of charity,[37] unless the devisees are clerical exempt religious; [38] 2) pious foundations,[39] unless these have been established in the churches, even parochial, of exempt religious; [40] 3) property which constitutes or belongs to non-collegiate ecclesiastical corporations, such as hospitals, orphanages, seminaries, schools, and other institutions which have a religious or a charitable purpose; [41] 4) money given in trust to individual clerics or religious with the stipulation that it be used for religious or for charitable purposes,[42] and 5) property of ecclesiastically incorporated lay associations, even when these associations are established in churches of exempt religious.[43]

In addition to the foregoing supervisory rights, the local ordinary enjoys immediate administrative powers over the following units of church property: 1) property which is strictly diocesan in character,[44] as opposed to those possessions which belong to parishes [45] and other subordinate canonical corporations within the territory of the ordinary; [46] 2) property which constitutes the *mensa episcopalis;* [47] 3) alms given to a church entrusted to re-

[37] Canon 1515, § 2.

[38] Cf. canon 198, § 1. In this latter case, the major superiors of clerical exempt religious have the right of supervision.

[39] Canons 1545; 1546, § 1; 1547. A pious foundation is property given in any manner to a canonical corporation with the stipulation that the annual income of the property is to be used perpetually, or at least over a long period of time, for the performance of pious or charitable works.— Canon 1544, § 1.

[40] In this latter instance, the right of supervision vests in the ordinary of the exempt religious.—Canon 1550.

[41] Cf. canons 1489, §§ 1-3; 1491, § 1; 1492.

[42] Canon 1516, § 2.

[43] Canons 690, §§ 1-2; 691, §§ 1-5.

[44] Canon 335, § 1.

[45] Comyns, p. 84.

[46] Abbo-Hannan, II, 725.

[47] Canon 1483, § 1. The *mensa episcopalis* signifies the benefice of the residential bishop.

ligious, in those cases in which the religious do not own the church; [48] 4) property of the cathedral church; [49] 5) alms which have been donated for an unspecified charitable use; 6) bequests contained in wills, in conformity with canon 1517, §§ 1-2; 7) the revenue accruing from the levying of taxes; [50] 8) the property of divided or extinct parishes,[51] and 9) property which the ordinary administers in virtue of legal prescription, acquired according to the norms of canons 1508-1512.[52]

Unless an equivalent provision has been lawfully made by law or particular custom, every local ordinary must, for the proper discharge of his supervisory and administrative responsibilities, establish in the see city a diocesan council of administration which is to consist of the ordinary as president and two or more qualified men who are, if possible, experts also in civil law, selected with the advice of the board of diocesan consultors.[53] When important administrative acts are to be performed, the local ordinary is to consult, without fail, the council of administration; however, the members of this council have only an advisory capacity, unless their consent is specifically enumerated in the general law or in virtue of the articles of foundation.[54]

[48] Canon 630, § 4.

[49] The local ordinary is the co-administrator with the cathedral chapter of the cathedral church and its possessions.—Cf. canon 1182, § 1. In those dioceses, as in the United States, which have no cathedral chapters, the co-administration of the cathedral church does not devolve upon the board of diocesan consultors. Such a right is not given by the Code, which states in canon 427 that the board of consultors is to assist in the government of the diocese.—Cf. Comyns, p. 93.

[50] Such taxes are the seminary tax (canons 1355, 2°; 1356, §§ 1-3; 1357, § 1), cathedratic tax (canon 1504), the extraordinary subsidiary tax (canon 1505), and the tax which may be imposed upon a church, a benefice, or some other ecclesiastical institute on the occasion of its foundation or consecration (canon 1506).

[51] Canons 1427, § 3; 1500.

[52] Canon 1519, § 1.

[53] Canon 1520, § 1.

[54] Canon 1520, § 3.

C. Subordinate Administrators of Church Property

In addition to the establishment of a diocesan council of administration, the local ordinary is to appoint administrators for those churches or pious institutions which by law or in virtue of the articles of foundation do not have an administrator; [55] thus, each canonical corporation will have its own administrator.

The administrators of church property are required to fulfill their responsibility with the diligence of a good householder; they must, therefore:

1) guard against the loss or damage of the property;

2) observe the requirements of both canon and civil law, as well as the requirements specified by the founder or the donor, or imposed by legitimate authority;

3) collect the income and profits diligently and promptly, safeguard them, and use them in accordance with the intent of the founder or with established laws or norms;

4) invest the surplus revenues of a church for the benefit of the church itself, after obtaining the consent of the ordinary;

5) keep an accurate account of receipts and expenditures;

6) arrange in proper order the documents and deeds on which the property rights of the church are indicated, and file them in the archives of the church or in a suitable and adequate safe; and, if possible, deposit authentic copies of them in the archives or safe of the chancery office.[56]

Both ecclesiastical and lay administrators are required to submit an annual report to the local ordinary of their administration of all churches, including the cathedral church, or of a canonically established pious place or of a confraternity, with

---

[55] Canon 1521, § 1. An instance where the common law itself provides administrators is found in canon 454, § 1, by virtue of which the rector of a parish church is constituted the administrator thereof. Cf. also canon 1182, § 1.

[56] Canon 1523, 1°-6°. In the Archdiocese of Santa Fe, "all deeds and abstracts to church property must be recorded by the pastor in the respective county at the proper clerk and assessor's office. Title, survey, and plat of property should be made in duplicate, the original to be sent to the Chancery Office, a copy to be kept in the parish."—Statute 241, § 2, *Seventh Synod of the Archdiocese of Santa Fe.*

every contrary custom ruled out and rejected.[57] If under particular law a report must also be submitted to others specifically designated, the local ordinary or his delegate must be included among these, and any exoneration from this obligation is of no juridical value to the administrators.[58]

Administrators of church property are estopped from filing a suit or from entering a defense to a suit in the name of the Church unless they have obtained written permission therefor from the local ordinary, or at least, in a case of emergency, from the rural dean, who shall immediately apprise the ordinary of the permission given.[59] If they fail to obtain the required permission for this or for any other act which exceeds the limits or the method of ordinary administration they act invalidly.[60] Furthermore, the Church is not responsible for contracts entered into by administrators who lacked the permission of the competent superior, except when and to the extent that it has profited therefrom.[61]

It is from the foregoing provisions of Canon law, as well as

[57] Canon 1525, § 1.

[58] Canon 1525, § 2. The administrators of certain religious communities are included among those who must submit this report to the local ordinary; the controlling law on this point is found in canon 535, §§ 1-3. Cf. also McManus, *The Administration of Temporal Goods in Religious Institutes,* pp. 155 ff.

[59] Canon 1526. Since the law makes no distinction, this prohibition is operative even in the case of a suit in an ecclesiastical court.

[60] Canon 1527, § 1. The following are considered acts of ordinary, as opposed to extraordinary, administration: the collecting of debts, rents, interest, or dividends; the making of contracts and disbursements necessary for the ordinary maintenance of the church and its personnel; the accepting of ordinary donations. Acts of extraordinary administration include all acts of alienation; the acceptance or refusal of a gift or bequest; the purchase of land; the construction of new buildings or extensive repairs on old buildings; the opening of a cemetery; the investment of all capital, whether liquid or stable; the establishment of a school or any other similar parochial institution; the taking up of special collections.— Abbo-Hannan, II, 731. In addition, the respective synodal or extra-synodal enactments are to be consulted.

[61] Canon 1527, § 2.

from the provisions incident to acts of alienation to be considered
in the subsequent Article hereinbelow, that one arrives at the
canonical determination of when and to what extent an administrator or agent acts within the scope of his authority and in
what instances he exceeds the limits thereof. It is worth noting,
with reference to agency, that as at Anglo-American law, so too
at Canon law, one who is capable of executing a given act can,
generally also, act through the agency of another.[62]

ARTICLE 2. ALIENATION OF CHURCH PROPERTY

It is in the field of contractual law that the Church in the
United States has most contact with Anglo-American law and
jurisprudence. Wishing to forestall as many conflicts as possible
between Canon law and the law of whatever country or jurisdiction is involved, the Church has ordained that whatever the
secular law of the territory provides in the matter of contracts,
generally and specifically, either by name or otherwise (*sive
nominati sive innominati*), is to be observed as enacted by Canon
law in ecclesiastical matters with the same effects, unless it is
contrary to the divine law or unless other provision is made by
Canon law.[63]

The classical concept of contract among canon lawyers, as well
as moral theologians, is expressed as "*duorum vel plurium consensus in idem placitum*," a meeting of minds. However, since
Canon law adopts and canonizes the secular law of contracts,
and inasmuch as the notion and concept of contracts is part of

---

[62] "Potest quis per alium quod potest facere per seipsum."—Reg. 68, R.J.,
in VI°.

[63] Canon 1529. Nominate (*nominati*) contracts include contracts of sale,
rent, lease, etc. The so-called innominate (*innominati*) contracts belong
to the fourfold class of *do ut des, facio ut facias, do ut facias, facio ut des*.
Anglo-American law does not make the foregoing distinction; it does,
however, recognize implied contracts and quasi-contracts. The former are
those where an actual contract in which a part or all of the offer or acceptance has not been put into express words is nevertheless inferred from
the conduct of the parties, and they are consensual; quasi-contracts are
those in which an obligation is imposed by law without regard to the intention of the parties, and they are nonconsensual.—12 Am. Jur., Contracts, §§ 8-10.

the secular law in this matter, it follows that Canon law adopts, for our purposes, the Anglo-American concept of contracts. The canonical concept, the classical definition, constitutes a moral contract. Anglo-American law, however, while recognizing the necessity of consent, is careful to include among the constitutive elements of the concept of contracts the notion of protection: "A contract is a promise or set of promises for the breach of which the law gives a remedy, or the performance of which the law in some way recognizes as a duty." [64]

Section 1. New Mexico Law

Anglo-American law requires that certain contracts be made in writing, if they are to be enforceable. The English Statute of Frauds,[65] passed in 1676, is in force in New Mexico [66] by virtue of the adoption of the common law of England.[67] Among the provisions dealing with contracts, the Statute of Frauds rules that a contract for the sale of any interest in land must be in writing.[68] The purpose of this provision is to prevent fraud,[69] and a court of equity will intervene and order performance when the refusal to intervene on account of the Statute of Frauds would permit a fraud to be committed.[70]

[64] *Restatement of the Law on Contracts* (St. Paul: American Law Institute, 1933), § 1.

[65] 29 Car. II, c. 3.

[66] Harris v. Hardwick, 18 N.M. 303, 137 P. 581 (1913).

[67] Maljamar Oil & Gas Corp. v. Malco Refineries, 155 F.2d 673 (C.C.A. N.M. 1946); Ades v. Supreme Lodge, Order of Ahepa, 51 N.M. 164, 181 P.2d 161 (1947).

[68] Sections 21-3-3, 70-1-4, 1953 N.M. Comp. Laws; Maxwell Land Grant Co. v. Dawson, 151 U.S. 586, 14 S.Ct. 458, 38 L.Ed. 279 (1894), reversing 7 N.M. 133, 34 P. 191 (1893). Cf. also 49 Am. Jur., Statute of Frauds, §§ 26-100.

[69] Kingston v. Walters, 14 N.M. 368, 93 P. 700 (1908).

[70] Holton v. Reed, 193 F.2d 390 (C.C.A.N.M. 1951). The New Mexico Supreme Court has held that the equity jurisdiction conferred upon it by the general government is the same as that possessed by the Chancery of England, and is subject to neither limitation nor restraint by state legislation.—Huneke v. Dold, 7 N.M. 5, 32 P. 45 (1893).

Contracts must be determined according to the *lex loci*, or the law of the place where they were made, unless there be a contrary proviso,[71] and it is not a proper function of the courts to relieve either party to a contract from its binding effect where it has been entered into without fraud or imposition and is not due to a mistake against which equity will afford relief.[72]

Any person, persons, or body politic, holding, or who may hold, any right or title to real estate in New Mexico, be it absolute or limited, in possession, remainder, or reversion, may convey the same in the manner and subject to the restrictions prescribed in law.[73] The right of alienation is one of the chief elements of property values, and is possessed by all citizens alike.[74]

With the exception of the legislative enactment of 1880, referred to hereinbefore,[75] whereby realty belonging to any religious, charitable, or educational corporation could not be sold or mortgaged except by consent of a judge of the Supreme court,[76] there have not been, nor are there now, any restrictions in New Mexico directly affecting the free exercise of the Church's right to alienate ecclesiastical property. And although the right of eminent domain shall never be so abridged or construed as to prevent the legislature from taking the property and franchises of incorporated bodies and subjecting them to the public use, the same as the property of individuals,[77] no person shall be deprived of life, liberty, or property without due process of law; nor shall any person be denied the equal protection of the laws.[78]

[71] Leitensdorfer v. Webb, 1 N.M. 34 (1853), affirmed 61 U.S. (20 How.) 176, 15 L.Ed. 891 (1858).

[72] In re Tocci, 45 N.M. 133, 112 P.2d 515 (1941).

[73] Sect. 70-1-3, 1953 N.M. Comp. Law.

[74] Territory v. Delinquent Tax List of Bernalillo County, 12 N.M. 139, 76 P. 307 (1904).

[75] Cf. *supra,* pp. 103-104.

[76] 1880 N.M. Laws, ch. 2, § 5. This restriction was repealed by 1909 N.M. Laws, ch. 23, § 1.

[77] N.M. Constitution, Art. XI, § 18; State ex rel. Biel v. Royal Neighbors of America, 44 N.M. 8, 96 P.2d 705 (1940).

[78] N.M. Constitution, Art. II, § 18.

Section 2.   Canon Law

At Canon law, not every transaction involving an outlay of money or property can be regarded as an act of alienation. The field of transactions in which the laws on alienation are operative is the restricted sphere of what constitutes a canonical corporation's stable capital,[79] as distinguished from the liquid assets thereof. Canon lawyers usually define stable capital as including all those assets which constitute the permanent basis of the financial structure of a canonical corporation,[80] assets which are not in ordinary circulation.[81] It is that capital which has been legitimately set aside to remain intact and to serve as a source of regular income.[82]

Within the framework of the foregoing qualification, the term "alienation" admits of a very wide sense, and includes any and all contracts whereby the financial condition of the Church is legally jeopardized.[83] Such contracts or acts of alienation by which a third person acquires any right to the real or personal property of a canonical corporation include: sale, exchange, gift, donation, mortgage, leases and rentals extending for a period of time longer than nine years, negotiation of loans, allowing passive easements or servitudes, renouncing active easements or servitudes, going surety for others, contracting debts, compromising and yielding lawsuits, and pawning church goods.[84]

---

[79] Heston, *The Alienation of Church Property in the United States,* The Catholic University of America Canon Law Studies, n. 132 (Washington, D.C.: The Catholic University of America Press, 1941), p. 72 (hereinafter cited Heston).

[80] Coronata, II, 493.

[81] Cf. Vermeersch-Creusen, II, 595.

[82] Heston, p. 73.

[83] *Ibid.,* p. 70. "The term *alienation* includes not only purchases or transfers of property, but includes as well any contract, debt, or obligation. The Canon Law regards all transactions, which may render the financial condition of the Institute, Province, or religious house less secure, as alienations."—Letter of Apostolic Delegate, U.S., to all Religious Superiors (Private), 13 Nov. 1936 (Bouscaren's Digest, II, 161).

[84] Cf. canons 1529-1543; Heston, pp. 69-70. Sale, exchange, and donation of church property constitute alienation in the restricted sense; the other

Without prejudice to the provisions of canon 1281, § 1 [requiring the permission of the Holy See for the valid alienation or transfer of images and relics of great importance], to alienate imperishable church property, whether movable or immovable, there is required: 1) a written appraisal of the property made by reliable experts; 2) a justifying reason, i.e., some urgent need, the evident advantage to the Church, or the promotion of piety; 3) the permission of the competent superior, without which the alienation is invalid.[85] Furthermore, other opportune precautions needed for the forestalling of loss to the Church are not to be overlooked, but shall be specified by the respective superior according to the circumstances of the case.[86]

Property is not to be alienated for a price less than that specified in the appraisal.[87] Moreover, the alienation should be executed by way of public auction, or at least it should be advertised, unless circumstances suggest a different course, and the property is to be awarded to the one who, all things considered, makes the higher bid.[88]

The competent superior whose permission is required for the validity of the acts of alienation is determined by the estimated value of the property in question, as set by the experts.[89] The Code provides that if the property involved be a precious object, or if its value exceeds 30,000 lire or francs, the permission of the Holy See is required.[90] However, on July 13, 1951, the Sacred Consistorial Congregation reduced that limit to 10,000 gold

---

contracts above-enumerated spell out alienation in a wider sense. For the purpose of this study, however, the foregoing distinction is purely academic.

[85] Canon 1530, § 1, 1°-3°. Since the canon speaks of an appraisal to be made *"a probis peritis,"* it follows that at least two such experts are required.

[86] Canon 1530, § 2.

[87] Canon 1531, § 1.

[88] Canon 1531, § 2.

[89] Code Comm., 24 Nov. 1920—*A.A.S.* XII (1920), 577; Bouscaren's Digest, I, 729.

[90] Canon 1532, § 1, 1°-2°.

francs,[91] and on October 18, 1952, it declared this sum to be the equivalent of 5,000 U.S. dollars.[92]

If the value of the property does not exceed 1,000 lire or francs [$167], the local ordinary is competent to grant the permission after he has heard the council of administration, unless the property is of very slight value and the interested parties give their consent.[93] And if the value of the property involved lies between 1,000 and 30,000 lire or francs [i.e., between $167 and $5,000], the local ordinary is competent to grant the permission, provided that he shall have obtained the consent of the cathedral chapter (board of diocesan consultors), of the council of administration, and of the interested parties.[94]

The formalities required under the rules of canons 1530-1532 must be observed not only in connection with the alienation of church property in the restricted sense, but also in the making of any contract which may jeopardize the condition of the Church.[95] Thus, for example, if there be a legitimate reason for church

[91] S.C.Consist., 13 July 1951—*A.A.S.*, XLIII (1951), 602; Bouscaren's Digest, III, 212.

[92] S.C.Consist. (Private), 18 Oct. 1952.—Bouscaren's Digest, IV, 391. The bishops of the United States, by virtue of their quinquennial faculties, are authorized to permit, in an urgent case, alienation up to $10 thousand. They must, however, advise the Holy See within the year of the use of this faculty.—Cf. Bouscaren's Digest, I, 66; III, 581. The Apostolic Delegate is authorized to allow alienations of property belonging to religious institutes up to the value of $500 thousand.—Letter of the Apostolic Delegate, U.S. (Private), 3 April 1947 [Bouscaren's Digest, III, 368; *The Jurist*, VII (1947), 339].

[93] Canon 1532, § 2. The sum of 1,000 lire or francs is to be taken as a sum equal to one-thirtieth of $5,000, or approximately $167.—S.C.Consist. (Private), 18 Oct. 1952 (Bouscaren's Digest, IV, 392).

[94] Canon 1532, § 3. If one of the above-mentioned bodies refuses its consent, the ordinary cannot supply it (S.C.Conc., 14 Jan. 1922—*A.A.S.*, XIV (1922), 160; Bouscaren's Digest, I, 730). Nor can the local ordinary validate an act of alienation which was invalid because of non-observance of the required formalities (S.C.Conc., 18 May 1919—*A.A.S.*, XI (1919), 382; Bouscaren's Digest, I, 727).

[95] Canon 1533.

property to be pledged or mortgaged, or if debts must be contracted, the competent superior must demand that a previous hearing be given to all interested parties, and he must see to it that the debt be liquidated as soon as possible.[96] For this reason, the annual rate of amortization payments shall be designated in advance by the competent superior.[97]

Contracts leasing church-owned land must be made according to the provisions of canon 1531, § 2, i.e., the land may not be leased except by way of public auction or other public announcement, unless special circumstances suggest a different course of action. Furthermore, provisions must always be made for the protection of boundaries, adequate maintenance, and payment of rent, with appropriate guarantees for the observance of these provisions.[98]

In the leasing of ecclesiastical goods, the norm of canon 1479 must be observed (which forbids the holder of a benefice to receive payment of the rent for over six months in advance from leased property of the benefice) and in addition the regulations following:

[96] Canon 1538, § 1. A pledge (*pignus*) under Anglo-American law is a contract of bailment whereby the bailee remits a chattel to the bailer in surety for a debt.—Cf. Cleary, *Canonical Limitation on the Alienation of Church Property*, The Catholic University of America Canon Law Studies, n. 100 (Washington, D.C.: The Catholic University of America Press, 1936), p. 99. A mortgage (*hypotheca*) at English common law was a contract whereby a debtor, to secure payment of his debt, conveyed realty in the form of a conveyance in fee to the mortgagee, subject to the payment of the debt as a condition subsequent. The performance of this condition gave the mortgagor a right to re-enter and to the restoring of his estate. Default in the payment gave the mortgagee an absolute title to property conveyed. Gradually, however, the Chancery granted the mortgagor an equity of redemption, whereby the mortgagee was required to institute foreclosure proceedings. A further relaxation permitted the mortgagee to recover only the amount of his loan. It is this view which most States have adopted, viz., that a mortgage merely gives the mortgagee a lien on the conveyance.—Cf. Stenger, *The Mortgaging of Church Property*, The Catholic University of America Canon Law Studies, n. 169 (Washington, D.C.: The Catholic University of America Press, 1942), pp. 66-71.

[97] Canon 1538, § 2.

[98] Canon 1541, § 1.

1) If the value of the lease exceeds 30,000 lire or francs [$5,000] and the term of the lease is more than nine years, the permission of the Holy See is required; if the term does not exceed nine years, the provision of canon 1532, § 3, must be observed [i.e., the local ordinary's permission is required, together with the consent of the board of diocesan consultors, the consent of the council of administration, and the consent of any interested parties].[99]

2) If the value is between 1,000 and 30,000 lire or francs [between $167 and $5,000] and the term exceeds nine years, the same provision of canon 1532, § 3, must be observed; if the term does not exceed nine years, canon 1532, § 2, applies [i.e., there is required the permission of the local ordinary after consultation with the council of administration, as well as the consent of the parties interested].[100]

3) If the value does not exceed 1,000 lire or francs [$167] but the term is longer than nine years, the same provision of canon 1532, § 2, must be observed; if the term does not exceed nine years, the lease can be made by the competent administrators after notifying the ordinary.[101]

With reference to remedies against irregular alienation, the Code provides two types of actions for recovery, depending on whether payment for damages or restitution of status be sought. First of all, the Church can file suit by way of personal action at law against the person who alienated church property without the observance of the requisite formalities and against his heirs; if the alienation was invalid, the Church can enter suit against anyone in possession of the property by way of asserting its right over the property alienated, but the purchaser retains his right against the one guilty of irregular alienation.[102]

A suit contesting an invalid alienation of church property may be entered by the one who alienated it, by his superior, by the successor of either in office, and by any cleric assigned to the

---

[99] Canon 1541, § 2, 1°.

[100] Canon 1541, § 2, 2°.

[101] Canon 1541, § 2, 3°.

[102] Canon 1534, § 1.

church which sustained the loss.[103]   Lastly, it should be observed that if the invalidly alienated property is recovered, personal action against the alienator is extinguished.[104]   Like Anglo-American law,[105] Canon law does not allow cumulative action for both restitution and damages.

ARTICLE 3.   SPECIAL PROVISIONS AFFECTING CHURCH
PROPERTY IN NEW MEXICO

Section 1.   Zoning Laws

For the purpose of promoting health, safety, morals, or the general welfare of the community, the legislative or governing bodies of incorporated cities, towns, and villages in New Mexico are empowered to regulate the height, number of stories, size of buildings and other structures, the percentage of lot that may be occupied, the size of the yards, the density of population, the location and use of buildings, structures, and lands for trade, industry, residence, or other purposes.[106] The given municipality may be divided into districts and the governing body may then enact regulations [107] to govern or restrict the erection, construction, alteration, or use of buildings or lands.[108] These regulations, however, do not become effective until after a public hearing in relation thereto, at which all parties in interest and citizens alike have an opportunity to voice their feelings.[109]

Although these regulations, restrictions, and boundaries may

[103] Canon 1534, § 2.

[104] Cf. Heston, p. 146.

[105] "Damages and restitution are alternative remedies, only one of which will be given as remedy for a breach of contract."—*Restatement*, § 384.

[106] Sect. 14-28-9, 1953 N.M. Comp. Laws. It is interesting to note that it was not until 1926 that the United States Supreme Court expressed its plenary approval of zoning laws.—Village of Euclid v. Ambler Realty Co., 272 U.S. 365, 47 S.Ct. 114, 71 L.Ed. 303 (1926) [hereinafter cited Ambler Case].

[107] The test for determining the validity of each regulation is its substantial relation to the public health, morals, and general welfare of the community.—Ambler Case, at 395.

[108] Sect. 14-28-10, 1953 N.M. Comp. Laws.

[109] Sect. 14-28-12, 1953 N.M. Comp. Laws.

be changed, modified, or repealed, a written protest against such change, modification, or repeal from a minimum of twenty percent of the property owners in the area will estop the amendments from becoming effective in the absence of a favorable vote of three-fourths of all the members of the governing body of the municipality.[110]

A Zoning Commission may be appointed by the municipality to make proper recommendations concerning regulations to be enforced in the various districts thereof,[111] and the local governing body may provide by ordinance for the enforcement of such regulations, a violation of which is a misdemeanor.[112]

Section 2. Building Laws

The city council and board of trustees of incorporated municipalities in New Mexico have the power to prescribe the thickness and the strength of the walls of buildings and the manner of their construction within the municipality, as well as the power to establish fire limits.[113]

Moreover, the governing body of an incorporated municipality has the power to require the removal from within the city limits of any building or structure which has become so ruined, damaged, or dilapidated as to be a menace to the comfort, health, peace, or safety of the public.[114]

Section 3. Tax Exemption

The power of taxation is inherent in the state,[115] and is a legislative function without any limitation except such as are imposed by constitutional provisions.[116]

[110] Sect. 14-28-13, 1953 N.M. Comp. Laws.

[111] Sect. 14-28-14, 1953 N.M. Comp. Laws.

[112] Sect. 14-28-17, 1953 N.M. Comp. Laws. Zoning legislation is a proper subject of police power.—Ambler Case, at 387.

[113] Sect. 14-28-2, 1953 N.M. Comp. Laws.

[114] Sect. 14-28-3, 1953 N.M. Comp. Laws.

[115] Flynn, Welch & Yates v. State Tax Commission, 38 N.M. 131, 28 P.2d 889 (1934).

[116] First State Bank of Mountainair v. State Tax Commission, 40 N.M. 319, 59 P.2d 667 (1936).

All tangible property in New Mexico is subject to taxation in proportion to its value, and should be taxed, unless it be specifically exempted by the Constitution or its authority.[117] Thus, taxation is the rule, and exemption is the exception; exemptions are never presumed, for the burden is on claimant to establish clearly his right to exemption, and the intention to make exemption must be expressed in clear and unambiguous terms in statutes and constitutional provisions.[118] The granting of an exemption from taxation is the freeing from a tax liability which others may be subject to, the freeing or lightening of the burden of the taxpayer, or the relieving or lessening of the load carried.[119] In a word, it is the freeing from the burden of enforced contribution to the expenses and maintenance of the government.[120]

The exemption granted to church property, public libraries, educational and charitable institutions, and cemeteries not used or held for private or corporate profit, proceeds upon the theory of the public good accomplished by them, and of the peculiar benefits derived by the public in general from their conduct.[121]

Specifically, in New Mexico there are three types of tax exemptions in favor of property used for religious, charitable, and educational purposes which might be considered germane to this study. They are the exemptions from Compensating or Use Tax, Inheritance Tax, and Property Tax. The first two are statutory exemptions, the third is established by constitutional provision.

With reference to Compensating or Use Tax, the storage, use, or other consumption of the tangible personal property of any religious, educational, charitable or eleemosynary institution, in the conduct of their regular religious, charitable, educational, or

---

[117] Sims v. Vosburg, 43 N.M. 255, 91 P.2d 434 (1939); Dillard v. State Tax Commission, 53 N.M. 12, 201 P.2d 345 (1948); Storrie Project Water Users Ass'n. v. Gonzales, 53 N.M. 421, 209 P.2d 530 (1949); Town of Atrisco v. Monohan, 56 N.M. 70, 240 P.2d 216 (1952).

[118] Flaska v. State, 51 N.M. 13, 177 P.2d 174 (1947).

[119] State ex rel. Salazar v. Humble Oil & Refining Co., 55 N.M. 395, 234 P.2d 339 (1951).

[120] Asplund v. Alarid, 29 N.M. 129, 219 P. 786 (1923).

[121] State v. Locke, 29 N.M. 148, 219 P. 790 (1923).

eleemosynary functions, is specifically exempted [122] from a tax of two (2%) percent of the sales price thereof.[123]

Exempted from Inheritance Tax is

> any portion of the estate of any decedent passing by will to or for the use of . . . any corporation or association, organized and operated exclusively for religious, charitable, scientific, literary or educational purposes, if no part of the net earnings of the corporation or association enures to the benefit of any private stockholder or individual; and all of such property so passed shall be used for the purposes of said corporation or association within the State of New Mexico . . .[124]

The New Mexico Constitution provides, in regard to Property Tax, that

> . . . All church property, all property used for educational or charitable purposes, [and] all cemeteries not used or held for private or corporate profit . . . shall be exempt from taxation.
>
> Provided, however, that . . . property acquired by churches, property acquired and used for educational or charitable purposes, and property acquired by cemeteries not used or held for private or corporate profit . . . by outright purchase or trade, where such property was, prior to such transfer, subject to the lien of any tax or assessment for the principal or interest of any bonded indebtedness shall not be exempt from such lien, nor from the payment of such taxes or assessments.[125]

Where the provisions of the Constitution specify certain property to be exempted from taxation, such provisions necessarily exclude other property not therein mentioned.[126] That of course,

[122] Sect. 72-17-4, 1953 N.M. Comp. Laws. "Tangible personal property" is, by statutory definition, property which may be seen, weighed, measured, felt, touched, or is in any other manner perceptible to the senses.

[123] Sect. 72-17-3, 1953 N.M. Comp. Laws.

[124] Sect. 31-16-1, 1953 N.M. Comp. Laws.

[125] N.M. Constitution, Art. VIII, § 3, as amended November 3, 1914 and November 5, 1946.

[126] State v. Board of Trustees of Town of Las Vegas, 28 N.M. 237, 210 P. 101 (1922).

is most consistent with the established principle that taxation is the rule and exemption the exception, and presents no difficulty. But the matter of ascertaining, in any given situation, what property *de facto* is "used for educational or charitable purposes" or what property can be said to be "church property" raises some interesting questions.

It is necessary to note, first of all, that ordinarily an exemption provision must receive a strict construction, and that no claim of exemption should be sustained unless it lies within the express letter of the necessary scope of the exemption clause.[127] Thus, one who claims exemption from a tax must bring himself clearly within the exemption provision.[128] However, in an interesting case [129] decided in 1933, the New Mexico Supreme Court noted that the canon of strict construction is very general, often

[127] Samosa v. Lopez, 19 N.M. 312, 142 P. 927 (1914); Peisker v. Unemployment Compensation Commission, 45 N.M. 307, 115 P.2d 62 (1941); Robert E. McKee, General Contractor, Inc. v. Bureau of Revenue, 63 N.M. 185, 315 P.2d 832 (1957).

[128] Iden v. Bureau of Revenue, 43 N.M. 205, 89 P.2d 519 (1939).

[129] Temple Lodge No. 6, A. F. & A. M. v. Tierney, 37 N.M. 178, 20 P.2d 280 (1933) [hereinafter cited Temple Lodge Case]. A Masonic Lodge, a corporation, sued to enjoin the collection of taxes assessed upon the Masonic Temple owned by it in Albuquerque. The assessed property consisted of certain lots, and the Masonic Temple thereon, consisting of lodge halls, club rooms, offices, dining room, cloakrooms, etc., used as the meeting place for the members of the appellant lodge, another Masonic Lodge, a Chapter of Royal Arch Masons, a Commandery of Knights Templar, a Temple of the Order of the Mystic Shrine, and for the organizations De Molay, Job's Daughters, Eastern Star, and White Shrine; the facilities of the building being primarily for the use of Freemasons and their families to carry on the functions, work, and objects of Masonry. Plaintiff's single contention was that said property was "used for educational or [and] charitable purposes," within the meaning of N.M. Const., art. 8, § 3, and accordingly was exempt from taxation. Defendant's contention was that the use to which the assessed property was devoted did not exclude a certain amount of social enjoyment and gratification; that the educational advantages were not open to non-members; that the charity was ordinarily and preferably, though not necessarily or entirely, confined to members and their families; that the real object of this lodge and the main use of its property was fraternity, rather than charity or

helpful, sometimes of little use.[130] The court declared that while the appellee invoked the familiar doctrine of strict construction,[131] where the exemption was for the promotion of religious, educational, charitable, or similar objects deemed beneficial to the state, and for affording a *quid pro quo,* an exception had frequently been declared.[132]

The Temple Lodge Case constitutes a significant precedent in that it underlies the fact that the Constitution does not require that such property be used exclusively for purely educational or charitable purposes.[133] Wrote Chief Justice Watson:

> The broad expression "used for educational or charitable purposes" necessarily imposes upon the court a severe task of interpretation. It is easy to instance purposes clearly within it. It is not difficult to suggest instances which would reduce to absurdity a rule too liberal . . . The line of demarcation cannot be projected. It can take shape only by the gradual process of adjudicating this or that purpose or use on the one side of it or on the other, or by change in the constitutional criteria.
>
> . . . Charity and education are no less effective, and sometimes more so, when their austere qualities are coated and hidden by fraternal and social intercourse. The strictness herein demanded by appellee might open a serious question as to whether some of the more successful and useful churches could qualify as religious societies.[134]

Property used for educational purposes continues to enjoy exemption from taxation only as long as the property is used for such purposes.[135] Two decisions wherein the court ruled that the property in question did not possess educational characteristics warranting exemption may here be cited. In one case, a

---

education. From a judgment in favor of the defendant, the plaintiff appealed. Judgment of the lower court was reversed.

[130] Temple Lodge Case, at 184.

[131] Temple Lodge Case, at 183.

[132] Temple Lodge Case, at 184.

[133] Temple Lodge Case, at 185.

[134] Temple Lodge Case, at 187-188.

[135] Berger v. University of New Mexico, 28 N.M. 666, 217 P. 245 (1923).

sorority chapter house, used primarily as a dormitory and boarding house for university students, was held not used for "educational purposes," and therefore was not exempt from taxation.[136] It pleased the court to find that the culture afforded by college sorority life is not "educational," so as to exempt the property in question from taxation, even though the sorority was incorporated to encourage scholarship.[137]   In the second case, a dwelling house and lot which were owned by a church and which were rented were not exempt from taxation as "property used for educational purposes," notwithstanding the fact that the church had acquired and held the property for sixteen years for the purpose of establishing and maintaining a girls' school.[138]

With reference to charitable uses, the use of the property, not its owner's declared objects and purposes, determines the right to exemption thereof from taxation as used for charitable purposes.[139]   A Lodge, using a building on its property primarily as a lodge home and center for carrying on its charitable and benevolent purposes, was held to be entitled to exemption from taxation, even though it rented rooms in the building to lodge members and prospective members.[140]   The exemption from taxation extends to any hospital used for charitable purposes, even though service is given to some patients who pay for it.[141]

There remains the question of what is meant by "church property" in the constitutional provision for tax exemption. The only

[136] Albuquerque Alumnae Ass'n. of Kappa Kappa Gamma Fraternity v. Tierney, 37 N.M. 156, 20 P.2d 267 (1933).

[137] *Loc. cit.*

[138] Trustees of Property of Protestant Episcopal Church in N. M. v. State Tax Commission, 39 N.M. 419, 48 P.2d 786 (1935).

[139] Albuquerque Lodge No. 461, B. P. O. E. v. Tierney, 39 N.M. 135, 42 P.2d 206 (1935).

[140] *Loc. cit.*

[141] 1912-1913 N.M. Attorney General Reports, 36: ". . . I understand that [St. Joseph's Sanatorium, Silver City,] . . . is primarily of a charitable character and, whether much or little charitable work is done, I believe that it falls within the constitutional exemption and that its property, used for charitable purposes, cannot be taxed."

case [142] tried by the New Mexico Supreme Court on that head was a hard-fought one. The writer suggests that the judgment was arbitrary, and submits that the court in this case gratuitously reversed its policy of a liberal construction as adopted in the Temple Lodge Case, and now applies the canon of strict construction.

The Constitution provides that "all church property" [143] shall be exempt from taxation. In the Holy Faith Case, the court drew a distinction between "all church property" and "all property of churches." [144] It established that, since the Constitution does not employ the latter phraseology, use, and not ownership, is the test of whether church property shall be exempt.[145] Accordingly, the phrase "church property" was construed to mean property required for the use of the church, that is, property used for religious worship and instruction.[146]

In appealing to the *quid pro quo* theory as a justification for exempting property from taxation, the court observed that the teaching and inculcating of religious ideas is beneficial to the state; that the theory necessarily rests upon the assmption that the property of the church will be held and used by the church for those purposes for which the church was incorporated and

---

[142] Church of the Holy Faith, Inc. v. State Tax Commission, 39 N.M. 403, 48 P.2d 777 (1935) [hereinafter cited Holy Faith Case; references thereto are from the Pacific Reporter]. The Church of the Holy Faith, a Protestant parish church in Santa Fe, a corporation organized for religious and charitable purposes, entered suit contesting tax assessment. The property involved was a dwelling house and the lot upon which it was situated. Acquired by devise, it was rented by appellant and the proceeds turned over to the parish church and used as all other funds of the corporation, that is, for religious and charitable purposes. From a judgment of the District Court of Judge Otero sustaining defendants' demurrer and dismissing the complaint, plaintiff appeals. Judgment of the lower court was affirmed in a 3 to 2 split: Justices Bickley, Sadler, and Hudspeth for the majority, Justices Zinn and Watson dissenting.

[143] N.M. Constitution, Art. VIII, § 3.

[144] Holy Faith Case, at 782.

[145] Holy Faith Case, at 784.

[146] Holy Faith Case, at 784.

exists; and that insofar as the property of the church is not so employed, there is no *quid pro quo*.[147]   And yet, the court recognized that "appellant is a corporation organized for religious purposes"; [148] it stipulated for the fact that "all of its funds are devoted to religious and charitable purposes through the religious and charitable activities of the parish church"; [149] and it further agreed that the property in question was rented by appellant "and the proceeds turned over to the parish church and used as other funds of the corporation are used, that is, for religious and charitable purposes." [150]

The majority opinion concluded that

> The property in question is not being used for religious purposes and therefore is not "church property," and also that said property is not being used for "charitable purposes" and is therefore subject to taxation. The fact that the rents accumulated from such property are used for religious or charitable purposes does not alter the situation.[151]

In a brilliant dissenting opinion, in which Justice Watson concurred, Justice Zinn wrote:

> . . . I find the plain meaning of the intended exemption in the phrase "all church property." This phrase does not require metaphysical or logical subtleties to interpret it.
>
> I look to our Constitution and there seek the thought which it expressed to the people of New Mexico who ratified it. I give to it the meaning found in the minds of its makers who are the people who adopted it. "All church property" is plain language, and to the mind of the citizen who voted for its adoption it had but one meaning, simply all property belonging to the church, or all property of the church . . .
>
> Now what did the people of New Mexico understand to be the meaning of the phrase "all church property"? "All" as an adjective means "the whole of," and used as in the Constitution it refers to the amount, quantity, or extent. All

[147] Holy Faith Case, at 784.

[148] Holy Faith Case, at 777.

[149] Holy Faith Case, at 778.

[150] Holy Faith Case, at 778.

[151] Holy Faith Case, at 784.

year includes every day thereof. "All church property," to
the mind of the citizen who voted for the adoption of the
Constitution, includes every piece of property belonging to
the church . . .[152]

[152] Holy Faith Case, at 786. "Ecclesiastical property" at Canon law
means all temporal goods, corporeal (both movable and immovable) and
incorporeal, real and personal, which belong either to the Universal Church,
to the Holy See, or to individual canonical corporations.—Canon 1497, § 1.
And since the Catholic Church is, by divine institution, a juridically perfect society independent of the state, it follows that church property cannot, without the consent of the Church, be subject to taxation imposed by
civil authority.—Schmalzgrueber, *Ius Ecclesiasticum Universum* (5 vols. in
12, Romae, 1843-1845), lib. III, tit. 49, n. 1 ff. In this country, however,
there is not—and by the Constitution of the United States there cannot
be—any official recognition of any religious denomination as an organization with powers that are not derived from civil authority.

CONCLUSIONS

1. The Spanish codes of law took for granted and presumed that the Church has an inherent right to acquire, hold, and administer property as means necessary to its primary end. The elementary concern of the civil law in matters of ecclesiastical property was to provide that the Church's possessions be fully guarded and that its rights thereto and dominion thereof be guaranteed. Since the Code of the Indies constituted mere exceptions to the civil law of the mother country, and inasmuch as the former nowhere attempted to abrogate, or derogate from, the right of the Church to temporal goods as recognized by the latter, it follows that the Crown recognized that right in its colonies as well. (Cf. pp. 17-32.)

2. In general, legal title to the Franciscan-held properties in New Mexico resided in the Crown until such a time as the latter formally ceded its ownership thereof to the Holy See through the Franciscans. No title passed from the Spanish sovereign by mere order of survey, permission to settle, or dedication. This only conferred an equitable right to demand a title, and what was ceded when is a question of fact. (Cf. pp. 32-57.)

3. With reference to the nature of a corporation, Anglo-American jurisprudence follows the English common law in accepting the Fiction Theory of Savigny who, in turn, endeavored to sustain his theory from the commentaries of Innocent IV. Although not the originator of the Fiction Theory, Innocent IV nonetheless took the first step in the *marche vers la personnification.* (Cf. pp. 59-99.)

4. New Mexico law provides for the establishment of non-profit corporations aggregate and sole, both of which, following Anglo-American jurisprudence, fall within the category of private corporations. (Cf. pp. 100-110.)

5. The present non-profit corporation law allowing for the association for religious and charitable purposes seems satisfactorily to secure for the incorporation of parishes and dioceses a reasonable assurance that the canonical concept of these two in-

stitutions will not be jeopardized. The charter provisions and by-laws of such corporation aggregate could contain safeguards whereby *de facto* the control of the corporation would not devolve on lay trustees. Such a corporation aggregate would constitute a safe mode of tenure of church property. (Cf. pp. 134-136.)

6. The disadvantages of the sole corporation are that it is a matter of conjecture how the New Mexico statute would be constructed with reference to the nature of tenure by the sole incorporator; and that upon a vacancy in the incorporator's office the fee is in abeyance and no one is duly qualified to transact business during the interregnum. (Cf. pp. 134-138.)

a) The first disadvantage is common to all corporations sole at Anglo-American law; it could not be forestalled by statute, but it is submitted that a court would probably admit parol evidence of Canon law to explain the nature of tenure and ownership of church property according to ecclesiastical law. (Cf. p. 142.)

b) The second drawback could very easily be precluded by statutory amendment. (Cf. pp. 142-143.)

c) Aside from these difficulties, a corporation sole under New Mexico law offers a safe method of holding church property in a manner approved by the Holy See. This mode of tenure forever protects title to church property by passing it from predecessor to successor by simple operation of law. In practice, the only formality required would be presentation of proof of the fact of succession. (Cf. p. 143.)

7. Because of its very nature the Church cannot take, or hold an interest in, property for objects other than educational, charitable, and religious. Since "evangelization" and "preaching the gospel" are in New Mexico valid objects of bounty to adequate guarantees, so likewise would be a grant for the purposes of Catholicism. (Cf. pp. 144, 147-148.)

8. The Spanish *ganancial* system, or community property laws, in vogue in New Mexico, will govern and indirectly affect charitable donations *inter vivos* when the grantor is married. (Cf. pp. 145-147.)

9. At Canon law, anyone who is entitled by the natural and ecclesiastical law to dispose freely of goods may relinquish them in favor of religion or charity not only by direct donation but by

testamentary disposition as well. New Mexico jurisprudence violates the Church's right to succeed to legacies, bequests, and devices by holding that the right to make a will is not a property right or a natural or inherent right, but is purely a statutory right subject to the legislature's complete control. In practice, however, the rights conferred by statute are favorable, and the doctrine of *cy pres* is operative to a generous extent. (Cf. pp. 147-159.)

10. Exemptions from Compensating or Use Tax, Inheritance Tax, and Property Tax are granted in New Mexico in favor of education, charity, and religion. But in regard to Property Tax, New Mexico law imposes the burden of taxation upon that part of ecclesiastical property which it judges to be used not for purposes of religious worship and instruction. In so doing, it violates the Church's right to immunity which frees all possessions of canonical corporations from tributes, assessments, and taxes imposed by the secular law. (Cf. pp. 187-195.)

BIBLIOGRAPHY

SOURCES

Acta Apostolicae Sedis, Commentarium Officiale, Romae, 1909-1928; Civitate Vaticana, 1929-

Acta et Decreta Concilii Plenarii Baltimorensis Tertii, A.D. MDCCCL-XXXIV, Baltimorae: Typis Joannis Murphy et Sociorum, 1886.

Acts of the Legislative Assembly of the Territory of New Mexico, 1875-1876, Santa Fe: Manderfield & Tucker, 1876.

Acts of the Legislative Assembly of the Territory of New Mexico, 1878, Santa Fe: Manderfield & Tucker, 1878.

Acts of the Legislative Assembly of the Territory of New Mexico, 1880, Santa Fe: R. W. Webb, 1880.

Acts of the Legislative Assembly of the Territory of New Mexico, 1889, Santa Fe: New Mexican Printing Co., 1889.

Acts of the Legislative Assembly of the Territory of New Mexico, 1905, Santa Fe: New Mexican Printing Co., 1905.

American Jurisprudence, 58 vols. and Indices, Rochester, N.Y.: Bancroft-Whitney Co., 1935-1952.

Archives of the Archdiocese of Santa Fe, Chancery Office, Santa Fe, New Mexico.

Bulario de la Iglesia Mejicana: Documentos Relativos a Erecciones, Desmembraciones, etc., de Diócesis Mejicanas, compiladas por Jesus Garcia Gutierrez, Mexico, D.F.: Editorial "Buena Prensa," S.A., 1951.

Bullarium Franciscanum Romanorum Pontificum . . . , notis illustratum studio et labore Fr. Joannis Hyacinthi Sbaraleae, 3 vols., Romae: Typis Sacrae Congregationis de Propaganda Fide, 1759-1765.

Canon Law Digest, The, 4 vols., Milwaukee: Bruce Publishing Co., Vol. I, 1934, Vol. II, 1943, Vol. III, 1954, edited by T. Lincoln Bouscaren; Vol. IV, 1958, edited by T. Lincoln Bouscaren and James I. O'Connor.

Chavez, Angelico, *Archives of the Archdiocese of Santa Fe: 1678-1900,* Washington, D.C.: Academy of American Franciscan History, 1957.

Codex Iuris Canonici, Pii X Pontificis Maximi iussu digestus, Benedicti Papae XV auctoritate promulgatus, Romae: Typis Polyglottis Vaticanis, 1917.

Códigos Españoles, Concordados y Anotados, Los, 14 codes in 12 vols., Madrid: La Publicidad, 1847-1851.

Colección de Leyes, Decretos, Reglamentos, Circulares, Ordenes, Acuerdos y Estudios Relativos a la Desamortización y Nacionalización de los Bienes de Corporaciones, formada por el Lic. G. Labastida, con autorización de la Secretaría de Estado y del Despacho de Hacienda y Crédito Público, Mexico, D.F.: Palacio Nacional, 1893.

Concilii Plenarii Baltimorensis II in Ecclesia Metropolitana Baltimorensi a die VII ad diem XXI Octobris A.D. MDCCLXVI habiti et a Sede Apostolica Recogniti Acta et Decreta, 2. ed., Baltimorae: Joannes Murphy, 1880.

Constitutions of Pope Nicholas III, Clement V, and Innocent XI Clarifying the Rule of the Friars Minor, The, translation authorized and distributed by the Very Reverend Ministers Provincial, O.F.M. in the United States, Chicago: Franciscan Herald Press, [no date].

Corpus Iuris Canonici, editio Lipsiensis secunda, post Aemilii Richteri curas . . . instruxit Aemilius Friedberg, 2 vols., Lipsiae, 1879-1881.

Corpus Juris Secundum, 95 vols. and Indices, Brooklyn, N.Y.: The American Book Co., 1936-1951.

Council Journal of the New Mexico Territorial Legislative Assembly, 1878, in ms. [Available at the office of the Secretary of State, Santa Fe, New Mexico.]

Decretales Gregorii Papae IX, suae integritati una cum glossis restitutae cum privilegio Gregorii XIII, Pont. Max. et aliorum Principum, Romae, 1582.

Decretum Gratiani, emendatum et notationibus illustratum una cum glossis restitutae cum privilegio Gregorii XIII, Pont. Max. et aliorum Principum, Romae, 1582.

Hernaez, Francisco J., *Colección de Bulas, Breves y Otros Documentos Relativos a la Iglesia de América y Filipinas,* 2 vols., Bruselas: Vromant, 1879.

Jaffé, Philippus, *Regesta Pontificum Romanorum ab condita Ecclesia ad annum post Christum MCXCVIII,* ed. 2. correctam et auctam auspiciis Gulielmi Wattenbach curaverunt S. Loewenfeld, F. Kaltenbrunner, P. Ewald, 2 vols., Lipsiae, 1885-1888.

Laws of the State of New Mexico Passed by the Legislature, 1951, [no place of publication]: Ward Anderson Printing Co., Inc., 1951.

Laws of the State of New Mexico Passed by the Legislature, 1957, Santa Fe: Schifani Brothers Printing Co., 1957.

Laws of the Territory of New Mexico Passed by the Legislative Assembly, 1851-1852, Santa Fe: Collins & Co., 1852.

Laws of the Territory of New Mexico Passed by the Legislative Assembly, 1853-1854, Santa Fe: Collins & Co., 1853.

Laws of the Territory of New Mexico Passed by the Legislative Assembly, 1856-1857, Santa Fe: Office of the Democrat, 1857.

Laws of the Territory of New Mexico Passed by the Legislative Assembly, 1860-1861, Santa Fe: Juan T. Russell, 1861.

Laws of the Territory of New Mexico Passed by the Legislative Assembly, 1863-1864, Albuquerque: Hezekiah S. Johnson, 1864.

Laws of the Territory of New Mexico Passed by the Legislative Assembly, 1866-1867, Santa Fe: Manderfeld & Tucker, 1867.

Laws of the Territory of New Mexico Passed by the Legislative Assembly, 1867-1868, Santa Fe: Manderfeld & Tucker, 1867.

Laws of the Territory of New Mexico Passed by the Legislative Assembly, 1871-1872, Santa Fe: A. P. Sullivan, 1872.

Legislación Mexicana: Colección completa de las disposiciones legislativas expedidas desde la independencia de la República (1687-1889), ordenada por Manuel Dublan y Jose Maria Lozano, edición oficial, 19 vols., Mexico, D.F.: Imprenta del Comercio, 1876-1890.

Liber Sextus Decretalium D. Bonifacii Papae VIII suae integritati una cum Clementinis et Extravagantibus earumque glossis restitutus, Romae, 1582.

Magnum Bullarium Romanum, a Beato Leone Magno usque ad S.D.N. Benedictum XIII . . . , editio novissima, 8 vols., Luxemburgi, 1727.

Mansi, Joannes, *Sacrorum Conciliorum Nova et Amplissima Collectio,* 53 vols. in 60, Parisiis, 1901-1927.

Moore, John B., *Digest of International Law,* 8 vols., Washington, D.C.: Government Printing Office, 1906.

New Mexico Digest, 1852 to Date, 6 vols. and Cumulative Annual Pocket Parts through 1958, St. Paul: West Publishing Co., 1948-1958.

New Mexico Statutes 1953, Annotated, edited by John W. Tranberg and Arie Poldervaart, 12 vols. and Pocket Supplements through 1957, Indianapolis: The Allen Smith Co., 1954-1957.

Potthast, A., *Regesta Pontificum Romanorum inde ab anno post Christum natum MCXCVIII ad annum MCCCIV,* 2 vols., Berolini, 1874-1875.

Recopilación de Leyes de los Reynos de las Indias, mandadas imprimir y publicar por la Magestad Católica del Rey Don Carlos II, 9 Books in 4 vols., 2. ed., Madrid: Antonio Balbas, 1756.

Regula et Constitutiones Generales Ordinis Fratrum Minorum, Romae: Curia Generalis Ordinis, 1953.

Report of the Attorney General of New Mexico, 1878, in ms. [Available at the office of the Attorney General, Santa Fe, New Mexico.]

Report of the Attorney General of New Mexico, 1943-1944, Santa Fe: [no specification], [no date].

Report and Opinions of the Attorney General of New Mexico, 1912-1913, Santa Fe: New Mexican Printing Co., 1914.

Revised Statutes of the United States Passed at the Forty-Third Congress, 1873-1874, embracing the statutes of the United States in force on December 1, 1873, 2. ed., Washington, D.C.: Government Printing Co., 1878.

Scott, Samuel P., *Las Siete Partidas,* translation and notes by Samuel P. Scott, New York: Commerce Clearing House, Inc., 1931.

Seventh Synod of the Archdiocese of Santa Fe, celebrated on December 2, 1958, by His Excellency, Most Rev. Edwin V. Byrne, D.D., Archbishop of Santa Fe, Saint Francis Cathedral, Santa Fe, Albuquerque: House of Moulton, 1958.

Statutes at Large of the United States of America, Washington, D.C.: Government Printing Office, Vol. XX, 1879; Vol. LXII, 1949.

REFERENCE WORKS

Abbo, J. - Hannan, J., *The Sacred Canons: A Concise Presentation of the Current Disciplinary Norms of the Church*, 2 vols., rev. ed., St. Louis: B. Herder Book Co., 1957.

Adams, E. B. - Chavez, A., *The Missions of New Mexico, 1776: A Description by Fray Francisco Atanasio Dominguez with other Contemporary Documents*, translated and annotated by Eleanor B. Adams and Fray Angelico Chavez, Albuquerque: University of New Mexico Press, 1956.

Alaman, Lucas, *Historia de Mexico*, 5 vols., Mexico, D.F.: Editorial Jus, 1942.

Augustine, Charles, *A Commentary of the New Code of Canon Law*, 8 vols., Vol. II, 3. ed., St. Louis: B. Herder Book Co., 1919.

Ballinger, Richard A., *A Treatise on the Property Rights of Husband and Wife, Under the Community or Ganacial System, Adapted to the Statutes and Decisions of Louisiana, Texas, California, Nevada, Washington, Idaho, Arizona, and New Mexico*, Seattle–San Francisco: Bancroft-Whitney Co., 1895.

Bancroft, Hubert H., *The Works of Hubert Bancroft*, 39 vols., San Francisco, Vol. XI, 4 tomes, *History of Mexico*, 1883; Vol. XVII, *History of Arizona and New Mexico*, 1889.

Bartlett, Chester J., *The Tenure of Parochial Property in the United States of America*, The Catholic University of America Canon Law Studies, n. 31, Washington, D.C.: The Catholic University of America, 1926.

Beste, Udalricus, *Introductio in Codicem*, 4 ed., Neapoli: M. D'Auria, Pontificius Editor, 1956.

Blackmar, Frank W., *Spanish Institutions of the Southwest*, Baltimore: Johns Hopkins Press, 1891.

Blackstone, William, *Commentaries on the Laws of England*, annotated by George Sharswood, 4 vols., in 2, Philadelphia: J. B. Lippincott Co., 1898.

Bonfante, Pietro, *Istituzioni di Diritto Romano*, 10. ed., Torino: G. Giappichelli, 1946.

Bouscaren, T. L. - Ellis, A. C., *Canon Law: A Text and Commentary*, 2. revised ed., Milwaukee: Bruce Publishing Co., 1951.

Brinz, A., *Lehrbuch der Pandecten*, Leipzig, 1895.

Brown, Brendan, *The Canonical Juristic Personality with Special Reference to its Status in the United States of America*, The Catholic University of America Canon and Civil Law Studies, n. 39, Washington, D.C.: The Catholic University of America, 1927.

Byrne, Harry J., *Investment of Church Funds: A Study in Administrative Law*, The Catholic University of America Canon Law Studies, n. 309, Washington, D.C.: The Catholic University of America Press, 1951.

Cappello, Felix, *Summa Iuris Canonici*, 3 vols., Vol. II, 4. ed., Romae: Apud Aedes Universitatis Gregorianae, 1945.

———, *Summa Iuris Publici Ecclesiastici,* 5. ed., Romae: Apud Aedes Universitatis Gregorianae, 1943.

Cleary, Joseph F., *Canonical Limitations on the Alienation of Church Property,* The Catholic University of America Canon Law Studies, n. 100, Washington, D.C.: The Catholic University of America, 1936.

Comyns, Joseph J., *Papal and Episcopal Administration of Church Property,* The Catholic University of America Canon Law Studies, n. 147, Washington, D.C.: The Catholic University of America Press, 1942.

Coronata, M. Conte a, *Institutiones Iuris Canonici,* 5 vols., Vol. II, 4. ed., Taurini-Romae: Marietti, 1951.

Cuevas, Mariano, *Historia de la Iglesia en Mexico,* 3 vols., 3. ed., El Paso: Editorial "Revista Católica," 1928.

Defouri, James H., *Historical Sketch of the Catholic Church in New Mexico,* San Francisco: McCormick Brothers, 1887.

Dignan, Patrick J., *A History of the Legal Incorporation of Catholic Church Property in the United States,* New York: Kenedy & Sons, 1935.

Doheny, William J., *Church Property: Modes of Acquisition,* The Catholic University of America Canon and Roman Law Studies, n. 41, Washington, D.C.: The Catholic University of America, 1927.

Duff, Patrick W., *Personality in Roman Private Law,* Cambridge: University Press, 1938.

Ehler, S. - Morrall, J., *Church and State Through the Centuries,* London: Burns and Oates, 1954.

Ferrara, Francesco, *Teoria delle Persone Giuridiche,* 2. ed. riveduta, Napoli: Eugenio Marghieri, 1923.

Fletcher, William M., *Cyclopedia of the Law of Private Corporations,* 20 vols., revised and permanent edition, Chicago: Callaghan & Co., 1931.

Gierke, O., *Das deutsche Genossenschaftsrecht,* 4 vols., Berlin, 1868-1913.

Gillet, Pierre, *La Personnalité Juridique en Droit Ecclésiastique spécialement chez les Décrétistes et les Décrétalistes et dans le Code de Droit Canonique,* Malines: W. Godenne, 1927.

Godfrey, John, *The Right of Patronage According to the Code of Canon Law,* The Catholic University of America Canon Law Studies, n. 21, Washington, D.C.: The Catholic University of America, 1924.

Gomez, Rafael Hoyos, *Las Leyes de Indias y el Derecho Eclesiastico en la América Española e Islas Filipinas,* Medellin, Colombia: Ediciones Universidad Católica Bolivariana, 1945.

Gomez del Campo, Jorge Martinez, *El Despojo de los Bienes Eclesiasticos en Mexico: Estudio Histórico y Jurídico,* Mexico, D.F.: [no specification], 1940.

Goodwine, John A., *The Right of the Church to Acquire Temporal Goods,* The Catholic University of America Canon Law Studies, n. 131, Washington, D.C.: The Catholic University of America Press, 1941.

Guilday, Peter, *A History of the Councils of Baltimore,* New York: The Macmillan Co., 1932.

Hall, Frederic, *The Laws of Mexico: A Compilation and Treatise Relating to Real Property, Mines, Water Rights, Personal Rights, Contracts, and Inheritances,* San Francisco: A. L. Bancroft Co., 1885.

Hannan, Jerome D., *The Canon Law of Wills,* The Catholic University of America Canon Law Studies, n. 86, Washington, D.C.: The Catholic University of America, 1934.

Hawes, Horace, *The Missions of California and the Rights of the Catholic Church to the Property Pertaining to Them,* argument before the Supreme Court of California, San Francisco: Daily Evening News Office, 1856.

Heintschel, Donald E., *The Medieval Concept of an Ecclesiastical Office,* The Catholic University of America Canon Law Studies, n. 363, Washington, D.C.: The Catholic University of America Press, 1956.

Heston, Edward L., *The Alienation of Church Property in the United States,* The Catholic University of America Canon Law Studies, n. 132, Washington, D.C.: The Catholic University of America, 1941.

Innocentius IV (Sinibaldo dei Fieschi), *Commentaria in Quinque Libros Decretalium,* Venetiis, 1570.

Jhering, R., *Geist des Römischen Rechts,* Leipzig, 1891.

Kanen, Charles F., *Kanen's New Mexico Corporation Laws,* Albuquerque: Morning Journal Press, 1910.

Kent, James, *Commentaries on America Law,* 4 vols., edited by O. W. Holmes, 13. ed., edited by Charles M. Barnes, Boston: Little, Brown, & Co., 1884.

Kerr, Robert J., *A Handbook of Mexican Law,* Chicago: Pan American Law Book Co., 1909.

Madden, Marie, *Political Theory and Law in Medieval Spain,* New York: Fordham University Press, 1930.

Martin, Thomas O., *Adverse Possession, Prescription and Limitation of Actions. The Canonical "Praescriptio,"* The Catholic University of American Canon Law Studies, n. 202, Washington, D.C.: The Catholic University of America Press, 1944.

Mayer, Brantz, *Mexico: Aztec, Spanish, and Republican . . . , and Notices of New Mexico and California,* 2 vols., Vol. II, Hartford: S. Drake & Co., 1851.

Mendieta, Fray Geronimo de, *Historia Ecclesiástica Indiana,* edited by Joaquin Garcia Icazbalceta, Mexico, D.F.: Antigua Librería, 1870.

Michoud, Leon, *La Théorie de la Personnalité Morale et son Application au Droit Français,* 3. ed., míse au courant par Louis Trotabas, 2 vols., Paris: Librairie Générale de Droit et de Jurisprudence, 1932.

Mode of Tenure: Roman Catholic Church Property in the United States, a Survey by the Legal Department of the National Catholic Welfare Conference, Washington, D.C.: National Catholic Welfare Conference, 1941, and Supplement — 1954.

Mora, Jose Maria Luis, *El Clero, El Estado y la Economía Nacional,* Mexico, D.F.: Empresas Editoriales, S.A., 1950.

Moreno, Angel Cruz, *Influencia de la Legislación de Indias en el Derecho Agrario Mexicano,* Mexico, D.F.: Universidad Nacional Autonoma de Mexico, 1950.

Munday, James E., *Ecclesiastical Property in Australia and New Zealand,* The Catholic University of America Canon Law Studies, n. 387, Washington, D.C.: The Catholic University of America Press, 1957.

Murphy, Joseph P., *The Laws of the State of New York Affecting Church Property,* The Catholic University of America Canon Law Studies, n. 388, Washington, D.C.: The Catholic University of America Press, 1957.

McManus, James E., *The Administration of Temporal Goods in Religious Institutes,* The Catholic University of America Canon Law Studies, n. 109, Washington, D.C.: The Catholic University of America, 1937.

Panormitanus (Nicholaus de Tudeschis), *Commentaria in Quinque Libros Decretalium,* 5 vols. in 7, Venetiis, 1588.

Pino, Pedro B., *Noticias Históricas y Estadísticas de la Antigua Provincia del Nuevo Mexico . . . 1812,* adicionadas por el Lic. D. Antonio Barreiro en 1839, y ultimamente anotadas pro el Lic. D. Jose A. de Escudero, Mexico, D.F.: Imprenta de Lara, 1849.

Philibert, Sister M., S.L., *Bishop Lamy, The Castrense, and the Court of Judge Baker,* Denver: Denver Catholic Register Press, 1955.

Pollock, F. - Maitland, F., *History of English Law,* 2 vols., 2. ed., Cambridge: University Press, 1909.

Prescott, William H., *History of the Reign of Ferdinand and Isabella,* 2 vols., Vol. I, 3. ed., New York: American Publishers Corporation, 1838.

Prince, L. Bradford, *A Concise History of New Mexico,* Cedar Rapids, Iowa: The Torch Press, 1912.

Read, Benjamin M., *Illustrated History of New Mexico,* translated from the 2. Spanish ed. by Eleuterio Baca, Santa Fe: New Mexican Printing Co., 1912.

Restatement of the Law on Contracts, St. Paul: American Law Institute, 1933.

Reynolds, Matthew G., *Spanish and Mexican Land Laws: New Spain and Mexico,* St. Louis: Buxton & Skinner Co., 1895.

Ruffini, Francesco, *La Classificazione delle Persone Giuridiche in Sinibaldo dei Fieschi (Innocenzo IV) ed in Federico Carlo di Savigny (1898),* in *Scritti Giuridici Minori,* 2 vols., Vol. II, Milano: A Giuffrè, 1936.

Salpointe, J. B., *Soldiers of the Cross: Notes on the Ecclesiastical History of New Mexico, Arizona and Colorado,* Banning, California: St. Boniface School, 1898.

Savigny, F. K., *System des heutigen Römischen Rechts,* Berlin, 1840.

Schmalzgrueber, Franciscus, *Ius Ecclesiasticum Universum,* 5 vols. in 12, Romae, 1843-1845.

Schmidt, Gustavus, *The Civil Law of Spain and Mexico,* New Orleans: Thomas Rea, 1851.

Schroeder, H. J., *Disciplinary Decrees of the General Councils,* St. Louis: B. Herder Book Co., 1937.

Schulz, Fritz, *Classical Roman Law,* Oxford: Clarendon Press, 1954.

Schwabe, M., *Rechts-subject und Nutzbefugnis,* Basel, 1901.

Simpson, Lesley B., *The Encomienda in New Spain,* Berkeley: University of California Press, 1929.

Smith, Herbert A., *The Law of Associations, Corporate and Incorporate,* Oxford: Clarendon Press, 1914.

Stenger, Joseph B., *The Mortgaging of Church Property,* The Catholic University of America Canon Law Studies, n. 169, Washington, D.C.: The Catholic University of America Press, 1942.

Tierney, Brian, *Foundations of the Conciliar Theory: The Contribution of the Medieval Canonists from Gratian to the Great Schism,* Cambridge: University Press, 1955.

Twitchell, Ralph E., *The Leading Facts of New Mexican History,* 5 vols., Cedar Rapids, Iowa: The Torch Press, 1911-1917.

Vance, John T., *The Background of Hispanic-American Law,* New York: Central Book Co., 1943.

Van Hove, Alphonsus, *Prolegomena ad Codicem Iuris Canonici,* editio altera auctior et emendatior, Mechliniae-Romae: H. Dessain, 1945.

Vareilles-Sommières, G. de, *Les Personnes Morales,* Paris, 1902.

Vera, Fortino H., *Apuntamientos Históricos de los Concilios Provinciales Mexicanos,* Mexico, D.F.: Tipografía Guadalupana, 1893.

Vermeersch, A. - Creusen, J., *Epitome Iuris Canonici,* 3 vols., Vol. II, 6. ed., Mechliniae-Romae: H. Dessain, 1940.

Wernz, F. - Vidal, P., *Ius Canonicum ad Normam Codicis Exactum,* 7 vols. in 8, Romae: Apud Aedes Universitatis Gregorianae, Vol. II, 3. ed., 1943; Vol. IV, Pars II, 1935.

Wiggins, Urban C., *Property Laws of the State of Ohio Affecting Church Property,* The Catholic University of America Canon Law Studies, n. 367, Washington, D.C.: The Catholic University of America Press, 1956.

Woywod, S. - Smith, C., *A Practical Commentary on the Code of Canon Law,* 2 vols., revised by Callistus Smith, revised and enlarged edition, New York: Joseph F. Wagner, Inc., 1948.

Zamacois, Niceto de, *Historia de Mejico,* 19 vols., Mexico, D.F.: J. F. Parres y Comp., 1877-1882.

Ziegler, A. K., *Church and State in Visigothic Spain,* The Catholic University of America Theological Studies, n. 32, Washington, D.C.: The Catholic University of America, 1930.

Zollmann, Carl, *American Civil Church Law,* Columbia University Studies in History, Economics, and Public Law, Vol. 77, New York: Columbia University and Longmans, Green & Co., 1917.

ARTICLES

Chavez, Angelico, "Santa Fe Church and Convent Sites in the Seventeenth and Eighteenth Centuries," *New Mexico Historical Review,* XXIV (1949), 85-93.

Feenstra, R., "L'Histoire des Fondations," *Tijdschrift voor Rechts-geschiedenis–Revue d'Histoire du Droit,* XXIV (1956), 381-448.

Hammond, G. - Rey, A., "The Crown's Participation in the Founding of New Mexico," *New Mexico Historical Review,* XXXII (1957), 293-309.

Keleher, W. A., "Laws of the New Mexico Land Grant," *New Mexico Historical Review,* IV (1929), 350-371.

Lacas, M. M., "The Encomienda in Latin-American History: A Reappraisal," *The Americas,* VII (1952), 259-288.

Machen, Arthur W., "Corporate Personality," *Harvard Law Review,* XXIV (1910), 253-267.

Maitland, Frederick W., "The Corporation Sole," *The Law Quarterly Review,* XVI (1900), 335-354.

Ramona, Sister Mary, S.C.N., "The Ecclesiastical Status of New Mexico (1680-1875)," *The Catholic Historical Review,* XIV (1928-1929), 525-568.

Scholes, France V., "Problems in Early Ecclesiastical History of New Mexico," *New Mexico Historical Review,* VII (1932), 32-74.

——, "Church and State in New Mexico: 1610-1650," *New Mexico Historical Review,* XI (1936), 9-76, 145-178, 283-294, 297-349; XII (1937), 78-106.

Tittmann, Edward D., "The First Irrigation Lawsuit," *New Mexico Historical Review,* II (1927), 363-368.

Ullmann, Walter, "The Delictal Responsibility of Medieval Corporations," *The Law Quarterly Review,* LXIV (1948), 77-96.

Vermeersch, A., "De communi monasterii possessione," *De Religiosis et Missionariis Supplementa et Monumenta Periodica,* V (1913), (20)-(23).

Warner, Louis H., "Conveyance of Property, the Spanish and Mexican Way," *New Mexico Historical Review,* VI (1931), 334-359.

PERIODICALS

Americas, The, Washington, D.C., 1946-

Catholic Historical Review, The, Washington, D.C., 1915-

De Religiosis et Missionariis Supplementa et Monumenta Periodica, Brugis, 1905-1919; *Periodica de Re Canonica et Morali, utilia praesertim Religiosis et Missionariis,* Brugis, 1920-1927; *Periodica de Re Morali, Canonica, Liturgica,* Brugis, 1927-1936, Romae, 1937-

Harvard Law Review, Cambridge, 1887-

Jurist, The, Washington, D.C., 1941-

Law Quarterly Review, The, London, 1885-

New Mexico Historical Review, Albuquerque, 1926-

Tijdschrift voor Rechtsgeschiedenis–Revue d'Histoire du Droit, The Hague-Brussels, 1918-

ABBREVIATIONS

A.A.S.—*Acta Apostolicae Sedis.*

A.L.R.—American Law Reports Annotated.

A.L.R.2d—American Law Reports Annotated, Second Series.

Ala.—Alabama Reports.

Am. Dec.—American Decisions.

Am. Jur.—*American Jurisprudence.*

Am.S.R.—American State Reports.

Ann.Cas.—American and English Annotated Cases.

App.D.C.—United States Appeals, Circuit Court of Appeals, District of Columbia.

App. Div.—Appellate Division, New York.

Ark.—Arkansas Reports.

Atl.—Atlantic Reporter.

Atl.2d—Atlantic Reporter, Second Series.

C.—*Codex Iustinianus* (Justinian's Code).

C.A.—United States Court of Appeals.

Cal.—California Reports.

Cal. App.—California Appeals.

Cal. App.2d—California Appeals, Second Series.

C.C.A.—United States Circuit Court of Appeals.

C.J.S.—*Corpus Juris Secundum.*

Co.—Coke's English Reports.

Code Comm.—Response of the Pontifical Commission for the Authentic Interpretation of the Code of Canon Law.

Cra.—Cranch's United States Supreme Court Reports.

D.—*Digesta* (Justinian's Digest).

D.C.—United States District Court.

Eng.—English Reports.

F.—Federal Reporter.

F.2d.—Federal Reporter, Second Series.

Fla.—Florida Reports.

F.Supp.—Federal Supplement.

Ga. App.—Georgia Appeals.

Gild. (N.M.)—Gildersleeve's New Mexico Reports.

Gray (Mass.)—Gray's Massachusetts Reports.

How.—Howard's United States Supreme Court Reports.

Humphr. (Tenn.)—Humphrey's Tennessee Reports.

Ill.—Illinois Reports.

Ill. App.—Illinois Appeals.

Ind.—Indiana Reports.

208

John. (N.M.)—Johnson's New Mexico Reports.
K.B.—King's Bench Reports.
Ky.—Kentucky Reports.
La.—Louisiana Reports.
La. Ann.—Louisiana Annual Reports.
La. App.—Louisiana Appeals.
L.Ed.—Lawyers' Edition United States Supreme Court Reports.
L.R.A.—Lawyers' Reports Annotated.
L.R.A.(N.S.)—Lawyers' Reports Annotated, New Series.
Mass.—Massachusetts Reports.
Mart. (La., N.S.)—Martin's Louisiana Reports, New Series.
Mart. (La., O.S.)—Martin's Louisiana Reports, Old Series.
Md.—Maryland Reports.
Minn.—Minnesota Reports.
Misc.—Miscellaneous Reports, New York.
Mont.—Montana Reports.
N.C.—North Carolina Reports.
N.E.—Northeastern Reporter.
N.E.2d—Northeastern Reporter, Second Series.
N.J.Super.—New Jersey Superior Court Reports.
N.M.—New Mexico Reports.
N.M.H.R.—New Mexico Historical Review.
N.W.—Northwestern Reporter.
N.W.2d—Northwestern Reporter, Second Series.
N.Y.—New York Court of Appeals Reports.
N.Y.S.—New York Supplement.
N.Y.S.2d—New York Supplement, Second Series.
Ohio N.P.(N.S.)—Ohio Nisi Prius Reports, New Series.
Ohio St.—Ohio State Reports.
Ore.—Oregon Reports.
P.—Pacific Reporter.
P.2d.—Pacific Reporter, Second Series.
Pa. Super.—Pennsylvania Superior Court Reports.
Pet.—Peters' United States Supreme Court Reports.
Pick.(Mass.)—Pickering's Massachusetts Reports.
Reg.—Regula Juris.
R.I.—Rhode Island Reports.
R.J.—*Regulae Juris.*
S.C.—South Carolina Reports.
S.Ct.—Supreme Court Reporter of Decisions of United States Supreme Court.
S.C.Conc.—Sacra Congregatio Concilii (Sacred Congregation of the Council).
S.C.Consist.—Sacra Congregatio Consistorialis (Sacred Consistorial Congregation).
S.E.—Southeastern Reporter.

S.E.2d—Southeastern Reporter, Second Series.
So.—Southern Reporter.
So.2d—Southern Reporter, Second Series.
S.W.—Southwestern Reporter.
S.W.2d—Southwestern Reporter, Second Series.
Tenn.—Tennessee Reports.
Tenn. App.—Tennessee Appeals.
Tex.—Texas Reports.
U.S.—United States Reports.
U.S.App.D.C.—United States Appeals, Circuit Court of Appeals, District of Columbia.
VI°—*Liber Sextus Decretalium Bonifacii Papae VIII.*
Wash.—Washington Reports.
Wheat.—Wheaton's United States Supreme Court Reports.
Wis.—Wisconsin Reports.
X.—*Decretales Gregorii Papae IX.*

INDEX OF ANGLO-AMERICAN CASES CITED

(Numbers refer to page numbers herein)

ALPHABETICAL INDEX

BIOGRAPHICAL NOTE

Manuel J. Rodriguez was born in Espanola, New Mexico, on January 16, 1930. He received his primary and secondary education in the Espanola Municipal Schools and at St. Michael's High School in Santa Fe, New Mexico. Upon graduation from the latter in 1946, he entered the Immaculate Heart of Mary Seminary, attending classes also at St. Michael's College, both in Santa Fe. In 1948 he enrolled at the Pontifical Gregorian University (North American College), Rome, where he received the degree of Bachelor of Philosophy in 1950. He was ordained to the sacred priesthood in Rome on January 17, 1954. In June of the same year he was awarded the degree of Licentiate in Sacred Theology by the Pontifical Gregorian University, and upon returning to this country he was assigned to the Chancery Office of the Archdiocese of Santa Fe, of which he is Vice Chancellor and Vice Officialis. In September, 1956, he entered the School of Canon Law of The Catholic University of America, where he received the degree of Bachelor of Canon Law in June, 1957, and the degree of Licentiate in Canon Law in June, 1958.